Who We Were Meant to Be

Who We Were Meant to Be

Rediscovering Our Identity as God's Royal Priesthood

by
MATTHEW BURDEN

WIPF & STOCK · Eugene, Oregon

WHO WE WERE MEANT TO BE
Rediscovering Our Identity as God's Royal Priesthood

Copyright © 2021 Matthew Burden. All rights reserved. Except for brief quotations in critical publications or reviews, no part of this book may be reproduced in any manner without prior written permission from the publisher. Write: Permissions, Wipf and Stock Publishers, 199 W. 8th Ave., Suite 3, Eugene, OR 97401.

Wipf & Stock
An Imprint of Wipf and Stock Publishers
199 W. 8th Ave., Suite 3
Eugene, OR 97401

www.wipfandstock.com

PAPERBACK ISBN: 978-1-6667-0874-5
HARDCOVER ISBN: 978-1-6667-0875-2
EBOOK ISBN: 978-1-6667-0876-9

All Scripture quotations, unless otherwise indicated, are taken from the Holy Bible, New International Version®, NIV®. Copyright ©1973, 1978, 1984, 2011 by Biblica, Inc.® Used by permission of Zondervan. All rights reserved worldwide. www.zondervan.com

The "NIV" and "New International Version" are trademarks registered in the United States Patent and Trademark Office by Biblica, Inc.®

Scripture quotations indicated as (NRSV) are from New Revised Standard Version Bible, copyright © 1989 National Council of the Churches of Christ in the United States of America. Used by permission. All rights reserved worldwide. nrsvbibles.org

Scripture quotations indicated as (NASB) taken from the (NASB®) New American Standard Bible®, Copyright © 1960, 1971, 1977, 1995, 2020 by The Lockman Foundation. Used by permission. All rights reserved. www.lockman.org

For my church family –
Second Baptist Church of Calais, Maine

Stand at the crossroads and look;
ask for the ancient paths,
ask where the good way is, and walk in it,
and you will find rest for your souls.
—JER 6:16

Table of Contents

Acknowledgments — ix
Abbreviations — x

Introduction — 1
1. Overview: The Priesthood of All Believers — 7

~ PART ONE: Biblical and Theological Foundations ~

2. Creation: The Cosmic Temple of God — 19
3. Human Identity: The Royal Priests of Eden — 35
4. The Temple: Rituals of Cosmic Reconciliation — 49
5. Christ's Ministry: The Messianic Priest-King — 59
6. Christ's Passion: The Priest-King's Coronation Rites — 77
7. New Creation: The Early Christian Perspective — 93

~ PART TWO: Life in the Royal Priesthood ~

8. The Church: Worship in the Living Temple — 109
9. The Service: Rites of the Royal Priesthood — 123
10. Holiness: The Call of the Priestly Life — 136
11. Desire: How to Train Yourself to Be Godly — 154
12. Disciplines: The Practice of Christian Training (Part 1) — 169
13. Disciplines: The Practice of Christian Training (Part 2) — 185
14. Prayer: Royal Authority and Priestly Service — 199
15. Union: Participating in the Divine Nature — 219
16. Mission: The Earth Shall Be Filled — 232

Appendix: On Reading Patristic Sources — 247
Bibliography — 251

Acknowledgments

I would like to thank my church family at Second Baptist Church for their support and encouragement in the midst of my reading, writing, and reflecting. Special thanks goes to the faithful viewers of my midweek Bible study videos during the pandemic summer of 2020, who followed along with my early efforts to put these thoughts on royal priesthood into some semblance of order. I am also tremendously grateful for the work of my email-list reading group, who reviewed my chapters as I produced them. They courageously waded through some very rough drafts along the way. I am particularly thankful for the contributions and comments of Rev. Dr. Al Fletcher, Rev. Dr. Sheila Heneise, and my father-in-law, Rev. Jim Spurrier. Any errors in this book, whether of fact, style, or perspective, are not attributable to them, but are wholly my own. My highest thanks goes to my wife Rachel and my three children, who not only patiently made space for my long hours of research and writing, but were a constant source of encouragement throughout the process.

Abbreviations

THE FOLLOWING ABBREVIATIONS REPRESENT *major collections of primary sources:*

ANF — *The Ante-Nicene Fathers.* Edited by Alexander Roberts and James Donaldson. 10 vols 1885–87. Reprint, Peabody, MA: Hendrickson, 1994.

NPNF[1] — *The Nicene and Post-Nicene Fathers*, Series 1. Edited by Philip Schaff. 14 vols. 1886–89. Reprint, Peabody, MA: Hendrickson, 1994.

NPNF[2] — *The Nicene and Post-Nicene Fathers*, Series 2. Edited by Philip Schaff and Henry Wace. 14 vols. 1890–1900. Reprint, Peabody, MA: Hendrickson, 1994.

OTP — *The Old Testament Pseudepigrapha.* Edited by James H. Charlesworth. 2 vols. 1983. Reprint, Peabody, MA: Hendrickson, 2009.

PG — Patrologia graeca. Edited by J.-P. Migne. 162 vols. Paris: n.p., 1857–86.

Introduction

LET'S BEGIN WITH A little music, shall we? Imagine for a moment that you've grown up thinking that the melody line of Beethoven's "Ode to Joy," from his Ninth Symphony (which many Christians know as the tune of "Joyful, Joyful, We Adore Thee"), was the sweetest, most profound work of music the world had ever known. Imagine that you had been taught that it was incomparably more beautiful than any other piece of music, from any other culture, at any time in history. And for those who know it, it certainly is sweet, profound, and beautiful. But for this little mental exercise to work, I need to underscore that the story you have been told about this piece of music has the *melody line* in mind, and only the melody line: that bold sequence of joyful notes that you know how to hum or plunk out on a piano, but without any harmonies or accompanying parts. Imagine that you have never heard "Ode to Joy" in its full orchestral setting.

This, I want to suggest, is how many of us learned the message of God's salvation plan: set forth in the barest, plainest, simplest terms, terms that anyone who heard could immediately put into practice. The melody line went something like this: (1) we have all sinned, and we need forgiveness for those sins; (2) Jesus died for us to provide that forgiveness; (3) by accepting him as Lord and Savior, we can be forgiven; (4) which means that we get to have an eternal life of joy with God instead of an eternity of suffering the consequences of our sins. There you have it: problem, solution, application, and resolution. It's so concrete and easily explainable that it's fit for a five-minute boardroom presentation: the salvation plan of the God of the universe, simple enough to write on a three-inch tract.

Before we begin to ask the obvious question of whether there might be just a little bit more to the story than those bare-bones facts, let's pause for a moment to admire the elegance and effectiveness of that simple melody. This plan-of-salvation story contains within itself a world of beauty, passion, and theological depth. Each point listed above can be the subject of volumes upon volumes of beautiful, articulate, soul-stirring reflections (and, indeed, they all have been, many times over). This little story has revolutionized the world, launched whole movements, transformed lives, and carried on the triumphant song of faith in Christ through many ages when the world would rather have silenced that song. Nothing in this book will take anything away from the glorious, world-turned-upside-down melody of personal salvation through Jesus Christ. Rather, what I hope to do is to surround that melody with some of the harmonies with which it was always meant to be heard, themes from Scripture that we have simply not tuned our ears to hear in quite the way the Composer intended.

Go back to our little musical exercise: you love the melody line of "Ode to Joy," but all you have ever heard is that melody. You have been sitting in the concert hall of God's gospel presentation, but the only one on stage is a single violinist, playing out those old, familiar, soul-stirring notes. Now, it's not that it isn't a beautiful melody, and it's not that the violinist is lacking anything in their performance technique. But that is not at all how Beethoven meant for his song to be heard. The melody is the heart of it, to be sure, but any composer would tell you that you are not really hearing the melody if you are separating it out from how it was meant to be heard.

This has been my experience with learning the gospel. I have loved that melody line for my whole life from as early as I can remember loving anything. It has been the soundtrack of my existence, and I would not trade it for anything else. But starting in my early adulthood, I began to get the sense that there was something missing. Now, I am not saying that any part of the salvation plan outlined above is incorrect; it does not lack for coherence, beauty, or transformational power. But I began to feel like there was more to the song than just that melody. There were parts that I was not quite hearing yet, and the echo of their absence began to ring around my life's concert hall.

I would read my Bible and notice that there were a lot of hanging notes, wandering musical themes, dancing rhythms that I did not know how to fit with my beloved melody line. Yet it was clear that those wandering themes meant something awfully important to the writers of Scripture, because they kept coming up, over and over again. I began to see that although I was listening to the lead violinist play out the melody, there were a lot more chairs on the stage than I knew what to do with. Other parts were written into this song, places for instruments to add marvelous harmonies to my melody, but I couldn't quite make out how they all fit together. I could not yet hear the harmonies. I found myself bemused, and sometimes frustrated, by the pieces of the puzzle that didn't quite seem to fit. Here are a few of the head-scratchers that kept me pondering things for years:

Why does the apostle Paul insist on talking about the goal of God's plan as being some kind of cosmic reconciliation of the entire universe? If my familiar old melody is written in terms of individual salvation (even if understood within the communal reality of the body of Christ), is it possible to reconcile that with a vision of Christ bringing together all things in heaven and on earth?

And what's the point of all the elements of the biblical story of God's plan that don't really seem essential for my four-point outline version? Why did Jesus spend so much of his time preaching about the kingdom of God instead of clearly proclaiming salvation by the forgiveness of sins?

And what about some parts of the story that just don't make a lot of sense? Why should all the rest of creation be affected by sin's curse just because humanity messed up? After his resurrection, why did Jesus have to leave in the ascension, instead of sticking around? Why are we called to pray, when God already knows what we're going to pray and is powerful enough to do everything without us anyway?

Now, as you read those questions, you might think that you could give some pretty solid answers to them. A lot of scholars and teachers have done a great deal of work in making sense of each of the questions above. But some of those scholars have begun to get the nagging notion, as I have, that those answers are hard to cram into the simple melody line we already know so well. They appear to be complementary notes to the melody, sprinkled here and there throughout the song. But they themselves are not notes about personal salvation through the forgiveness of individual sins. They are tied into something a bit different: something broader, vaster, and wilder than what we have long imagined.

If you look at my list of questions again, you might also think that it's just the random flotsam of a haphazard theological mind. The questions don't actually seem to fit together into any kind of coherent theme—after all, what do prayer, the ascension, Jesus preaching about the kingdom, and some mysterious cosmic reconciliation have to do with each other?

What I am going to do in the following pages is try to convince you that, in point of fact, all those scattered puzzle pieces are connected to each other in a grand, unified theme that runs in harmony to the melody we know and love so well. Those random questions, and many others besides, all point toward answers that reveal a harmony line of immense beauty and power. They all cohere together in a big-picture story of what God has been doing in his world since the very beginning, and when we begin to understand that big picture, we'll start to hear more of the song in the way our Composer intended.

Our imaginary concertgoer is still there, listening to the melody being played on solo violin. For me, this was the song of my American, evangelical, Baptist heritage: the life-giving refrain of personal salvation in Jesus Christ. But over the years, as I listened and prayed and studied, I began to hear other parts filling in around that sound. I heard the drums of contemporary Bible scholars, sounding out the rhythm of the kingdom of God; I heard the soaring brass of the early church fathers playing a fanfare of New Creation; the strings and woodwinds of Eastern Christian theology and Western devotional classics sounding out runs and arpeggios of union with God; and over it all, the tidal wave of voices from the chorus of all the Scriptures, singing about creation and priests and kings. The melody I loved was still there, in the center of the song, but now it was made more radiant by all that surrounded it, like a jewel in its setting. For someone who has only ever heard "Ode to Joy" plunked out one note at a time on a piano, hearing it as Beethoven intended, in its full orchestral glory, is a revelation of almost mystical wonder.

In this book, I hope to be able to train your ears to hear this harmony, because I truly believe that this is—at least in part—the way the salvation plan of God was always meant to be heard. This is the story of how God's plan encompasses not only you and me, but everything that he has made. I'm going to present it as the story of three interwoven themes: creation, temple, and kingdom, and of our place in that great story—God's royal priests of the New Creation. These three themes cohere into a unified harmony that plays alongside the melody of personal salvation, and overlays it with new layers of beauty.

Most readers, I suspect, will find this path of discovery to be a joyful adventure. The truth is, many of us have already learned some of the other harmonies that also accompany the melody line, harmonies which provide some of the depth and beauty of our Christian experience: for instance, the communal life of the body of Christ, the adventure of discipleship, and the long and lovely road of sanctification unto holiness. Each of these is a complementary sequence of notes, meant to fit together gracefully with the grand theme of personal salvation in Christ. The harmony I'll be tracing out for you, then, is simply one more in a line of harmonies that you may have already begun to hear.

One more clarification, which I hope by this point is obvious, but it's worth stating outright: I'm not arguing *against* the old story, the melody line of personal salvation in Christ. To shift the metaphor, I'm arguing that we've been staring at the center of a vast stained-glass window for centuries. That central picture is in the center for a very good reason, and no one would suggest that you could understand the real meaning of the window by removing the center. Rather, what I'm suggesting is that we can only understand the scope of the window's artistry if we look at the whole picture in light of the center.

Professional theologians sometimes have an irksome habit of demanding that their personal interpretive scheme is the only permissible way to understand the entire story of God's plan; but I'm not going to do that. I believe that the themes I'm talking about here are integral parts of God's great symphony, but not the whole. So while I won't be talking about lots of classic doctrines like justification, sovereignty, repentance, or conversion, that's not an indication that they're not a central part of the symphony; it's only because that's not the part of the stained-glass window I happen to be describing.

My goal is simply to focus on the question of our identity as God's royal priesthood, and to trace the meaning of that identity in the big-picture story of God's plan of redemption for the entire created order. And my hope is that, by the end of it, we'll be able to understand just a bit of what Scripture means when it says that the mystery of God's will, purposed in Christ, was "to bring unity to all things in heaven and on earth" (Eph 1:10).

This, then, is the story of a mighty chorus that you may have never heard in full before, but which your heart was made to join in exultant, jubilant song.

1

Overview: The Priesthood of All Believers

EVERY NOW AND THEN, you run into a thought that sticks like a splinter in your brain—a Bible verse that jumps out at you in a whole new way, or a new insight that just springs up, demands attention with nagging insistence, and reveals a whole new way of considering things. One of those odd epiphanies happened to me when I was studying the ways in which early believers prayed.

Let me introduce this idea with a certain picture in mind: we have all seen lovely little paintings or sketches of a child learning to pray, kneeling beside her bed with her eyes closed and her hands folded. It's a quintessential portrait of humble piety and childlike faith, is it not? Well, now imagine the child's parents rushing into the room, hauling her up, and rebuking her: "No, child, you mustn't pray like that! Stand on your own two feet!"

I think you will agree that the image is a bit jarring. But that is essentially the picture of a great swath of early Christian prayer, and it made me reconsider some of my preconceptions about how I prayed. The normal posture for prayer throughout much of the early church was to stand, often with one's arms upraised. Of course, they could also kneel, bow, or even prostrate themselves, but only on certain occasions or for certain types of prayers. On some days, kneeling was actually forbidden. Standing was considered the base position for prayer in much of early Christianity. That may not seem all that significant at first glance, but it was different enough from my normal practice that it made me pause.

You see, this was not how I had learned to pray. Whenever I was invited to join in prayer in church, it usually came prefaced with, "Let's all bow our heads." Most Western Christians, if forced to make a guess as to the normal posture for Christian prayer, would probably say "kneeling," "heads bowed, eyes closed, hands folded," or some combination of those elements. There is a long tradition which holds that bowing or kneeling is the way we ought to pray. In my Baptist tradition there is not a lot of kneeling, but it's still seen as perfectly appropriate. Most people just bow their heads and close their eyes. If you are feeling particularly spiritual, you can go further than just bowing your head, and slouch your whole upper body over until your elbows are resting on your knees. But that's about as far as we go. Still, it shows an attitude of submission and contrition: in the presence of Almighty God, we bow.

In light of our current habits, the early church's preference for standing in prayer was a startling contrast to me. But to those who know their Bibles well, it might not come as much of a surprise—to pray standing was a very common way of praying in Jewish culture (see, for example, 1 Sam 1:26; 1 Kgs 8:22; Matt 6:5; Mark 11:25). So maybe, one might think, Christians just inherited an interesting Jewish practice as an incidental cultural relic. But it's not quite that simple. This was not just a matter of a traditional practice; it apparently meant a great deal to the early church. In fact, according to the records of the first ecumenical council (Nicea, AD 325), the very council that produced many of the standard formulations of Trinitarian theology and Christology which we still hold today, Christians were not to kneel in prayer on Sunday—not at all, not ever during worship or prayer on the Lord's Day.[1] The fact that they forbade kneeling indicates that these postures were imbued with significant symbolic meanings. Kneeling in prayer, at least sometimes, was seen as inappropriate because of the message it conveyed.

To many Christians, this seems almost inexplicable. Why on earth would kneeling in prayer be inappropriate? All of a sudden, I found that I was holding a puzzle piece that changed the scope of the picture for me. Not only could I not find a place in my tidy, Americanized version of Christianity to fit it in, but its color and shape suggested there was a vast swath of the picture I hadn't even yet imagined.

Kneeling in prayer suggests an attitude of humility and of sorrow for one's sin. There wasn't any place in my melody-line tune (personal salvation through the forgiveness of sins) where I could fit a note which suggested that expressing humble sorrow for one's sins was inappropriate. If

---

1. First Ecumenical Council, Canon 20 (*NPNF*[2] 14:42).

salvation was all about forgiving my individual sins, and if the fundamental story of my identity as a Christian was that of a sinner saved by grace, then there was no possibility of suggesting that an attitude of contrition was out of place. So what to do with this puzzle piece that didn't fit anywhere? What to do with this jarring musical note? It suggested there was another thread of notes out there somewhere, a line of harmony I had never quite heard before, that must put its main emphasis on something quite different than my familiar story of personal sin, guilt, and shame.

You may think at this point that I'm reading an awful lot into one piece of historical minutia. But at the point that I came across this interesting early Christian trait, I had already spent years studying the works of the early church fathers and mothers (a field known as patristics). It was from these very generations of Christians that we had received much of the gold standard of Christian doctrine—ways of understanding foundational truths like the Trinity, the nature of Christ, the meaning of the atonement, the shape of the biblical canon, and so on. So if those same Christians were operating on a different view of sin and human identity than I was, then I wanted to know about it, because I had every reason to believe that they might just be onto something important.

As it turned out, that puzzle piece about standing in prayer spoke a great deal about Christian identity. In short, it comes down to this: they stood in prayer not only because of traditional practices handed down to them, but because it was a position of dignity, honor, and authority. To kneel on certain days (like Sundays), they believed, was to misrepresent our identity and so deny the truth about ourselves. That truth was that we were far more than just sinners saved by grace. We were created to be the kings and queens and priests of God's creation, crowned with the royal splendor of his reign, and we were called to stand proudly in that identity. Kneeling in prayer was appropriate when making confessions, but while kneeling spoke to the influence of sin in our lives, standing spoke to the very manner of our making.

This, I think you will agree, is a far cry from the sin-guilt-repentance cycle that we modern Christians often find ourselves living. Humble contrition of sin is a good and godly thing to express, but it does not reflect the deepest level of our identity. It speaks only about the curse of our fallenness, but not the grandeur of our created nature, made in the image of God. As Basil, one of the greatest of those early church fathers, grandly proclaimed: "O human, are a ruling being!"[2]

The Big-Picture View

Let me give you the basic idea that we will explore together, and then we will spend some time looking at how Scripture and early Christian beliefs paint the picture of God's great plan and our place within it. The basic premise is this: we are going to take seriously—just as the early Christians did—the Bible's language about our role as God's royal priesthood. Many Christians just gloss over the priesthood of all believers as if it's merely a nice idea, with no practical application beyond congregational polity. But that's not the way the Bible portrays it, nor the way that Christian orthodoxy originally understood it. We need earnestly to consider the notion that we were created to be both royal and priestly, and to take seriously what Scripture says about how we exercise those roles as part of God's great plan.

There are seven basic ideas here, all rooted in Scripture and early Christian beliefs, which we will explore at some length in the following chapters:

1. All creation was intended to be a temple in which God dwells, in a loving journey of ever-greater unity with his creatures. This was to culminate in an eternal unity of heaven and earth as the temple of God's reign.

2. We human beings were made as the priests of this creation-temple, as well as the designated, authoritative, ruling ambassadors of God's reign within it.

3. Our fall into sin put us into a position in which we need individual salvation through the forgiveness of sin and the defeat of its consequences (the familiar "melody line" of the gospel). But the fall also ruptured the unity of God's creation-temple. Because its priests have rebelled, creation is a desolated temple, and the intended union of heaven and earth has been severed.

---

2. Basil, *First Discourse on the Origin of Humanity* 8, in *On the Human Condition*, 37.

4. The Old Testament system of temple worship intentionally echoed the pattern of the creation-temple and prepared the way for the restoration of humanity's offices through Christ.

5. Jesus Christ's incarnation, ministry, death, resurrection, and ascension are all essential pieces of his work in serving both as the true King and great High Priest, as well as the active divine agent of New Creation.

6. Jesus' redemptive work is not limited to the salvation of individual humans, but extends also to the communal and cosmic levels by creating a new humanity and restoring it to its role as royal priests of the New Creation.

7. This New Creation, which has begun with humans but will one day encompass all creation, will ultimately culminate in the creation's intended goal: the union of heaven and earth.

A few of the terms and phrases used above may sound a little strange to some ears, but as we will see, they are rooted not only in the theology of the early church, but in Scripture itself. Many of us have become accustomed to following a single narrative thread through the Bible, and as a result we have sometimes failed to notice that there are other threads running alongside. Some of these ideas are now just beginning to return to the center of the way we conceptualize the grand sweep of the plan of God. A growing chorus of Bible scholars have written books on these themes within the past decade; this present work seeks to add to that conversation by grounding it in the theological vision of the patristic age and by offering practical applications to our daily Christian lives. This vast biblical metanarrative—all creation as the temple of God, and its cosmic restoration through Christ—is not a new development in theology; it is a return to the original vision, and it has a great deal to say about how we live our lives.

Some of the greatest theologians of the early church saw the sequence of biblical beliefs listed above as standing at the very center of our faith. New Creation was just as important an idea for them as the idea of being saved from our sins. But it is not the case that the two ideas were viewed separately; rather, they were part of one whole, grand, overarching story of God's work in Christ. If your individualized story of salvation in Christ through the forgiveness of sins was one side of the coin, then the story of communal and cosmic restoration was seen as the other side.

Your personal salvation is a single line in a grand epic of God's work to rescue his entire creation, and if you don't bother to read the whole epic, then you're not really going to understand the glory and magnitude of the place that your redemption plays in the overarching story. God's salvation, then, is as near as your own soul and yet as vast as the entire universe.

But why, you may ask, should we bother listening to what the theologians of the early church thought? After all, many in my tradition have tried to trace a direct arc from the apostolic age to the Protestant Reformation a millennium and a half later, thus effectively skipping over all the major teachers of the patristic age. I believe, however (just as the Protestant reformers believed), that we need to listen to the fathers and mothers of the early church with great attention. The truth is, you are already deeply rooted in patristic theology, whether you know it or not. Every doctrine that orthodox, Bible-believing Christians hold to about the nature of the Trinity and the work of Christ found its precise expression in the work of early theologians like Athanasius and the Cappadocian Fathers. Yes, all those doctrines are also firmly rooted in Scripture as the unassailable bedrock of their truth, but it was the fathers who taught us how to read those Scriptures.

You will find that this book is essentially a presentation of some of the most fruitful themes of early church theology, which many of us modern folk have too often forgotten. The same voices that taught us about the nature of the Trinity and the atoning work of Christ also taught about creation as a temple, we humans as its priests, and the cosmic work of New Creation in the person of Jesus of Nazareth. We should listen to these early church voices, not only because they have taught us so reliably and so well in the past, but also because they grew up much closer to the cultural milieu of the Bible than you or I did. While contemporary biblical studies can unearth marvelous understandings of scriptural texts, which in some cases even bring us to a better sense of certain verses than the early church fathers had, we still live within the all-pervasive, unconscious influence of our own cultural systems. In a very real sense, we wear blinders when we sit down to read our Bibles. There are things in Scripture that we cannot see unless we have been trained to take our cultural blinders off. (An easy example is the way most Americans read the New Testament with a primary view toward themselves as individuals, when in fact much of it should be read in light of their communal identity in the body of Christ.) The theologians of the early church had their own blinders, too, but they were a different set of cultural blinders than ours, which means that they could see things in Scripture that you and I have a hard time seeing, even though they are right there in front of our faces. (For a more in-depth discussion of the use of patristic sources, see the appendix.)

You may also notice that in most of the instances when I refer to "New Creation," both words are capitalized. This is to distinguish it as a theological idea of particular importance, a core paradigm derived from patristic theology. It is important to note that New Creation designates not only a thing or a state of affairs, but the main story-arc of God's plan of redemption. In other words, New Creation is not just a different term for the new heavens and the new earth as described in Revelation 21–22; rather, it relates to the whole process by which God brings his creation to that point. It is God's new work of creation, accomplished through Christ and implemented through the Spirit.

But we're getting ahead of ourselves. Let's start with a bit of common ground, someplace where we already feel our feet on solid biblical grounding. We will begin by taking a look at a piece of the puzzle that many of us already hold in our hands: the old Reformation axiom of "the priesthood of all believers."

The Priesthood of All Believers

In most of the Christian circles in which I've lived, the idea of being God's royal priesthood has not been a major part of our self-conception. We are "sinners saved by grace," "children of God," "redeemed," and so on. But how many of us think of ourselves as "priests of the living God?" Nonetheless, in my particular branch of Christianity (and, I suspect, in a great many of the wider Protestant traditions) there's quite a bit of emphasis on a belief called "the priesthood of all believers." It is a phrase derived from those passages in which the people of God are described as "a kingdom and priests" (Rev 1:6; 5:10) or "a royal priesthood" (1 Pet 2:9).

For many Protestants, this idea leads to the understanding that each and every Christian is endowed with the same blessing of spiritual life in Christ, the same abiding presence of the Holy Spirit, and the same union with God in Christ Jesus our Lord. This forms the basis for our understanding of congregational life—no one is necessarily closer to God than anyone else; we are all redeemed, all with access to the same Spirit, all able to call on our heavenly Father without the need of any mediator but Jesus. In my denomination, this extends directly to our notion of church polity: since we all have access to God by the same indwelling Holy Spirit, it is the congregation itself, the body of Christ, which constitutes the highest authority for local church life.

But as lovely as such ideas might be, and as fruitful and liberating as they are in the lives of churches and individual Christians, our understanding of this crucial, Bible-based doctrine has also gotten a little bit twisted along the way. You see, many of the times that I have heard the priesthood of all believers described, it is used as a way of explaining why we Protestants are not Roman Catholics. "We don't have priests," we say, "because we believe in the priesthood of *all* believers." The priesthood of all believers, then, while it does give us a theological framework for congregational authority, is often used to explain why we don't call our pastors priests, in contrast to Catholics (and a few other denominations). Essentially, this doctrine has become a tool to use in debates half a millennium old.

But stop and think about this for a moment. In using the idea of the priesthood of all believers in this way, we have begun to look at the whole thing upside-down. We are now in the ironic position that when we explain the priesthood of all believers, instead of using the phrase to show that we are all priests, we are using it to explain why none of us are. In making a case for congregational polity rather than a priestly hierarchy, we have stumbled into a strange antireading that says "this is why we have no priests," when the phrase itself very clearly suggests "we are all priests."

Let me put it to you another way. Most of my interactions with this doctrinal catchphrase have put the emphasis on "all"—the priesthood of *all* believers. This is the case whether we are talking about congregational polity or about low-church Protestant distinctions from Catholicism. But what we very seldom do is shift the emphasis and ask ourselves, "What does it mean that we believe in the *priesthood* of all believers?" I would suggest that this latter reading is the one that the biblical authors want us to take seriously.

Let's imagine for a moment that we are asking a Protestant evangelical audience the following question: "If all believers are priests, what does that mean in practical terms?" I suspect, from my years of pastoring and studying within evangelical circles, that most people would be tempted to answer that question in terms of access. To be a priest means that you have access to God without an intermediary, like the priests in the Old

Testament. In contrast to God's people in pre-Christian times, who had to approach God through a human mediator (a priest), now through the mediation of Christ Jesus we have direct access to the presence of the Father.

That's a good answer, and undoubtedly true. The only problem is, it does not appear to be the answer that the Bible itself gives, or at least not the main answer. Whereas our tendency is to focus immediately on the privileges of being a priest (probably because our culture hardwires us to think in terms of rights above all else), the Bible moves first to a consideration of duties. In both 1 Peter and Revelation, the immediate application is about practical duties that we, as God's priests, undertake. First Peter 2:9 says that as his royal priesthood, we are called to declare his praises. Revelation 5:10 says that we are appointed to serve. Much of the second half of this book will be an exploration of the practical ways in which we serve as God's priests, fulfilling the duties of our office. But the bottom line is this: not only do we have the privileges of an office based on our fundamental identity, but we also have a mission, a task, a set of services to perform. Just like the Levitical priesthood in the Old Testament, we have a job to do here. And as we will see, it is a job that we have been prepared for since the very beginning, a job through which God is working out his great purposes.

A skeptic might, at this point, ask whether I'm perhaps making too much of a minor, passing image found only in a couple late references from the New Testament age. Isn't the royal priesthood idea, after all, just a reference back to God's use of the same turn of phrase for his chosen people, the Israelites, in Exodus 19:6 ("You will be for me a kingdom of priests")? And if so, aren't Peter and John really just saying that Christians are also heirs of God's covenant-family, as Old Testament Israel was? Maybe we risk pushing things too far if we are making the idea of royal priesthood a central aspect of our Christian identity.

This skeptical line of thought might be persuasive at first glance. But the history of Christian interpretation tells a different story. As it turns out, the priestly identity of humanity was indeed one of the central aspects of early Christians' understanding. They would have agreed that we are sinners saved by grace and children of God, but they also insisted, far more regularly than we ever do, that they served a priestly function in God's plan for the world, with all the duties that accompanied that office.

Creation, Temple, Kingdom—A Cord of Three Strands

To understand that priestly function, we will be looking at three interwoven themes throughout the Bible: creation, temple, and kingdom. I say that these themes are interwoven, because they very often tend to arise in conjunction with one another, both in Scripture and in early Christian theology. In terms of the way these themes connect with our life as Christians, we will be talking about them in terms of New Creation (touching on the first theme) and royal priesthood (the second and third themes).

This book is divided into two major sections: chapters 2–7, which give a detailed overview of the biblical and theological foundations of the seven points listed above, and chapters 8–16, which offer some practical reflections on what our royal/priestly identity means in the life of the local church and in our own daily lives. Some readers, particularly those not well acquainted with reading in-depth biblical and theological explorations, may find it necessary to skip directly to chapter 8. For most, however, the biblical analysis should prove a fruitful foundation on which to build a fuller understanding of the practical applications in later chapters.

When we examine the creation stories in Genesis, we will see that Adam and Eve, placed at the center of the original created order, were granted authority as the royal priests of creation. In the stories of Old Testament Israel, we will see how the traditions of tabernacle and temple reflect back to these themes of the created order, and also point forward to their coming restoration. In the Gospels, Jesus is portrayed in his divine nature as the active agent of New Creation, and in his human nature as the ultimate fulfillment of humanity's royal and priestly roles. The message he preaches, proclaiming the kingdom of God, is directly tied to the grand vision of the restoration of God's indwelling reign in his creation. And when we look at Acts, the Epistles, and Revelation, we will see how all these threads are bound up together in the wild realization that the New Creation has begun in Jesus and has been extended to us; that our original role as royal priests has been reestablished; that the kingdom of God is not merely a nice-sounding idea but includes the active administration of God's reign through his kingdom-officials; and that God's plan will indeed finally reach its glorious, eternal, intended end: the union of heaven and earth as the true temple of his glory, in which he dwells with his creatures and reigns as "all in all" (1 Cor 15:28).

That, friends, is the vision we are after: as near as our own souls, and as vast as the universe.

Part One

Biblical and Theological Foundations

2

Creation: The Cosmic Temple of God

WHY DID GOD CREATE the universe? After all, he didn't have to. Christian theology has always taught that God, existing eternally in the superpersonal reality of the Trinity, is the consummation of all perfection, in and of himself. He needs nothing else. The absence of everything else in the universe would not and could not detract from the infinite wholeness of love and delight which characterizes his being. As Maximus the Confessor wrote, "When God, who is absolute fullness, brought creatures into existence, it was not done to fulfill any need."[1] So why make anything at all?

In some respects, this is a question we cannot ever answer in full. Scripture permits us some views toward forming an answer, particularly regarding the purposes of God in creation. But the question itself often tempts people into speculating on God's inner motivations for creating, and here we would be well advised to remember our frailty and fallibility as we keep in mind "the incomprehensibility of deity to the human mind and its totally unimaginable grandeur."[2] If we are going to explore the theology of creation in the same way that early Christians did, then we must approach such questions not just as a mode of logic and exegesis, but as an exercise in humility. We come to the task not only as rational minds, but as finite creatures seeking to speak of their Creator. The fathers and mothers of the early church insisted that theology was a task only for those who could do it in the right *phronēma*—that is, with a

---

1. Maximus the Confessor, *Centuries on Charity* 3.46, quoted in Clément, *Roots*, 32.

2. Gregory of Nazianzus, Oration 28, 11, in *On God and Christ*, 45.

mindset saturated in prayer and devotion. We who undertake these paths must remember to walk them with humble awe, and in some cases, that means knowing when to stop and say, "Let the rest be adored in silence."[3]

This does not mean that all theology is off limits, or that we cannot use reason to explore the wonder and mystery of God's being. Only this: in our exploring, we must always keep with us the awestruck wonder of Scripture itself. Theology must be an act of worship as well as reason, marked at least as much by prayer as by thinking, reading, and writing. "If you are a theologian," said Evagrius, "you will pray truly; and if you pray truly, you are a theologian."[4] But be advised: "praying truly," in this context, does not refer simply to a few mumbled words or a couple minutes of speaking to God; it speaks of a whole life that is ordered intentionally Godward.

Now back to the main question: Why did God create the universe? We will make our way to a very particular answer, one of several valid answers one might give from Scripture and Christian tradition, an answer that focuses on God's purposes for his creation but leaves speculation about his motivations to the side. Here it is: God created the universe to be a temple. Now, that might sound far too vague to be helpful. But the very idea of temple is a layered image, rich in meaning, when taken in the context of Scripture. It designates a place where God's glory dwells, as well as a place of union in which God's creatures can grow in relationship with him. As such, it includes within itself some of the more common answers given to the question of why God created the universe. If one prefers an answer like "for his own glory," then the image of a temple, as a place for the display of God's splendor, fits the theme perfectly. Or if one prefers to say "God created the universe as an act of love," then here too a temple fits the theme, as the designated place from which God's presence would bestow his blessings on his people.

The temple image also includes a third aspect in addition to glory and love, which forms one of the crucial foundations of the patristic view of salvation: the theme of union. A temple exists for the purpose of maintaining a relationship, for gathering people together with one another and drawing them near to God. Maximus identified this aspect as one of the purposes behind creation: the universe was made for our delight in God and God's delight in us, "as [humanity] draws inexhaustibly upon

---

3. Gregory of Nazianzus, Oration 45, quoted in Clément, *Roots*, 45.

4. Evagrius, *On Prayer* 61, quoted in *Philokalia* 1:62; cf. Athanasius, *On the Incarnation* 57 (*NPNF*² 4:67).

the Inexhaustible."⁵ A temple exists as an invitation to a journey into the experience of greater union with God. And not only with God, but also with one another—a theme which the apostle Paul set at the center of his proclamation: that all people, Jews and gentiles alike, are drawn together into union in the temple of the body of Christ.

If the idea of God creating the universe for the purposes of drawing his creation into union sounds like a head-scratcher to you, it might be good to take another look at Ephesians 1:9–10: "[God] made known to us the mystery of his will . . . to bring unity to all things in heaven and on earth under Christ" (NIV). Or, as the NRSV puts it, "to gather up all things in him." The great purpose of God's will, as revealed in Christ, is to bring together all things in heaven and earth. One aspect of this, to be sure, is the picture of all creation submitting, whether willingly or not, to the lordship of Christ (1 Cor 15:24–28; Phil 2:9–11). But Colossians 1:20 suggests it is more than just a unity of submission that God is after: "to *reconcile to himself* all things, whether things on earth or things in heaven." So when we speak of God's goal for creation as being one of union, we are referring to more than just his reign as the universal King; rather, it is an invitation to enter into a restored relationship with our Creator, in which we are transformed "with ever increasing glory" (2 Cor 3:18). The patristic period had a great deal to say about our union with God—a great deal, in fact, that sounds wildly strange to our ears—and so in chapter 15 we will explore in greater depth what exactly "union" means.

But for now, we turn to our explorations of Scripture. In the symbolic worldview of the biblical writers, this idea of union was most easily and clearly understood with reference to the temple: the place where Creator and creation came together. In the next chapter, we will begin to survey the biblical evidence behind the idea of humanity's vocation as a royal priesthood. While one might have expected an exploration of temple themes to begin with the temple, we must press it back further, and begin with creation itself: creation as it was first made, and creation as it is revealed at the culmination of God's plan for it. The early church, you see, did not envision royal priesthood as just a nice metaphor, plucked at random from Israel's temple texts; they understood it to be an indication of the way we humans were made, a portrait that is painted from Genesis 1 to Revelation 22. Over and over again, the thinkers and writers of the

---

5. Maximus the Confessor, *Centuries on Charity* 3.46, quoted in Clément, *Roots*, 32.

early church insisted that we were priests because of the creation stories. Our priestly identity—and, yes, our royal identity, too—are rooted not only in what a couple passing New Testament verses say about us, but in the very manner of our making. We are priests, the early church believed, because that is exactly what we were meant to be from the very beginning.

The Cosmic Temple of Creation

From the opening pages of the Bible, Scripture presents God's work of creation as the construction of a temple. But wait, you might say—the Genesis accounts never refer to God's creation as a temple or a tabernacle, not even once. That's true so far as it goes, but we should keep in mind that many of us are not really that familiar with the religious culture of Old Testament Israel. Had we grown up in that system of worship, surrounded by its symbols, we probably would have seen allusions to the temple throughout Genesis 1–3, and echoes of creation and the garden of Eden in every part of the temple.

There is one place in Scripture where these connections lie close to the surface, and anyone can see them without too much trouble. Instead of starting at the beginning, though, one has to start at the end. It is rather like trying to see the meaning behind a work of sculpture: you would look at the completed product, after the artist's full conception had been realized, and not just by contemplating the first chisel-strokes on the original hunk of marble. To see what God intends for his creation, there is no better place to start than Revelation 21–22, where the union of the new heavens and new earth is portrayed in overlapping images of the temple and the garden of Eden.

Before we look at those chapters, though, it is useful to pause and take note of one tendency of early Christian reflection on God's work in creation, which offers a slight contrast to the way some modern Christians think about it. You may have already noticed that the way I have been phrasing God's purposes for creation is dynamic and developmental: God created the universe to be a temple in which he invites his creation into a journey of ever-greater union with him. In other words, God created his creation to grow and develop in a Godward direction. This should not come as a surprise, if we are suggesting that God invites his creatures into relationship with him. After all, it is the nature of relationships that one grows into them by a beautiful process of knowing and experiencing one another more deeply.

By contrast, I used to view my part in God's plan in static rather than dynamic terms. This static-state understanding of salvation had its own interpretation of the narratives of Eden and the fall: (1) we were in possession of God's perfect plan for us—an everlasting existence of bliss, in relationship with him; (2) we lost it through sin; and (3) God's plan was restored to us through the sacrifice of Christ, so that once again we are in possession of everlasting life and joy in God. In this way of thinking, the dynamic, journey-oriented elements of God's plan, like sanctification, are subordinated as footnotes to the fact that we are saved and going to heaven. It becomes a story of us swapping one status for another.

Much of the patristic tradition viewed the matter in more dynamic terms. It was not the case that Adam and Eve were in possession of the full consummation of God's plan, viewed as an unchanging status; rather, they were seen as having been placed at the beginning of a process of growth and spiritual maturation in the context of their relationship with God. He created a world, as it were, at the outset of a journey, and the intent was for it to grow into greater communion with him, with humanity as the agents and mediators of this process. With this in mind, there is good reason to begin our biblical study by looking at the end. If Eden was more of a launchpad than a final destination, then to understand God's work we need to look at the ultimate end, pictured for us in the visions of Revelation 21–22.

When we study the imagery of the new heavens and new earth in Revelation 21–22, we are immediately confronted with two overlapping sets of symbols: those referring to the temple, and those referring to Eden. John begins by pointing to Isaiah's prophecy of "a new heaven and a new earth" (Isa 65:17), but rather than designating two distinct realities, with heaven on one side and earth on the other, the most immediate symbol is a symbol of union. This is not simply another earth and another heaven, existing apart from each other, but the coming together of both into one new reality, fused by the presence of God himself. The first symbol John sees is that of the union between husband and wife: the new Jerusalem descends from heaven as a bride coming to meet her groom (Rev 21:1–3). This city, the place of union between heaven and earth, is described in detail in 21:9—22:4, first in terms of the temple, and then in terms of Eden.

The city "shone with the glory of God," a fulfillment of the way the shekinah glory of God inhabited the temple (v. 11). The twelve gates and twelve foundations show it to be the community of the whole people of God (vv. 12–14). When it is measured (an act that mirrors the temple-vision of Ezek 40–42), the city is found to be perfectly cube-shaped (vv. 15–16). These dimensions do not make much sense for a city, but they bear a powerful meaning in view of the temple: the holy of holies, the innermost sanctum where the presence of God rested, had the same proportions, being as long and wide as it was high. The entirety of the new Jerusalem is presented here as the holy of holies, where God dwells in the midst of his creation. Even the precious stones which make up the foundations and gates call to mind the ornamentation of the temple, such as the breastplate worn by the high priest (vv. 18–21).

John makes the temple connection plain in v. 22: "I did not see a temple in the city, because the Lord God Almighty and the Lamb are its temple." He then goes on to describe God's presence in terms of light and glory, very much in the way God's presence in the temple is described throughout the Old Testament (vv. 23–25). There is no need for a temple here, because the presence of God fills and indwells the whole city just as he did in the holy of holies of old. This is a vision of God's redeemed covenant community, restored and exalted to what it was meant to be: a temple of the glory of God, where he is united to his people with all the splendor and joy of a bride and a groom.

The vision does not end there, though. It shifts its focus from temple analogies to Eden analogies in Revelation 22. These symbols come in quick succession: first "the river of the water of life" in the middle of the city (vv. 1–2). One of the distinguishing features of Eden was its great river, which split into four and watered the nations of the earth. Another feature of Eden pops up in verse 2: the tree of life, now freely offered to all of God's people. And then in verse 3 John caps the Eden analogy by declaring, "No longer will there be any curse." The effects of the fall from Eden have been entirely undone in Christ. John sums it up with a quick note about the redeemed people of God who live there, and his words ring with the call and vocation of the royal priesthood: "His servants will serve him. They will see his face, and his name will be on their foreheads" (Rev 22:3–4). Each of these three phrases—serving God, seeing his face, his name on their foreheads—would have called to mind the way that priests sought God's presence in the temple and were marked on their foreheads with his divine name (Exod 28:36–38).

So, to sum up: the Bible's final vision of the consummation of God's plan shows the entirety of his created order (earth and heaven together) as a temple of his glory, and this temple is presented in terms of a fulfillment of Eden. If we take that clue, and go back to our original question—Why did God create the universe?—then the answer comes out clearly, shown in God's revelation of its ultimate destiny: God created the universe to be a temple, so that his beloved people may dwell in union with him. And since that very vision of Revelation 21–22 shows itself as the fulfillment of Eden, it is worth following the trail of clues to our next question: Is this vision of creation as a temple visible in Genesis 1–3 as well? After all, if God's intended design for creation was to be a vast, glorious, cosmic temple, then we should see signs of that identity in the creation stories themselves.

How to Read Genesis 1

People love to fight over Genesis. Here in our scientific age, many Christians come to the creation accounts with a theological agenda and a scientific conception already in mind, ready to swing their hammers until either the text or the science (or, preferably, both) neatly adheres to their ideas. Now, to be fair, such considerations are not inconsequential, and the creation accounts should be studied carefully in light of such things. But the trouble comes when the only questions we ask of the text are scientific ones. If you only ask technical questions about how the world came together, you are probably never going to see what was plainly obvious to many ancient interpreters: that Genesis is first and foremost a theological text, speaking of the meaning of creation at least as much as it spoke of the exact manner of its making.

We tend to focus on the question of how creation came about. What is the exact historical narrative of creation? How, scientifically speaking, did the world come into the form we recognize today? Again, those are not bad questions, but if we believe in the inspiration of Scripture, then we have to wrestle with the fact that those are probably not the main questions that Genesis 1–3 is trying to answer. The doctrine of inspiration includes the fact that God spoke through human authors in particular cultures, and the documents they wrote bear the marks of those cultures. In the case of Genesis, the culture in which the text was initially received was not nearly as interested in issues of scientific precision as our culture is. That does not mean that we are wrong to ask historical and scientific questions of the text, only that they are probably not the main point of the passages in question.

The argument that follows—for interpreting Genesis 1 as a temple text—is one that has been made by a number of Bible scholars recently. I should perhaps make clear that while I also propose Genesis 1 to be read as a temple text, in view of early church positions on the matter, I have no agenda toward promoting a particular historical or scientific view. That avenue of inquiry remains open and will not be touched upon here. The teachers of the patristic age had no trouble believing that Scripture could speak to several different levels of meaning at the same time. To study the text's theological meaning, then, is not to discredit its historical or scientific meaning. So while the primary meaning of Genesis 1 was often taken to be a theological allegory, many early church theologians also saw a valid historical narrative of creation in the text. Take, for instance, the closing books of Augustine's *Confessions*, written near the end of the fourth century, which include a detailed interpretation of Genesis 1 as a symbolic allegory of the human soul. In his writing, Augustine humbly acknowledges that no one can claim the infallible knowledge "that this and none other was the meaning which Moses had in mind when he wrote [these words]."[6]

The interpretation which we will examine, then, is offered in the same spirit of humble reflection that Augustine used. This interpretation is neither scientific nor allegorical, but it is theological. It seeks to answer the "why" question of creation, but not the "how." In that sense, it does not invalidate any historical or scientific view of the creation accounts, because it is answering a different set of questions altogether. As such, any Christian, regardless of their scientific views, should be able to consider the following interpretation and perhaps even hold it hand-in-hand with their own conceptions of science and history. A young-earth creationist and a theistic evolutionist would be equally able to consider and accept this theological window into the meaning of the creation accounts, because it founds itself on neither science nor history, but on the structure of Scripture itself.

---

6. Augustine, *Confessions* 12.24 (300–301).

The Creation Narratives as Temple Texts

As it happens, there is a good biblical argument that the creation narratives of Genesis were understood as temple texts. There are a few crucial pieces of evidence that we will examine with regard to the creation-as-temple thesis: (1) the argument from literary structure, comparing the format of Genesis 1 to the construction of the tabernacle at the end of Exodus; (2) the intentional reflections of Eden and the created order built into the tabernacle and temple; and (3) the possibility that God's "rest" on the Sabbath of creation week was understood in temple terms. Along the way, we will show that this evidence was recognized by early Jewish and Christian interpretations of Genesis. (A further line of evidence which is sometimes put forward in other works, but which we will not consider here, is a study of parallels between Genesis and other ancient Near Eastern temple texts.)

The first argument is one that has been around since biblical times. Ancient Jewish texts interpreted the construction of the tabernacle (the tent-like precursor of the temple) as a reenactment of the universe's creation. The tabernacle was meant to represent, in miniature form, the entirety of the cosmos. As one ancient midrash put it: "The tabernacle is equal to the creation of the world."[7] This understanding is not just found in rabbinical texts, but in the biblical prophets too, who speak of the world in the same terminology used to express the reality of God's abiding presence in the tabernacle and temple. In Isaiah's vision (6:1–3), the angels cry out, "The whole earth is full of his glory!" When we read such texts, we often interpret "glory" simply as an aesthetic word, an expression of radiant majesty, but ancient Jews likely would have thought of the temple as their first association for God's "glory," especially in the temple setting of Isaiah's story: it was a word that referred to God's presence in the holy of holies. The angels, then, were speaking of the whole world in temple terms.

At this point, it is worthwhile to pause and clear up a possible misconception. When we say, along with ancient rabbis and church fathers, that the universe was created as a temple, it is important to understand that this is a reference to the meaning of creation, and not to any structural features of its design. In other words, it is the cosmos itself that is the foundational reality of God's creation, of which the temple was a symbolic system intended to reflect and elucidate the meaning of that

---

7. Midrash *Tanh.* 11.2, quoted in Barker, *Temple Theology*, 17.

cosmos. It is not the case that God was so entranced with ancient Near Eastern temples that he decided to shape the universe according to that paradigm; rather, he used the symbolic systems of those cultures to communicate his intention for creation. So while we talk about the cosmos being a temple, we mean it primarily in terms of the underlying theological realities of God's intent for his universe.

Parallels in Literary Structure

Throughout the history of biblical interpretation, scholars have noted that there is an interesting pattern in Genesis 1. It is fairly obvious once you see it—so obvious, in fact, that it strikes many readers as an intentional structure. Tertullian describes this structure well: "God completed all his works in a specified order. At first, he laid them out in their unformed elements, so to speak. Then he arranged them in their finished beauty... He first gave [the earth] existence; then he filled it."[8] There are two stages of creation: making places, and then filling those places. The six days of God's creative activity in Genesis 1 are arranged, as it were, in two parallel columns. The first column, days one through three, describe God creating functional spaces. He makes broad areas or aspects of his creation, things like day and night, skies and waters, and finally, dry land (with vegetation considered as part of that functional space). In the second column—days four through six—God fills those functional spaces with elements that correspond to the matching day from the previous column (see the following chart for a visual layout of this pattern). So, for instance, day four, which matches day one in the previous column, describes the functional elements of sun, moon, and stars within the functional space of day and night. Day five shows the filling of the skies and waters with their functional elements—birds and water animals, respectively. And day six has God filling the functional space of the dry land and trees with animals and human beings.

The matching-column layout of Genesis 1 is striking when you see it. For some early Christian interpreters, this structure was taken as prima facie evidence that Genesis 1 was intended to be read with a primary layer of theological allegory.[9] Unfortunately, those allegorical interpretations could get pretty fanciful sometimes (for example, Augustine

---

8. Tertullian, *Against Hermogenes* 29 (ANF 4:493).
9. See, for instance, Origen, *On First Things* 4.1.16 (ANF 4:365).

turns the gathering of the waters into an allegory for the wicked desires of human souls). Nevertheless, there is a common thread that binds much early-church reflection on Genesis 1–3 together: the belief that its narratives describe humanity as having a priestly role; and if humanity is priestly, then the place where they are set must be a temple. As Lactantius put it plainly, God fashioned the first human to be "a priest of a divine temple."[10]

There is a good reason for why a priestly/temple connection was intuited from the structure of Genesis 1. In a parallel passage at the end of Exodus, the construction of the tabernacle is described using a similar textual structure. The two-columned layout of Genesis 1, with its description of functional spaces that are then filled with functional elements, is mirrored by the blueprint-style chapters at the end of the book of Exodus, describing exactly how God wanted the tabernacle to be designed. As even a casual reader of the Bible knows, those chapters are so full of painfully precise details that they can, at times, feel interminable. But it stands to reason that if God had such exact specifications for his tabernacle, it probably signified something important. My suggestion, gleaned from ancient Jewish and early Christian sources, is that the tabernacle did precisely that: it signified, in miniature form, the entire cosmos of God's creation.

There is a loose equivalent to the structure of Genesis 1 in the tabernacle plans of Exodus 36–39. In both cases, construction begins by building functional spaces—in creation, these are day/night, water/sky, and dry land; and in the tabernacle, Exodus 36 lays out detailed arrangements for the practical elements that produce functional spaces: the frames and curtains that form the walls of the tabernacle's rooms. Those rooms are the holy of holies (or most holy place), the sanctuary (holy place), and the courtyard just outside the tabernacle doors (the inner court, with its dual areas for the altar and the great basin).

With these functional spaces mapped out, they are then filled with functional elements. In the holy of holies, there was the ark of the covenant, with its cherubim and its special lid ("mercy seat"), which is made in Exodus 37:1–9. In the holy place, there was the table for the bread of the presence, the altar of incense, and the lampstand, which are made in Exodus 37:10–29. The inner court was dominated by the large bronze basin and the sacrificial altar, and their making is described in Exodus

---

10. Lactantius, *On the Anger of God* 14 (ANF 7:271).

38:1–8. Just as day/night were filled with their functional elements (sun, moon, stars), and water/sky with theirs (birds and water animals), and dry land/vegetation with theirs (land-dwelling animals), so also the set of functional spaces in the tabernacle is endowed with the functional elements proper to each. And here's the key point: several ancient sources directly relate these areas of the tabernacle with areas of created reality that they are meant to represent: the basin is the sea, the altar is the dry land, the sanctuary stands for the physical heavens, and the holy of holies for the heaven beyond space and time, where God dwells.[11]

There is still another parallel between the two passages which underscores their similarity: in each case, the description of creation/construction concludes with the identification of a functional agent within the temple. In the case of Genesis 1's cosmic temple, the functional agent is humanity—the climax of the account is the creation of Adam and Eve on the sixth day, who are endowed with dominion over all other creatures. And, as it happens, the climax of the chapters describing the tabernacle's construction also focuses on a functional agent: the priests. In Exodus 39, after all the instructions are given for the areas of the tabernacle and the elements within, there follows a detailed account of the commission and function of the priesthood.

In the final scenes of assembling and consecrating the tabernacle, there are even more reflections of creation. Exodus 39:43 sounds as if it is intentionally echoing the refrain of Genesis 1, in which God looks over the completed work and affirms it as good: "Moses inspected the work and saw that they had done it just as the LORD had commanded. So Moses blessed them." Then in Exodus 40:33, the final scene of tabernacle assembly concludes with: "And so Moses finished the work," echoing Genesis 2:2's phrase, "God had finished the work." Further, Exodus 40:17 tells us that the tabernacle was erected on the first day of the first month, which is perhaps yet another allusion to the creation of the world "in the beginning."

The similarity of structure between the two accounts is laid out in the following charts, following one of several traditional interpretations of the creation/tabernacle correspondence. In this conception, which undergirds much of the practice of ancient Jewish worship, the tabernacle lays out the created order with spaces for God, for heavenly creation, and for earthly creation. This corresponds roughly with Genesis 1's pattern

---

11. See Josephus, *Antiquities* 3.181, in *Complete Works*, 106–7.

of describing God in his eternal existence ("in the beginning"), and then narrating the creation of heavenly realities (the parallel works of Days 1 and 4), followed by the creation of earthly realities (Days 2, 3, 5, and 6).

Creation (Gen 1)	
Functional Spaces	**Functional Elements/Inhabitants**
"In the beginning"—infinite eternity, beyond space & time	God
Day 1: Heavenly cosmos, light/darkness	Day 4: Heavenly lights (sun, moon, stars)
Day 2: Water, sea, sky	Day 5: Birds, fish, sea animals
Day 3: Dry land (with vegetation)	Day 6: Land animals
Climax: Functional Agent Humanity	

Tabernacle/Temple Layout (Exod 36–40)	
Functional Spaces	**Functional Elements**
Holy of Holies—God's preexistent reality before time	Ark of the Covenant, cherubim, etc.
Sanctuary (corresponding to Day 1 of creation—the heavenly spaces)	Lampstand (corresponding to heavenly lights—Day 4), with table, incense, etc.
Inner court areas (corresponding to Days 2–3 of creation—earthly spaces)	Bronze basin (corresponding to the waters—Day 5)
Inner court areas (corresponding to Days 2–3 of creation—earthly spaces)	Altar for burnt offerings (corresponding to the dry land and animals—Day 6)
Climax: Functional Agent Priests	

On its own, this rough parallelism might not seem all that convincing, were it not for the evidence that the tabernacle and temple were expressly designed to call to mind the cosmic temple of creation, and were understood that way in ancient Jewish teachings. Consider, for example, the Jewish historian Josephus:

> If anyone, without prejudice and with judgment, looks upon these things, he will find they were all made in way of imitation and representation of the universe. Moses distinguished the tabernacle into three parts and allowed two of them to the priests, as a place accessible and common [the sanctuary and inner court], he denoted the land and the sea, these being of

general access to all [the basin/altar area]; but he set apart the third division for God [the holy of holies], because heaven is inaccessible to men.[12]

In Josephus's view, the parallelism between the tabernacle and the universe should be clear to all, and he sketches it out in three basic tiers: the inner court area with the basin and altar, which represent the sea and land of the physical earth; the sanctuary of the tabernacle, accessible to all priests, which stands for the physical heavens (indeed, he goes on later in the passage to associate the seven-branched lampstand with the seven heavenly bodies visible to the naked eye—the sun, moon, and five of the planets); and the holy of holies, reserved for God alone, representing God's heavenly existence beyond space and time. This gave to the worship of Israel a perpetual sense of ascent toward God in their worship, an idea that would carry over to much of the way that early Christians conceived of their worship.

Parallels between Eden and the Tabernacle/Temple

The second line of evidence concerns a number of intentional parallels between the garden of Eden and the tabernacle/temple. One easy parallel is simply to note that the tabernacle and temple were decorated as if they were representations of the garden of Eden. The Old Testament's temple designs include multiple images of trees, fruit, and animals (Exod 37:17–21; 39:24–26; 1 Kgs 6:18, 29–25; 7:17–22, 29, 36, 42; 2 Chr 3:16; 4:4, 13; Ezek 41:17–20, 25–26). The lampstand in the sanctuary was designed to look like a blossoming tree, which has often been taken as a reference to Eden's tree of life. Even the two great pillars outside Solomon's temple, wreathed in pomegranates, have been interpreted as references to the two trees of Eden (1 Kgs 7:15–22). Josephus records other ancient traditions of imagery within the tabernacle, including the detail that the great curtain between the sanctuary and the holy of holies was woven with intricate floral designs.[13] For a religion that is often associated with the prohibition of images in worship, it is striking just how many images appear in these texts. Their presence—pomegranates, palm trees, and the occasional animal—points directly back to the experience of Eden. In

---

12. Josephus, *Antiquities* 3.180–81, in *Complete Works*, 106–7 (material in brackets added); see also 3.123.

13. Josephus, *Antiquities* 3.126, in *Complete Works*, 103.

fact, Ezekiel, whose temple visions also record the presence of these images, in another passage refers to Eden as a "sanctuary," a term usually referring to the tabernacle or temple (28:13, 18).

Both the temple and Eden also feature cherubim—understood in ancient Judaism as throne-angels (Pss 80:1; 99:1; Isa 37:16; Ezek 10:20; cf. Josephus, *Antiquities* 3.137)—whose appearance signifies the presence of God, much as a flag flying at Buckingham Palace tells one when the Queen is in residence. Cherubim were among the main decorations inside the holy of holies, but Exodus 26:31 tells us that they were also pictured on the great curtain, so their images would have been prominent in the sanctuary as well. The cherubim at the gates of Eden (Gen 3:24) show the garden to be a place of divine residence, just as in the holy of holies. One ancient Jewish document, *Jubilees* (2nd century BCE) says it plainly: "the garden of Eden was the holy of holies and the dwelling of the Lord."[14] In another place, *Jubilees* implies again that Eden is to be understood as a holy sanctuary, applying the same purity requirements to Eve's condition there as to Israelite women at the temple courts.[15]

Further, the terminology used for Adam and Eve's life in the garden of Eden is strikingly similar to language used for priestly service. In Genesis 2:15, God puts Adam in Eden and tells him to "cultivate and keep" it. These two verbs are fairly common and occur throughout the Old Testament, often rendered as "serve" rather than the more specific "cultivate," and "guard" rather than "keep." The duties of priests and Levites at the tabernacle and temple are often referred to in the same way—serving the Lord and guarding/keeping the sanctuary.

Yet another shared image of Eden and the temple is that of rivers. One of the dominant features of the garden is that it is the source of a great river, which then splits into four major rivers to water the regions of the earth. But where, you might ask, is the parallel image of rivers in the temple? There is no river at all there, neither in the tabernacle of the exodus years, nor in Solomon's Temple in Jerusalem. But there are rivers connected to the temple—not in the physical, historical buildings, but repeatedly in liturgical and prophetic references. Intriguingly, two of the major visions of the temple both include rivers as part of their imagery (Ezekiel's vision in Ezek 40–47, and John's in Rev 21–22; cf. Ps 36:8–9; *Odes of Solomon* 6.8). Ezekiel actually sees a river pouring out from the

---

14. *Jub.* 8.19 (*OTP* 2:73); cf. *1 En.* 25 (*OTP* 1:26); Ephrem the Syrian, *Hymns on Paradise* 3 (90–96).

15. *Jub.* 3.9–12 (*OTP* 2:59).

temple and bringing life to the regions to which it flows (47:1–12), much as the river of Eden flows out and brings water to the nations. And while the physical structure of Solomon's Temple did not feature a river, the flowing water necessary for purification rites (called "living water" in Jewish usage) would likely have been a very present feature.

God's Rest

Our third line of evidence is based on a particular reading of God's "rest" as described at the end of God's creative work (Gen 2:1–3). Scholars through the ages have debated what these verses signify, because they present an obvious theological problem: Why would an omnipotent deity need to rest? Perhaps, some have speculated, the idea of rest simply refers to a cessation of activity. But if so, it is not entirely clear why such importance is given to the occurrence: Why should God bless the seventh day, make it holy, and declare its observance a lasting ordinance for his people, if it simply marks an absence of activity? There are lots of good answers to these questions, including the possibility that God was intentionally setting a precedent designed for the good of mankind and the flourishing of humanity's relationship with him. Jesus, after all, teaches that "the Sabbath was made for humans" (Mark 2:27). There is also the rich theological parallelism between God's rest on the seventh day of creation and Jesus' "rest" in death on the Sabbath of Holy Week, an idea of which we will have more to say in chapter 6.

But the Old Testament itself testifies to another use of the "rest" of God: it is the way God's abiding presence in the temple is described. Consider what Solomon says at the dedication of the temple: "Now arise, Lord God, and come to your resting place . . ." (2 Chr 6:41; cf. 1 Chr 28:2; Ps 132:8, 14; Isa 66:1). This is true not only of the Old Testament, but of temple texts in ancient Near Eastern cultures more generally: a god or goddess was said to rest in their temple, as if enjoying the fruits of their labor after having completed a work. Within the background of that cultural context, it seems plausible that this is how God's rest in Genesis 2 would have been understood. God had finished his work of creation, and now he rested—that is, he took up residence in his new temple, to dwell there and enjoy the fruits of his labors, as it were. The universe, then, would have been his temple, and Eden his holy of holies.

3

Human Identity: The Royal Priests of Eden

IN ANTHONY HOPE'S CLASSIC 1894 adventure novel, *The Prisoner of Zenda*, the soon-to-be-crowned king of Ruritania (a fictional European country), is abducted and locked away in a castle. But thanks to the heroics of a lookalike English visitor, the king is eventually released from his chains and restored to his throne. *The Prisoner of Zenda* is a winsome, compelling rescue story, made all the more dramatic because the prisoner was royalty and the wellbeing of an entire nation hung in the balance.

When we describe the essence of the gospel, we sometimes tend to focus on the pivotal transition of the climax: the prisoner is set free! We sinners are now saved, thanks to the grace of our Lord Jesus Christ. That is, without question, the heart of the gospel as it applies to our individual Christian lives. But to leave it there is to leave out something rather important. It is like telling the story of *The Prisoner of Zenda* without ever mentioning the fact that the man who was rescued was royalty, and that in freeing him, he was put back in a position to reign. It's still a fun little caper with a dramatic and beautiful conclusion, but we've lost a bit of what makes the story so grand to begin with. The ancient Christian view of salvation thought it important to include some of those details that we so often leave out: that we human beings, the prisoners who were freed, had been intended to be the priestly kings and queens of God, and in our salvation, we are restored to the glories of our former office.

The Image of God and Our Royal Identity

So far, we have looked at arguments for regarding creation as a temple of God. This perspective is much more than just a curiously different view of creation—some early Christian writers saw it as an essential proof for the status they claimed for human beings. That is, if creation is the temple of God, then that fact bears tremendous meaning for understanding who we were meant to be. Human beings were the royal priests of creation, and the fathers and mothers of the early church saw this identity woven throughout Scripture. As Clement of Alexandria wrote of the Spirit-led Christian: "He is, then, the truly kingly man; he is the sacred high priest of God."[1]

Just as priests were the functional agents of God's sanctuary, described at the end of the tabernacle-assembly chapters in Exodus, so too humans are the functional agents set in the sanctuary-garden at the end of the creation narrative of Genesis. Temples and priests went together in the ancient Near Eastern cultures of Old Testament times, and so if creation was a temple, then it stands to reason there would be a priestly class established to serve within it. But what about the royal part of "royal priesthood?" Clearly, there is more to the story than simply a priestly identity, as important as that is. When one considers the identity of human beings as portrayed in the creation stories, it is impossible to miss this royal element. A great many Bible scholars have noted these themes, particularly in regard to the "image of God" language used in Genesis 1:26–27, but for our purposes we will simply touch on them briefly. It should be apparent to everyone who reads Genesis 1 that humanity is endowed with a vast measure of authority: human beings are expressly told to "subdue" the earth and "rule over" its creatures (1:28; cf. 1:26). Later, Adam is given the task of establishing names for the animals, thus underscoring his status of being in charge of all of them.

One of the signposts pointing to our royal identity comes in the repeated refrain of humanity being made "in the image of God," an idea expressed three times within the span of two verses (Gen 1:26–27). Theologians throughout the ages have theorized as to what exactly this "image" language means in a practical sense. Many classic interpretations point to the way that we, apart from all other animals, exhibit characteristics that reflect the character of God: reason, creativity, moral awareness, and so on. Even as all creation shows evidences of God's being, character, and

---

1. Clement of Alexandria, *Miscellanies* 7.7 (*ANF* 2:533).

nature (Rom 1:28), it is especially so with humans, who reflect aspects of the divine Maker in ways that other creatures simply do not.[2] The parallel usage of the phrase in Genesis 5:3, in relation to the birth of Adam's son Seth, suggests that humanity reflects the likeness of God as a child would its parent.

Another possible aspect of the image of God, and one that is a direct corollary to the creation-as-temple idea, is the fact that temples in the ancient Near East included an image as an essential part of their structure and function. Usually, of course, this is viewed in the Bible as a bad thing, and these images are called idols, but such reproaches apply only in the case of false gods, wherein humans are lured into the destructive fantasy of setting their worship upon inanimate objects. In God's creation-temple, it is not a senseless idol of wood or stone that has been set up, but a living, breathing reflection of the character of God himself, and here the image is not the worshiped one, but the worshiper.

There is yet another interpretation of the image of God which has connections to ancient Near Eastern cultures. In an age far before any of our modern technologies, the administration of a king's reign in his outlying provinces had to be overseen by officials. These officials would bear seals of the king's symbol or of his very likeness, so that the areas they administered would know that they bore the authority of the king himself. As such, these image-bearers of the king were seen as directly exercising the sovereign rule of the royal court, even though the king himself happened to be elsewhere. Ignatius of Antioch, one of the earliest church fathers, may allude to this idea in the way he opens his epistles, regularly describing himself as "Ignatius the Image-Bearer." If this sort of cultural identity does indeed lie behind the terminology of "the image of God," then it, too, would tend toward an interpretation of human beings as bearers of God's royal authority, just as God's commission for them to subdue the earth and rule over the animals would seem to suggest.

Early Christian writers put a great deal of emphasis on the idea of humanity being made in the image of God, in ways that spoke not only of each human being's inherent value, but as monuments of God's grandeur too glorious to fully describe. Consider what Gregory of Nyssa, one of the Cappadocian fathers of the fourth century, said about this:

> Know to what extent the Creator has honored you above all the rest of creation. The sky is not an image of God, nor is the

---

2. See Athanasius, *On the Incarnation* 3 (NPNF² 4:37).

> moon, nor the sun, nor the beauty of the stars.... You alone have been made in the image of the Reality that transcends all understanding, the likeness of imperishable beauty, the imprint of true divinity, the recipient of beatitude, the seal of the true light.... There is nothing so great among beings that it can be compared with your greatness."[3]

Lest one worry, however, that this view of things is a trifle too anthropocentric, focusing attention on the glory of humanity rather than of Christ, it should be noted that many early church fathers made it a point to use the language of image in a slightly different way than we sometimes do. While it has become common parlance in theological circles to refer to humans simply as "the image of God" (often in the Latin, *imago Dei*), there was a consistent thread of early Christianity which chose to say such things only in a very particular way, and would not directly equate the image of God with human beings. While it is possible, biblically speaking, to say that humans *are* the image of God (see, for example, 1 Cor 11:7), the use of the term in Scripture more commonly reserves that ascription for Christ: he *is* the image of the invisible God (Col 1:15; 2 Cor 4:4; cf. Heb 1:3), and we humans are made *in* the image of God (Gen 1:26–27; 9:6). That little word "in" was a common marker for early Christianity's discussion of human identity, so while speaking of the image of God puts us in a position of glory, "in" puts us in a position of submission to Christ. It is our great and glorious calling to be, in Martin Luther's famous words, "little Christs," radiating the likeness of him who actually is the full, visible form of God (Rom 8:29; 1 Cor 15:49; 2 Cor 3:18). Thus, while early Christians took the rhetoric of humanity's identity to lofty heights, they also took care to note that Christ's glory was incomparably greater, and, in fact, our glory is quite simply drawn from him, the Image Absolute.[4]

Prophet, Priest, and King?

At this point, it would be good to pause and consider a brief excursus, because the following question might be present in some readers' minds: Why are we only focusing on priesthood and kingship, and not on the

---

3. Gregory of Nyssa, *Second Homily on the Song of Songs*, quoted in Clément, *Roots*, 79.
4. See Athanasius, *On the Incarnation* 11 (*NPNF*[2] 4:42).

office of prophet as well? Wasn't Jesus, from whom our identity and purpose derives, known to be "prophet, priest, and king?" So why aren't we also exploring the office of prophecy in our human identity?

The triad of prophet, priest, and king is so well known in the Christian tradition as to be practically axiomatic. The only trouble is that it is not really a biblical paradigm. As near as we can tell, it was first coined by Eusebius of Caesarea in the fourth century. While it is true that Jesus was the definitive climax of all three roles, grouping them together as a triad blurs the lines a bit. It makes us expect to find "prophet" as a parallel category to "priest" and "king," and blinds us to the fact that throughout Scripture, priesthood and kingship exist in a special relationship with one another. Priesthood and kingship emerge, over and over again, as a linked set of dual roles. One sees it not only in the New Testament passages we have examined ("royal priesthood," "kingdom and priests"), but also in major characters like Melchizedek, in the rituals of the people of Israel (such as anointing, reserved for kings and priests), and in expectations of the Messiah (as in the messianic prophecies of Zechariah, which keep both the royal house of David and the office of high priest constantly in view). Prophets are important, and Christ was certainly the ultimate fulfillment of the prophetic office, but the prophet's role does not seem to be fundamental to human identity in the same way that priesthood and kingship are. The office of prophet was exercised by particular humans toward other humans, as empowered by God. The priestly and kingly parts of our identity, by contrast, have to do with the very way we were created, and how we relate not only to other humans, but to the totality of God's creation.

A Microcosm of All Creation

This leads us to an important reflection. Humanity's roles are dual (priestly and royal) because of the unique position of human beings in God's creation. In the patristic conception, human beings stand in the middle, between God and the rest of creation, and the role that we call priestly is simply an aspect of our task of mediating creation's worship toward God, and the role that we call royal is an aspect of our task of mediating God's sovereignty toward creation. We are not royal priests just because God arbitrarily decided to festoon us with the cultural offices of the ancient

Near East; rather, those identities are windows to the fundamental reality of our position in God's created order.

Consider the entire scope of God's creation: stars, comets, cherubim, planets, oceans, animals, seraphim, mountains, trees, etc. If you were to make a single metaphysical distinction to group all of these things into two broad categories of how they are constituted (that is, what they are made of), what would it be? You might start by trying to divide God's creations between living beings and nonliving, but that doesn't really address the issue of what each created thing is made of. Or you may try to make a distinction between those creations here on our planet and those in outer space, but the same issue arises again, and in this case, you also run into trouble with the angels. It won't quite do to say that angels are in outer space in the same way that stars and comets are. No, one quickly realizes that the only distinction that neatly organizes all of God's creation into two big categories (regarding what they are made of) is something like material versus spiritual. The terms one could use here are somewhat fluid, but all Christian doctrine has always agreed that God's creations are made either of physical matter and energy (the entirety of our visible universe) or of spirit (angels, demons, etc.). This material/spiritual distinction is the only one that covers all the bases of everything God has made.

Now, here's the thing: there is one creature in all of God's created order that does not fit that paradigm. The problem is not that it's something other than matter or spirit; the problem is that—unlike everything else that exists—it is both. We are talking, of course, about human beings. Humans exist in this startlingly unique position of being material/spiritual hybrids (but hybrids who retain the fullness of both their material and spiritual existence). No other creations of the physical universe—not mountains, not the sun, not any animals—are spiritual beings in the same way that humans are, with the ability to relate to God in a conscious and intentional way. On the other side of the coin, no other creations of the angelic realm are material beings in the same way that humans are. Angels have no natural kinship with the physical world, but we do. We are utterly, staggeringly unique. Everything else in the entire universe falls into one of these two categories, except us.

In this sense, then, humanity stands at the center of God's creation, as the only creature with one foot planted in both the physical and spiritual worlds. If that sounds like a strange idea, it's good to remember two things. First, it's a notion that's firmly grounded in the doctrines that

Christians have always believed; it is simply implicit in the way we understand the nature of the created order. And second, it fits the biblical conception of humanity's nature. This is essentially the same paradigm you find portrayed in Psalm 8:5-8—humans are created "a little lower than the angels" and yet we are rulers, with all physical creatures "under [our] feet." We stand in between angelic and animal creation, and we humans are "crowned . . . with glory and honor."

Early Christian writings, speaking of our spiritual and physical aspects, regularly refer to humans as "a microcosm of the cosmos" (a turn of phrase that shows up not only in theological treatises, but in the communal prayers of the early church, perhaps derived from earlier Jewish usage).[5] In other words, each one of us is a tiny representation of what the whole creation is: both physical and spiritual. In Origen's words, each of us is "a universe in miniature."[6] Here's how Gregory of Nazianzus, another of the Cappadocian fathers, explains it:

> The great Architect of the universe conceived and produced a being endowed with both natures, the visible and the invisible. . . . Thus in some way a new universe was born, small and great at one and the same time. God set this hybrid worshiper on earth to contemplate the visible world, and to be initiated into the invisible; to reign over earth's creatures, and to obey orders from on high. He created a being at once earthly and heavenly . . . flesh and spirit at the same time.[7]

Since we stand in this middle position in all creation, we are uniquely situated to act as representatives of the material world in the spiritual realm, and representatives of the spiritual realm in the material world. This puts us squarely in the sort of mediatory and representative role that priests held in the ancient world. Priests were the ones who represented humans before God, and God before humans. They bore the worship of the people into the presence of God, and bore the teachings, blessings, and judgments of God back to the people. They were the cosmic go-betweens, and that is exactly what humanity, in its very nature, appears to have been created to be. To call us go-betweens, though, risks treating too lightly what is a great and momentous role. We are the only creature

---

5. See *Apostolic Constitutions* 7.34.6; 8.9.8; 8.12.16 (*OTP* 2:679, 689, 692).

6. Origen, *Fifth Homily on Leviticus* 2, quoted in Clément, *Roots*, 78.

7. Gregory of Nazianzus, Oration 45, 7, quoted in Clément, *Roots*, 77; cf. John of Damascus, *Exact Exposition* 2.12 (*Writings*, 234-39).

who can walk in both worlds; or, to put it in temple terms, the only creature fashioned to serve at both the altar and the holy of holies. In order to preserve the awe-inspiring sense of what it means to be God's royal priesthood, Maximus the Confessor liked to turn the tables on the microcosm language, and insist that humanity was, if anything, a macrocosm!

This sort of position is not only priestly, but kingly. The two roles are really one role, understood in two aspects. We are priestly when we serve by offering the praises and bounty of the material world in worship and gratitude to God, and we are royal when we administer the practical outworking of the reign of God in the material world. (There are even indications that the royal part of our identity will one day extend over the angelic realm as well—as Paul says, "we will judge angels," 1 Cor 6:3). In each case, priestly and royal, these roles are simply an expression of our position as the microcosm set in the middle of the cosmos. At the risk of oversimplifying it, the priestly/royal dynamic can be understood as the two directions in which God's relationship with his creation is mediated through humanity: from creation upwards toward God, through humans as priests, and from God downwards toward creation, through humans as reigning agents of divine rule. (This is not a perfect encapsulation, but hopefully it serves to illustrate the principle in some small way.)

You begin to see, then, how this idea of royal priesthood is far more than just a poetic image from cultures long gone. It is not about the trappings and rituals of being a priest in the ancient Near East, and it is not about the status and practices of monarchs in biblical times. It is about who humanity is, vis-à-vis God and the world, and the priestly and kingly dimensions of our singular role are symbolic lenses by which we can understand our identity.

Growing into Our Identity

If one looks closely at Genesis, though, there is another aspect of our calling to consider. The shape of our identity as royal priests of creation was something that we were meant to grow into. Our office was a part of a grand process intended to draw us ever deeper into the knowledge and experience of God. It was an office of movement, including goals that would push us outward, a mission that would not have left humans in a settled state of bliss in the garden of Eden. Consider the fact that God's original commission to humanity was one that would require us to leave the garden: "Fill the earth and subdue it" (Gen 1:28). As we have seen, early Christian tradition associated the garden of Eden with the holy of holies, but the entire cosmos was the larger temple, and we had duties in it that would send us ever onward and outward.

This notion strikes some Christians as strange, because many of us may have assumed that Adam and Eve were in full and perfect possession of God's eternal will for their lives before they fell into sin. If they had not sinned, we tend to think, then they could have stayed in paradise forever. But this is not necessarily the picture Genesis paints, at least not if we take the commission of Genesis 1:28 seriously. It seems, rather, that as Adam and Eve grew into their roles, their work would have taken them (or their children) beyond the bounds of paradise, to help the rest of creation also grow into its identity as God's great temple.

Such an idea probably would not have struck early Christians as strange, because they tended to assume that Adam and Eve were created on a growth trajectory. The *Odes of Solomon*, a collection of early Christian hymns, includes a lovely line which describes humans in paradise as those "who grow in the growth of [God's] trees."[8] Adam and Eve's life in Eden was not regarded as a settled state, but as a starting-point from which they would grow. Athanasius assumed that even if they had remained in a state of holy bliss in Eden's paradise, God's plan for them would ultimately lead them toward the experience of blessedness now enjoyed in heaven itself.[9]

This is one of the main differences between patristic readings of the Eden narratives and some of the currently dominant readings, and it is worth taking a moment to understand it, because each position assumes a particular theological anthropology that shapes a great deal of the way we view the Christian life. Many early Christians viewed human nature as developmental, a dynamic essence with a call upon it to grow in a radically Godward direction. As such, their view of Christian experience has a great deal to say about such things as being transformed into Christ's glory (2 Cor 3:18) and participating in the divine nature (2 Pet 1:4). Some later Christian traditions, by contrast, view human nature more through the lens of a static reality, an essence which is either in the state of needing salvation or in the state of having obtained salvation, and such Christians tend to have a great deal to say about those parts of Christian experience

---

8. *Odes of Solomon* 11.19 (*OTP* 2:745).
9. Athanasius, *On the Incarnation* 3 (*NPNF*² 4:37).

which can be understood in terms of settled states, like legal justification. To call attention to this contrast is not to suggest that one is right and the other is wrong, since both perspectives are well-grounded in Scripture, but simply to draw attention to complementary aspects of theological anthropology which we might otherwise have missed.

The interpretation of the Eden narratives is one of the places where you can see this contrast clearly, because a great many patristic writers tell that story in a way that is unfamiliar to many modern Christians. They are not, to be clear, saying anything unbiblical, but they read certain assumptions between the lines of Genesis that are different from the assumptions that some later generations of Christians were inclined to see. Two of the most common such assumptions were (1) that Adam and Eve were created as moral infants—that is, although bodily adults, they were essentially still children in their spiritual life and moral understanding; and (2) that the tree of the knowledge of good and evil was intended to be a good gift of God, to be received when the time was right. By contrast, many later generations of interpreters take Adam and Eve to be rational adults in full possession of their powers, and the tree of knowledge is presented as a straightforward test of obedience, the fruit of which is toxic to one's spiritual life. The important thing to realize is that Genesis does not actually include any of that information one way or the other; these are all simply assumptions that we bring to the text. The patristic assumptions, far from being a strange reading from the margins of the early church, form a strong and significant tradition in some of the earliest and most authoritative theological writers.

The patristic story of Eden focuses not only on Adam and Eve's blessedness in the garden, but also on their calling and capacity to grow into ever-greater beatitude in the presence of God. Theophilus, an early apologist, says that Adam was created with "means of advancement ... [for] maturing and becoming perfect."[10] Similarly, Irenaeus describes the initial condition of humanity as "being yet an infant."[11] While this language may sound strange to our ears, there is a good deal of sense to it; after all, we Christians, even when we are adults, are also regarded as moral infants who are called to a progressive trajectory of "growing in the grace and knowledge of our Lord Jesus Christ" (2 Pet 3:18; cf. John 3:3–5; Eph 4:13–15; Col 1:28; Heb 5:12–13; Jas 1:4; 1 Pet 2:2), rather than

---

10. Theophilus, *To Autolycus* 2.24 (*ANF* 2:104).
11. Irenaeus, *Against Heresies* 4.38 (*ANF* 1:521).

being automatically endowed with full spiritual maturity at the moment of our conversion. If that is true of us, who have been given the Spirit of adoption and are mystically united to Christ as his body, how much truer would it have been of Adam and Eve, who as yet did not have any of those spiritual benefits? No one would suppose that Adam and Eve were created at a full state of spiritual maturity—their rapid fall into disobedience is evidence enough of that—and so we must suppose that the intent was for them to walk a long road of learning God's ways in ever-deepening relationship with him. Adam, writes Clement of Alexandria, was "naturally adapted for the acquisition of virtue," which requires a movement, by Adam's free choices, toward exercising those attributes of God's character in which he could participate.[12]

Basil, another of the great Cappadocian fathers, read the commission to humanity in Genesis 1:28 as "*grow* and multiply and fill the earth," assuming that it meant not only to be fruitful by having children, but to grow in a spiritual sense as well. Basil then went on to describe humanity's high calling toward maturity and godliness: "[Our Creator] allowed us to be artisans of the likeness of God," for by learning and exercising Christian virtues, empowered by the Holy Spirit, we become conformed to the divine image of Christ. "What is Christianity?" he asks. "Likeness to God as far as is possible for human nature."[13]

This view of Adam and Eve as developmental beings, whether you find it a compelling perspective or not, gives us an important window to consider the nature of our own calling, and will help us frame our minds for our later discussions of our experience of union with God. Humans were designed as developmental beings, not just physically, but spiritually as well, and we all inherited an open invitation, encoded in our spiritual wiring, to undertake the greatest pilgrimage of all: an ever-rising, upward adventure into the wisdom, knowledge, and grace of God, growing into greater union with our Creator.

This growth track view of the Eden narratives is also visible in the way many early Christian writers dealt with the tree of knowledge. Genesis does not tell us much about the tree, except that its fruit looks good and that breaking God's commandment by eating it would lead to death. But it does not answer the question of why the tree is even there in the first place. Many commentators have suggested it is simply a test of

---

12. Clement of Alexandria, *Miscellanies* 6.12 (*ANF* 2:502), wording updated.

13. Basil, First Discourse on the Origin of Humanity 12–17 (*On the Human Condition*, 40–45).

obedience, the first instance of God granting a commandment by which humans can live good and holy lives. That is certainly part of the answer, but that narrative can also lead some readers to unsettling questions of whether this sort of arrangement is even remotely fair. Suppose that I, as a father, announced to my children, "I'm leaving this pile of guns and knives right in the middle of the house, but you're not allowed to touch them, because they'll kill you." Now, if one of my children violated my command and died, most reasonable observers would not place the guilt of the incident on the child. As such, while some early church fathers did see God's command not to touch the tree as an example of his good and holy laws setting a test for our obedience, there was also a significant stream of early Christian reflection that took it a different way.

Some early Christian writers posited that the tree of knowledge was in fact a good gift of God, eventually intended for humanity's use when they had grown to the point of being able to receive it.[14] There are hints within the Genesis narrative that point to this being a plausible interpretation. One may begin by noting that "the knowledge of good and evil" is generally interpreted as a good thing—the ancient Jewish/Christian document *1 Enoch* simply calls it "the tree of wisdom."[15] In fact, Genesis shows God himself agreeing with the serpent's assessment (found in 3:5) that this fruit confers something of God's own character to the eater: "They have become like us," says God, "knowing good and evil" (3:22). Essentially, then, by eating the fruit, Adam and Eve have become more like God, according to whose likeness they were originally made (Gen 1:26). This might suggest that the fruit was a good and holy thing, since it is associated with God's own attributes, and it has granted to Adam and Eve a part of the heritage that was intended to be theirs from the beginning: the likeness of God. Their sin was in disobeying God's command and making use of it according to their own desires, rather than waiting in humble trust for God's plan to be made manifest.[16] Rather than being a cruel and capricious experiment, then, the tree of knowledge was something more akin to our experience of sexuality: an awesomely good, holy, and marvelous gift, but meant to be used at the right time and in the right way, according to God's gracious plan. Or, to use a temple analogy,

---

14. See John of Damascus, *Exact Exposition* 2.11 (*Writings*, 232–33), which explores two distinct sets of interpretations in patristic sources regarding the tree of knowledge.

15. *1 En.* 32.3–6 (*OTP* 1:28).

16. See *Epistle to Diognetus* 12.3 in Holmes, *Apostolic Fathers*, 716–17.

Ephrem the Syrian portrays the tree of knowledge as being like the great veil that leads to the holy of holies—an entrance into something so good as to be beyond our ability to describe, but at the same time, something so holy that it needs to be treated with tremendous care.[17] Indeed, the restriction on the tree of knowledge is very similar to later restrictions on touching the holiest things in the temple.

In any case, by disobeying God's command, Adam and Eve ruptured their relationship with God and derailed their intended growth into union with him. Now separated from God by their sin, they suffered the consequence of death, which early Christian theology saw not only as physical mortality, but as the corruption and decay of our spiritual natures, now cut off from the very source of all spiritual life, rather like a pond that stagnates and reeks of death after being cut off from its source of flowing water. Not only do we die physically as a result of our sin, and not only are we precluded from having eternal spiritual life, but we are also cut off from growing into the vibrant, marvelous destiny of being who we were meant to be here and now: vessels of God's glory, pouring forth "rivers of living water" (John 7:38).

Fallen Priesthood, Desolate Temple

The expulsion story of Genesis 3 is not just about us humans. It includes a curse on all physical creation: "Cursed is the ground because of you" (v. 17). This brokenness in nature is noted again in the New Testament when Paul says that the creation was "subjected to frustration" and is in a state of "bondage to decay" (Rom 8:20–21). To many readers, though, this fall of the natural world does not make a great deal of sense, nor does it seem particularly fair. Why should other parts of nature suffer for humanity's sin? If the problem of sin was my problem—a problem of my personal guilt, cutting myself off from God and resulting in spiritual death for me—then what did that have to do with an ocean or a mountain or an eagle? Why should they have to suffer for my crimes?

This is where the patristic view of humanity's priesthood, standing as the microcosm in the middle of the cosmos, comes to bear. Humans were priests of the temple of all creation. So when the priests abandoned their position, choosing their own way rather than God's, they left the temple desolate. For this reason, the fall has ripple effects throughout the

---

17. Ephrem the Syrian, *Hymns on Paradise* 3 (90–96).

entire created order. We were designed to fill a very particular role in the relationship between God and the cosmos, so when we shirked our position and fell away, that relationship between God and the cosmos was injured as well. If there are no priests serving in the temple, the temple cannot function in the way that was intended for it.

The whole cosmos suffers because of our sin, for we were made to be its kings and priests, and without us in our proper roles, it cannot live in the fullness of its proper relationship with its Creator. Rather as in C. S. Lewis's novel, *The Lion, the Witch, and the Wardrobe*, the harmony and order of all creatures can only be truly established when the Sons of Adam and Daughters of Eve reign from their thrones. But we, through our sin, have broken our upward unity with God, and so the downward unity that is meant to flow through us to all other things has also been ruptured. The cosmos is plunged into its experience of the curse, until the disease can be healed, the rupture reconciled, and God brings forth the New Creation.

4

The Temple: Rituals of Cosmic Reconciliation

WE HAVE ALL HAD the experience of being on the outside looking in. For many of us, we feel this most poignantly in our youth. Perhaps a group of friends has gathered for an activity of which we were left out. Perhaps the popular kids are enjoying their status without a second thought for those left watching from the wings. There is a poignant kind of sorrow with being on the outside. We know it well, because this is not just our individual experience, it is the story of our race. The expulsion narrative of Genesis 3 is the story of humanity's current condition. We are a race in exile, an exile of our own making. We stand on the outside, looking back at the sanctuary of Eden. But this, too—this feeling of being on the outside—is also part of the temple experience.

There is an emblematic story being told within the temple system of rituals, and for the vast majority of worshipers, it is a story of being on the outside looking in. In having a physical building which the worshipers were kept outside of, the temple served as a constant reminder that we humans were separated from God. Temples, in that way, are very different from our modern experiences of church. Unless you were a priest, you never got to go inside. You might be able to walk about in the courtyards of the temple, and perhaps even watch the rites of sacrifice at the great altar in front of the temple porch. But as for the temple building itself—the structure containing the sanctuary and the holy of holies—an ordinary worshiper simply could not go inside. This was a building that you only ever saw from the outside, and as such, it was a physical demonstration of being cut off from God. Even within the temple, the ordinary priests themselves could not set foot within the holy of holies; that was only for the high priest, and then only once a year.

Nevertheless, temples also offered an avenue toward restoring, in small and carefully guarded steps, the disrupted relationship between ourselves and God. It was not only a reminder of separation, but also a sign that that separation was not the original intent. Temples offered a way to set things right with God It is not enough to say that the temple system constitutes a symbol of being on the outside; we also must realize that it was an expression of love from a God who was working to draw us back to the point where, by his atoning grace, we could commune with him on the inside again.

In fact, many patristic writers thought they could hear this note of God's grace even in the painful stories of Adam and Eve being cast out of their sanctuary of Eden. The act of expulsion was more than just a punishment for sin; it was also thought to be an act of divine mercy. Humanity, in its sinful state, was cast out so that we might not partake of the tree of life in our sinful condition (Gen 3:22). "God . . . kept them back from eating of the Tree of Life, lest by eating of it and living forever, they would have to remain in a life of pain for eternity."[1] The tree of life was still meant for us, but now we were not in a state of being able to receive it. We would have to be outside for a time, in exile, but his sanctuary would still be there in our midst, a reminder that his plan to draw us to himself had never gone away.

If you look at the bookend accounts of the Bible—the temple texts of the garden of Eden and the new Jerusalem—you will notice a remarkable contrast with the actual temple. In these places, God is with his people in a very real way, and there is no physical building separating them from his presence. These accounts, revealing the foundation and the capstone of God's design, show that all the people are on the inside of the temple with God. It is no longer a symbol of separation, seen from the outside; now we are with God in the holy of holies, and the disrupted union has been restored.

This, then, is the meaning of the temple: it points toward the ultimate goal of God's plan for his creation, and that goal is *God with us*. In patristic theology, this goal is often described in terms of union. A temple was conceived of as the place where the realm of the divine intersected with the created order, and the innermost sanctum was the one physical

---

1. Ephrem the Syrian, *Commentary on Genesis* 2.35 (*Hymns on Paradise*, 223); cf. Irenaeus, *Against Heresies* 3.23.6 (*ANF* 1:457).

place in the world where God was present in a direct and unmediated way. This was what the garden of Eden was to the entire cosmos; and when Adam and Eve were shut out of Eden, they were closed off from their union with God in the holy of holies. The problem of the fall, symbolized and signified in the rites of the temple, is the problem of our disrupted union with God, and the whole symbology of the temple was pointing toward the ultimate restoration of that union.

Israel and All Humanity

This story of fall and exile is not just the story of Eden; it is the entire story of Israel writ large. God's great plan to draw humanity back into communion with himself would require him doing for us what we could not do for ourselves. Where we had disrupted that union, he would unite himself with humanity in the most intimate and earth-shattering way imaginable: the incarnation of Jesus Christ. And to get to that point, he readied a people to receive his presence, a people that he chose and loved out of all the nations of the world, a people who would symbolically enact the restoration of humanity's office as his royal priesthood.

One might ask what it means to call Israel "a kingdom of priests" (Exod 19:6), which is the same terminology that Peter and John use to refer to Christians in the New Testament. In a sense, Israel was simply being what all humanity had been intended to be, in the same way that their priests were being what God would call all Israelites to be: fully committed to his service with their whole lives. The priestly identity of humanity was held by a series of groups in ascending order, with the Israelite high priest at the summit. In essence, the high priest was perceived as the emblem of all Israel (bearing as he did the symbols of all twelve tribes on his breastplate), undertaking the identity intended for all until God restored it to all. In this sense, the high priest undertook the truly human vocation as a representative of the entire priestly clan; the priests as representatives of the tribe of Levi; the Levites as representatives of Israel; and Israel as representatives of all humanity.

Unfortunately, Israel's representation of all humanity can be seen not only in its glories but in its tragedies as well. Just as the story of our whole race is the story of our falling short of the glory of God and wandering in exile beyond the gates of Eden, so too Israel, throughout the Old Testament, repeats this cycle of fall and exile. You can see it in the exodus story, where sins of rebellion lead to a generation of exiled wandering beyond the boundaries of the promised land, and again in the stories of the dissolute and idolatrous monarchies, leading to the exile in Babylon. Yet the story of Israel is also a story of grace; exile never has the last word. It is a story of great restorations, of entering the promised land and of reinheriting the long-abandoned cities. So not only does the story of Israel encapsulate the story of our past, it also points forward, to the great restoration that was to come: the advent of the true High Priest who would unite humanity to God and usher in the New Creation.

Entering the Presence of God: The Temple as a Journey of Union

To understand the way temple worship worked, we must first understand that there were two movements associated with God's presence there: God's movement toward us, and our movement toward God as we responded to his gracious invitation. On the one hand, Israelites believed that God had come down, as it were, to enter their reality at this particular place and in this particular way. But on the other hand, it was also believed that entering the holy of holies constituted a symbolic entrance by humans into the eternal places where God dwelt, beyond the realm of space and time. There was an intimate connection between the holy of holies and the eternal throne room of God, and there humanity, in its divinely appointed office, could still be who we were meant to be, albeit in a symbolic and much diminished way.

This is an important point, because it is rather different from the way many Christians nowadays tend to think about entering the presence of God in our worship. We sometimes assume that this means God is present with us in a spiritual sense, there in our worship services at church. But the theology of the holy of holies added a further assumption to temple worship: not only was it a matter of God coming and being present with us in our place, it was, in a very real sense, a matter of us ascending into the very presence of God. When the high priest stepped behind the curtain of the holy of holies on the Day of Atonement, he was symbolically entering the eternal realm of God.[2] It was done in only a very limited and highly regulated fashion, thus showing that the experience was a signpost to the coming restoration of our access to the throne

---

2. See Clement of Alexandria, *Miscellanies* 5.6 (*ANF* 2:452–54).

of God, but not yet the full reality (Heb 9:7–8). The earthly tabernacle was a "copy" (Heb 8:5–6; 9:24), but the presence of God gave it more than a mere representative function: to enter the holy of holies was to step into the presence of God, the very same presence that abides on the throne in John's visions of heaven in Revelation.

This understanding is implicit in the design of the tabernacle itself, and later the temple as well. To process toward the holy of holies was, in a symbolic fashion, to ascend toward the throne room of God. This idea of ascension as the fundamental movement of worship is prefigured by Israel's worship on Mount Sinai, where the seventy elders ascended to meet with God and share his covenant feast (Exod 24), and it was later built into the structure of the temple in Jerusalem, where a series of steps led the priests upward as they ascended into the sanctuary, ever nearer the holy of holies.

The way the Bible speaks of the holy of holies and its furnishings all suggest that this was considered the throne room of God, or at least an entrance thereto. In it stood the ark of the covenant, overshadowed by cherubim, who by tradition are understood to be throne-angels (sometimes referred to as "angels of the presence"). The ark itself contained three sets of objects, each of which points again to the presence of God. The tablets of the Ten Commandments were there, as was customary for covenant contracts in the ancient Near East. There would be copies of the covenant given to both parties, so the fact that they were in the ark perhaps signified that these were God's copy, held within his very presence (the Israelites' copies, presumably, would be the records of the covenant as written in their Torah scrolls). There was also a jar of manna, which many early Christians took as a symbolic foreshadowing of Christ, the bread of life (see John 6:30–33). And there was Aaron's staff, which had budded, taken as a dual symbol for the tree of life and the cross of Christ.

The lid of the ark of the covenant, traditionally translated as "the mercy seat," did not come by the terminology of "seat" by accident. It was understood as the very throne of God (or a part thereof, such as his "footstool"), where he reigned in the midst of Israel (see, for instance, Pss 9:11; 99:1–5; cf. 1 Chr 28:2; Ps 132:7; Lam 2:1). Here we see again one of the many interweavings of the "temple" and "reign" ideas: not only was humanity both priestly and royal, but the place of God's presence was both his temple and the seat of his kingly power. God reigned from the holy of holies, and this was not understood in just a figurative way. It was an actual reign, with his authority mediated by his judges, prophets, and priests. This was why it was such a big deal when the Israelites asked to have a human king in Samuel's day: it was a rejection of God's very real reign in their midst (1 Sam 8:6–7). Yet, as with the fall itself, God can take even our rebellions and turn them into occasions for his grace. As Augustine said, "God judged it better to bring good out of evil than not to permit any evil to exist."[3] So the expulsion from Eden would lead to the restoration through Christ, and the devolution of Israel's kingship onto mere men would prepare the way for the messianic king to come one day, preaching a message of the reign of God.

The holy of holies was separated from the temple's sanctuary by a massive curtain (sometimes called the veil), woven of white linen along with blue, purple, and red wool. Ancient Jewish tradition tells us that these colors and materials were thought to represent the creation itself: the elemental makeup of all things.[4] It was almost as if the curtain was a physical expression of the "Let there be" moment of Genesis 1, when God, by speaking his word, sent creation spinning into existence. To step beyond the curtain, into the holy of holies, was in a sense to ascend past the barriers of space and time, to where the Lord dwelt "in the beginning." And to move the other way, from the holy of holies into the sanctuary, was to pass the barrier into a profusion of symbols of God's creative work, with all the decorations of Eden and the continual cycle of offering the fruits of the earth and the lives of animals back to God in worship.

We should also note that the high priest's outer garments (his ephod, breastpiece, and sash) were made from the exact same materials as the holy of holies's curtain (Exod 26:31; 39:2, 8, 29). In the time of the tabernacle, all the outer tent sheets also would have been made this way (Exod 26:1), but when the temple replaced those outer hangings with walls, only the great curtain and the priestly garments were made with these materials: white linen and blue, purple, and red wool. The high priest, then, was essentially wearing a portion of the great curtain. Within the symbolic language of the temple, the high priest was clothed in the physical representation of the place where God's presence intersects with our realm. Jewish tradition noticed this connection and suggested that it was not mere coincidence that the high priest was wearing a portion of the great curtain. A Jewish text of the first century BCE, *Wisdom of Solomon* (part of the biblical apocrypha), says "the whole world was on

---

3. Augustine, *Enchiridion on Faith, Hope, and Love* 27 (NPNF[1] 1:246).
4. Josephus, *Antiquities* 3.183; *War* 5.212–213 (*Complete Works*, 107, 848).

[Aaron's] long robe" (18:24).⁵ When he came out of the holy of holies, the high priest was coming out from the presence of God, crowned with God's own name, and clothed in the symbolic material of creation itself. To Christian eyes, this was a foreshadowing of the incarnation, played out in front of Israel each and every year. As Clement of Alexandria said, "The robe prophesied [Christ's] ministry in the flesh."⁶ Indeed, as we will show in the next chapter, there were ancient Christian traditions, going back to the New Testament itself, which associated the material of the great curtain with the body of Jesus Christ.

Sacrifice as a Symbol of Union

The core ritual of the temple was, of course, sacrifice. Many modern Christians focus their attention on sacrifices of atonement—those that match our central theological concern with the forgiveness of sins—but any reader of the Bible will know that there were many different types of sacrifices and offerings. There were burnt offerings, grain offerings, peace (or fellowship) offerings, sin (or purification) offerings, guilt offerings, drink offerings, thanksgiving offerings, wave offerings, and votive offerings (the first five are generally considered the main categories, with the remaining four being specific types within those categories). And those are only the regular cycle of offerings, brought by individual Israelites and offered through the ministry of the priests. There are further sacrifice and offering rituals associated with the major festivals of the Jewish calendar, with the Day of Atonement standing as the most important set of sacrifices in the annual cycle.

Sacrifice has to do with the forgiveness of sins, but that's not all it is. The gospel-tract version of Christianity ("You can have your sins forgiven through Christ's sacrifice so you can go to heaven") is true, but it misses a good deal of the relevant context. We need our sins forgiven, of course, but the end goal is not simply getting to go to heaven: rather, as the whole system of Israel's temple worship testified, the point of having one's sins forgiven was to get back into right relationship with God. And happily, being in right relationship with the God of eternity does include, as a natural consequence and a gift of grace, eternal life in his presence. But

---

5. See also Josephus, *Antiquities* 3.184 (*Complete Works*, 107).
6. Clement of Alexandria, *Miscellanies* 5.6 (*ANF* 2:453).

to speak of heaven as the end goal is to put the cart before the horse; God himself is the great goal, the *telos* of our creation.

The forgiveness of sins is the climactic turning point of the story in each of our lives, but it is not the whole story. When we reduce the gospel to sin and forgiveness, we have turned it into a problem-and-solution narrative that is pleasant and easy to understand, but a bit simplistic. The trouble lies in the fact that the gospel is much more like a grand romance than a problem-and-solution story. It is as if we were telling the story of Cinderella like this: "A girl lost her shoe at the ball, and through the kindness of a handsome prince, she got it back." That is definitely a true part of the story, but it's not the whole story. What about the romance, the marriage, the union to which the whole narrative rises? Our gospel story is about a God who created us to grow into a union of love with him—a destiny laid waste by our own rebellions—and about coming back into right relationship with him through the work of Christ. As a result, we are once again able to grow into union with him, experiencing, in ever-greater glory, the depths of his love throughout untold ages.

The story of sacrifice in the Old Testament points us in the same direction. Forgiveness of sins was the immediate aim of some of the offerings, but not the ultimate aim. The ultimate aim was the restoration of right relationship between God and his people, at least as much as could be experienced until the full atonement worked by the sacrifice of Christ. Even our English word "atonement" tells the story of this journey into union with God, for it is the word at-one-ment: something that makes things at one with one another. The other temple offerings, which often had nothing to do with sin, added to this dynamic, providing God's people with ways to offer thanksgiving and expressions of joy in their relationship with him, and to bear the fruits of their land back to their Maker.

The symbolic imagery of sacrifice tells a story of union with God. Fire was a common symbol for the presence of God, seen in the burning bush, the pillar of fire that guided the Israelites in the wilderness, and the tongues of flame that descended on the apostolic church at Pentecost. Deuteronomy 4:24 tells us, "Our God is a consuming fire" (see also Heb 12:29). It is worth noting that the imagery of sacrifice (at least in the case of burnt offerings) is an imagery of entering the flames and being consumed by fire. This may have spoken a symbolic message of union with God. In fact, one of the favorite metaphors of Christian life in patristic writings is that of an object being plunged into the flames until it is transformed and glows, with the fire's own nature burning inside it.[7] Sacrifice, then, had to do with the outpouring of blood and the forgiveness of sins, but it also had to do with being surrounded and suffused with the very symbol of the presence of God.

Sacrifice as Priestly Worship

There might also be another layer of meaning in the practice of offering sacrifices of various kinds. While the primary function seems to be as an act of restoring our right relationship with God, it may also be a way in which humanity began, in small ways, to reclaim its office of bearing the worship of creation back to God. In the practice of sacrifice, human beings were acting as mediators in God's cosmic temple, offering the bounty and the worship of the physical world back into God's own presence.

Consider for a moment the fact that sacrificial offerings were a regular part of biblical worship well before the institution of the tabernacle. In fact, it is sacrifice—not, as one might expect, prayers or songs—that constitutes the very first ritual of worship recorded in Scripture, when Abel and Cain present their offerings in Genesis 4. It is instructive to note that in all the sacrifice and offering stories in Genesis (including those that mention altars, the sites of such rituals), there is no reference to sin, guilt, or forgiveness (4:3–4; 8:20; 12:7–8; 13:18; 15:9–17; 22:1–18; 26:25; 31:54; 33:20; 35:1–7, 14; 46:1). One might be able to make a tentative case that issues of guilt or sin could be understood as a background context in the case of Genesis 8 or 15, but even if so, it still appears that the practice of sacrifice in Genesis had far more to do with bearing offerings to God in recognition of his gracious works on our behalf than it did with making atonement for sins. This accords with the priestly function of humanity: we, as part of our worship, bear the bounty of his works back to him and offer them up in praise of what he has done.

Indeed, to go back to the structure of the tabernacle, most of its furnishings and rituals include some act of bearing the fruits of estranged creation back into the presence of God. Within the elements of the sanctuary and inner court, one can find representative parts of all six days of creation being offered up. You have the light (the "fruit" of Day 1) from the candle flames, lamps, and the incense altar; the smoke of the incense filling the air (Day 2); the drink offerings, grain offerings, and bread of

---

7. See, for example, Pseudo-Macarius, *Fifty Spiritual Homilies* 4.14 (56).

the presence, made from the fruits of the earth (Day 3); the individual lights on the candlestand echoing the creation of the heavenly lights (Day 4); the washings with purifying water and the presentation of bird sacrifices (Day 5); and the presentation of land animals at the sacrifice altar (Day 6). Simply by doing the work of their ministry, the priests were enacting a drama of bringing all creation back into the presence of God in worship and thanksgiving.

In the view of many patristic writers, it was this understanding of priestly ministry that helped shape their understanding of what Christ had done for us. His sacrifice had been a work of atonement, with his outpoured blood covering the consequences of our sins, but it had also been an act of bearing humanity back into the presence of God. As the great High Priest and the new Adam, Jesus had taken human nature itself and brought it back to God. It was the first act in a grand and ongoing narrative, by which God was bringing forth his New Creation, culminating when, through the work of Christ he would enact the "universal restoration" (Acts 3:21 NRSV). Jesus, through his priestly identity, summed up Adam and Eve's vocation and the whole symbolic narrative of the temple, and bestowed on his followers the offices undertaken by the Levitical priests: to bear offerings, pray, study, and teach Scripture, exercise judgment, lead the worship of God's people, and help guide others into the inheritance of a clean heart and a right relationship with God.

With these foundational reflections on the priestly system in place, we will turn next to the New Testament development of these ideas. In our examination of the Old Testament, we have centered our attention on two loci: Adam and Eve's role in the garden of Eden (where patristic writers put so much of their focus), and the system of worship instituted in the tabernacle and temple. There is, of course, a great deal more that could be said from the stories of ancient Israel on both themes, royal and priestly, but at this point we will shift our focus ahead and consider the person and ministry of Jesus Christ. This is not a passing over of the rest of the Old Testament record, but rather an opportunity to view it from a particular perspective, as early Christian writers so often did. There will be more to see of Israelite kingship, of exile, and of Melchizedek and David and the prophets, but to do it in the patristic manner, we will press on to see it all through the lens of Christ and his church.

5

Christ's Ministry: The Messianic Priest-King

IN THIS CHAPTER, WE turn to an examination of the Gospels, the familiar story of Jesus' life and ministry, up to the events of his passion week. There are untold depths to be explored in these waters, but we are devoting our attention to just a few areas of interest. This chapter could easily form a book of its own, full of lengthy studies of Gospel passages, but for our purposes I will just point out the features of the landscape, like a tour guide at a scenic overlook, so that you can see the whole picture in all its splendor. Having studied the stories of Eden and the temple, we can expect to see familiar lines and movements in the story of Jesus, whom the New Testament proclaims to be both the new Adam and the great High Priest.

As we begin this survey of the life of Jesus, we should remind ourselves that there was a certain aesthetic sensibility to the way early Christians read the Bible. Not only did they expect to be able to discern truth from the plain sense of each portion of text, but they also expected to find an underlying beauty to the shape of God's plan. Believing that God's sovereign grace had guided the story of Scripture from Eden to the church, they thought that it was entirely reasonable to look for connections between the various parts, threads of the interweaving pattern that the Holy Spirit was pulling together into the image of Christ. As such, they were keen at discerning beautiful symmetries between different parts of the Bible. These observed symmetries may sometimes be speculative, but they are lovely and edifying, and thus well worth considering.

From Incarnation to Temptation: The Prologues to Jesus' Ministry

The birth narratives, and particularly Luke's, are saturated with images that point to Eden and the temple. But we will begin one step further back, and take a quick look at a temple feature which early Christian tradition associated with those narratives in a remarkable way: the great curtain of the temple, the veil that stood before the holy of holies. In the previous chapter, we examined some of the traditions that associated this veil with a representation of created reality, and specifically, the elemental matter of the physical universe. As the line that separated God from humanity in the temple space, it was considered an icon of the moment of creation itself, beyond which lay the timeless realms of the throne room of God. So for the high priest to emerge from the holy of holies on the Day of Atonement, moving past the curtain and garbing himself in garments made of the same symbolic material—this was a living performance of the incarnation: the divinely sent figure, clothing himself in the stuff of our creation, to walk among us as our sole mediator with God.

This curtain is directly associated with Jesus' physical body in the New Testament. In all three Synoptic Gospels, we are told that the curtain split down the middle the moment Jesus died on the cross (Matt 27:51; Mark 15:38; Luke 23:45). This is often interpreted as signifying the opening of a way to the Father, in the sense that Jesus' sacrificial death secures access for us into the presence of God, an access that before had only been granted to the high priest. That's certainly true, and is very likely part of the symbolism that the Gospels intend to convey. But there is also another layer of symbolism portrayed in the New Testament which makes the curtain itself equivalent to the physical body of Jesus Christ. In the view of ancient Christian tradition, the story of the curtain's tearing was not just about the effects of the tear, but about the meaning of the curtain itself. The curtain is a physical sign of Jesus' flesh, a symbol of his incarnation. Hebrews 10:20 appears to hold both readings together: the split curtain was taken to be the physical body of Christ, which opens a way of access to us: "a new and living way opened up for us through the curtain, that is, his body."

This brings us to an old and winsome story, much beloved in the early church: a sort of folk-hero retelling of Mary's life that we find in the second-century document called the *Protoevangelium of James* (sometimes called the *Infancy Gospel of James*). It was not actually written by

James, but it is one of the earliest noncanonical Christian documents we have, and it was widely appreciated in orthodox Christian circles. While it appears to have accrued some legendary features, making it historically dubious in some of its details, it is early enough that there may be lingering echoes of authentic memories in its narrative. For instance, it is from this document that we get the familiar tradition, often shown in paintings of the nativity, that the stable of Jesus' birth was in a cave, a detail also affirmed in other early sources.

In the *Protoevangelium*, we are told about the renovation of the temple undertaken during Herod's reign, and that the production of a new curtain was outsourced to a group of young Jewish women, all virgins (as seems plausible, given women's training at the loom and the purity restrictions of the temple), and further, that one of these virgins was Mary. She was given the task of weaving some of the curtain's sections made of purple and scarlet wool. In some paintings of the annunciation, Mary is shown near a loom or a spinning wheel, a detail which derives from this ancient tradition. In any case, we have this intriguing little story from the early Christian church that it was Mary herself who wove the temple's great curtain, just as the physical body of Christ was knit together in her womb. Whether historical or not, this story offers some insight into how early Christians thought about the incarnation and the temple-symbol of the great curtain. If nothing else, it adds a little bit of color to the symbolism we have already discussed: the curtain as a sign of Christ's incarnation, the point at which the divine and the human came together in the temple, and which clothed the body of the high priest.

While Matthew and Luke are the only Gospels which record the stories of Jesus' birth, John also gives us a beautiful prologue which presents the incarnation of Jesus Christ in terms borrowed from Old Testament temple traditions. John describes the incarnation as a tabernacle event: "The Word became flesh and made his dwelling among us. We have seen his glory..." (John 1:14). The verb translated as "made his dwelling" could be rendered more literally as "pitched his tent" or even "tabernacled" (see Sir 24:8). This, combined with John's use of the temple-vision language of "seeing his glory," should call every reader's mind to the tabernacle of Israel's wilderness days, when God's very presence dwelt in their midst.

Luke's nativity story afforded patristic writers a great many avenues of connection with the Old Testament accounts of Eden and the temple. When Gabriel announces the incarnation of Jesus in Mary's womb (Luke 1:35), he says, "The Holy Spirit will come on you, and the power of the

Most High will overshadow you." Here Gabriel uses language that evokes the holiest parts of the temple: the divine cloud and the ark of the covenant in the holy of holies (the same Greek word for "overshadow" being used of the cloud of God's presence in the transfiguration stories and of the statues of the cherubim over the ark of the covenant). To those with ears tuned to hear those allusions, Gabriel's statement was not just a practical explanation of how Mary's pregnancy would come about; it was signifying the manifest presence of God, as clearly there with Mary as in the holy of holies.

Other allusions follow: the angels' joyful announcement to the shepherds, with light spilling out of darkness, carries echoes of the moment of creation (Gen 1:3) and of the response of the angelic realm to seeing that moment, when "all the angels shouted for joy" (Job 38:7). Luke's details of the shepherds, stable, and manger all point to the presence of animals in the nativity story, which may also be an echo of creation. Just as Adam and Eve were made at the climax of the sixth day, on which God brought forth the land animals, and were then placed in a garden surrounded by animals, so also the new Adam is brought forth in the midst of animal creation. Indeed, almost as if to underscore these connections, Luke gives us a genealogy of Christ going back not only to Abraham (as Matthew's does), but all the way to Adam, the priest-king of the first creation. To make the identification of Jesus and Adam even stronger, Luke calls the latter "the son of God" (3:38). Luke also highlights the place of the temple in his narrative, from the initial announcement of God's coming redemption, given to the priest Zechariah as he prays in the temple, to the coming of Jesus himself to the temple after his birth (where he is spoken of by Simeon with the temple images of "light" and "glory"—2:32), and again when he was twelve, where the temple is portrayed as his true home (2:46–49).

The story then jumps ahead to Jesus' adulthood. He inaugurates his ministry by undergoing baptism in the Jordan River, a scene which, once again, carries echoes of creation. It is a story that can be viewed from many different angles, and it is probably best to regard the potential interpretations of this event as a sort of multilayered symbolism, rather than as a means of looking for one right answer. One can, with good reason, view Jesus' baptism as any of the following (and there are probably even more): an act of submission to the Father's will; of association with John the Baptist's ministry; of ceremonial washing before commencing priestly service; of anointing by the Spirit as king and priest; or of recapitulation of the stories of Israel passing through the Red Sea with Moses, Israel passing through the Jordan with Joshua, or the moment of creation itself. As any good test-taker knows, when offered a list of answers like this, it may be best to mark your guess as "all of the above." For our purposes, we are most interested in the ways this event stands as a recapitulation of creation and as a washing/anointing in preparation for royal and priestly offices.

Jesus' baptism has several symmetries with the creation narrative. You can see the work of the entire Trinity: God the Father speaking, the Word present as the active agent of the New Creation, and the Spirit descending over the waters. Both accounts close with statements of God's affirmation: "God saw that it was good" in Genesis 1, and "With him I am well pleased" in Matthew 3:17. Even Jesus' enigmatic answer to John's question in Matthew 3:14–15 carries echoes of creation. Rather than telling John to baptize him by simply saying, "Do it," he says, "Let it be so," calling to mind the many divine "Let there be" statements of Genesis 1. Jesus then says that he is seeking baptism "to fulfill all righteousness," a turn of phrase which potentially can be understood in the sense of "setting all things at right." And if that is the sense implied, then it speaks of the great hope of New Creation and the "restoration of all things" (Acts 3:21 NASB).

It is also worth noting that immediately after Jesus' baptism, Matthew shows Jesus being led into the wilderness "to be tempted by the devil" (4:1). There appears to be some intentionality behind setting up this episode of temptation, cast as a rematch of Genesis 3, and now the new Adam throws down the gauntlet to the serpent. In the Eden narratives, we see the creation accounts followed by the temptation of Adam and Eve; and in the Gospels we see a glimpse of the New Creation at Jesus' baptism, followed by his temptation. But in the latter case, Jesus does what Adam and Eve could not do, and triumphs by his obedience. If this parallelism is part of the intended symbolism of Jesus' baptism and temptation, then we have here a vision of God's work of New Creation, begun in the person of Jesus Christ.

Jesus' baptism may also speak rather directly to the idea of his consecration to priestly and royal service. Jesus did not fill any public office during his ministry years other than that of a wandering rabbi, and yet his followers later came to see him as both king and priest. The descent of the Spirit at his baptism was taken by the early church as an act of anointing (the moment when Jesus is revealed as "Christ," the anointed one), and they followed the pattern by including a ritual of anointing after their own baptisms as well.[1] In Luke's Gospel, Jesus goes directly from his baptism and temptation to the preaching of his first sermon, which begins with the words of Isaiah 61:1, "The Spirit of the Lord is on me, because he has anointed me . ." (Luke 4:18). It would be hard to read this reference to anointing without thinking of the Spirit descending on Jesus in the immediately preceding stories.

In the Old Testament, anointings were given only to priests and kings (as in Exod 30:30–31; 40:15; 1 Sam 9:16; 16:1). So if Jesus' baptism included an anointing, then in the symbolic language of Israel's rituals, Jesus must be king, or priest, or both. Luke also includes the detail that Jesus was thirty years old at the time, which was the age when young men from priestly families were consecrated for service. Priestly ordination was a ritual that included a ceremonial washing of the whole body (Lev 8:6). Thirty also happens to be the age at which David was enthroned as king, together with an anointing (2 Sam 5:3–4). So here at Jesus' baptism, we can see all three of the major themes we have been tracing: creation (in the symbolism of the baptism and temptation), priesthood (in the washing and anointing), and kingship (in the anointing).

Jesus as King and Priest

What exactly do we mean when we say that Jesus was both king and priest? The evidence is clear that messianic figures were expected to fulfill both functions; in fact, some ancient Jewish sources, unable to reconcile how one person could be both king and priest, appear to expect two messiahs, one for each office (a feature of messianic expectations in some Qumran documents and in *The Testament of Levi*). So how did the early church explain Jesus' claim to these two offices, neither of which he actually held during his earthly life (at least not in terms of an office within a recognizable social institution)?

In Scripture and early church tradition, each of these offices was linked to a historical anchor, a person in whose tradition Jesus followed—David and Melchizedek—and then also (in both cases) to Adam himself. In looking at the history of Jesus' royal claim, the figure of David is central. The New Testament indicates that Jesus' kingship derives from his connection to the Davidic line (indeed, Matthew's genealogy hints that

---

1. See Justin Martyr, *Dialogue with Trypho* 87–88 (ANF 1:242–44).

if the Davidic house still ruled Israel, then Jesus would, quite literally, be its king). Yet it is important to note that the Messianic king was not only expected to fulfill David's legacy, but to bring it to a far higher point than David himself had. David's own kingship pointed forward to the Messiah as its defining figure: the dynasty is brought to its climax in Christ, in whom it is established forever (2 Sam 7:12–13). The prophetic expectation was not just that a king from David's line would one day emerge, but that this king would complete all the promises given to Adam, Abraham, Moses, and David, and that his reign would usher in the day of the Lord. The coming king would not only be a restorer of a temporal dynasty but would establish the reign of God over all this rebel world as well. Jesus, in his works of ministry, stakes out an unshakable claim to be that very king.

Now for the priesthood: the historical character linked to Jesus' priestly office is Melchizedek. At first glance, he seems an odd choice. Not much is known about him, as he is referenced only twice in the Old Testament, and both times in passages that generate more questions than answers (Gen 14:18–20; Ps 110:4). Not even what we do know about him seems to tell us much—his name is not actually a name; it simply means "king of righteousness." Yet early Christians, following the interpretation in the book of Hebrews, placed great emphasis on the fact that Jesus was a priest from the order of Melchizedek. To some skeptics of previous generations, this was a mental leap that smacked of desperation. It was clear that the Messiah was supposed to fulfill a priestly office in some respect, but Jesus was not from the priestly tribe of Levi, so some other priesthood had to be ascribed to him. The only significant candidate was the enigmatic Melchizedek, whose order of priesthood had been mentioned in Psalm 110. It seems like a sleight-of-hand trick, a way of getting past the obstacle of Jesus' nonpriestly lineage by just ascribing his name to an ephemeral priestly order known only by a single member who lived 2,000 years before. What did it even mean, to be a priest in the order of Melchizedek? As far as anyone knew, there was no such order, no lineage, no ceremonies, and no consecrating rituals by which an aspiring priest might join. Nothing Jesus said ever mentioned Melchizedek or implied that he was a member of an established priestly order. So was this just a case of wishful thinking on the part of the early church, grasping at straws to explain a difficult question about Jesus' identity?

The answer, as we now know, is no. They were not simply making this up. As it turns out, the hints we have in the Old Testament are part of a broader stream of Melchizedek traditions in ancient Judaism. It was not the case that he was just an enigmatic historical figure of the distant past; he was actually the very character who exemplified some Jews' expectations of the Messiah in the generations before Jesus came. In the Dead Sea Scrolls, one particular segment (11Q13, the Melchizedek document) focuses on expectations for a priestly royal messianic figure called Melchizedek. He is expected to provide atonement and redemption for his people, and is even described in the terms of the very same passage of Isaiah 61 that Jesus claims for himself in his inaugural sermon. Among some Jews of the Second Temple period, there were expectations that a priestly messianic figure would arise, in the mold of Melchizedek himself, and that his priestly office would be carried out through his acts of exercising judgment over demonic forces, forgiving people of their sins, and proclaiming the good news of salvation (see 11Q13). If these are the parameters of Melchizedek's priesthood, laid down in the generations before Jesus' day, then it is Jesus, and only Jesus, who can truly be called a high priest in the order of Melchizedek, because he fulfills them all.

Jesus' Ministry and the Reign of God

The teachings and acts of Jesus as recorded in the Gospels constitute the most extraordinary story the world has ever known, and through all of it runs the intertwining threads of Jesus' royal and priestly identity. When he chooses twelve men as his disciples, he is reconstituting Israel, the original kingdom of priests. He appears to give them priestly authority at various points in the Gospels, such as the power to "bind" and "loose" (Matt 10:18; terms associated with authority in teaching and applying the commands of Scripture), and even to administrate the forgiveness of sins (John 20:23). He himself also practices many priestly activities: teaching Scripture, praying, bringing the unclean into a state of restored communion with God, and proclaiming forgiveness.

But what about the royal aspect? His main message was a proclamation of "the kingdom of God" (or "the reign of God"). A great deal of recent scholarly work has helped to illuminate what exactly this message signified, but for our purposes we are only considering a very basic angle on the question: What image would this rhetoric have brought to mind for his original audience? The reign of God was clearly an anticipated result of the coming day of the Lord, but we should remember that Jesus' hearers probably would not conceive of this reign as a nebulous idea of spiritual sovereignty. In Israel's Scripture and tradition, the reign of God was linked to a particular place and a particular structure. When Jesus proclaimed the kingdom of God, many of his audience would have been hearing his message in temple terms. "God reigns . . . he sits enthroned between the cherubim," as one temple hymn, Psalm 99, puts it. To declare the reign of God was to call to mind the holy of holies and the ark of the covenant, the very footstool of the throne of God. It was in that place that God's reign had been manifest in their midst. Keep in mind, though, that the holy of holies in Jesus' day was vacant—the ark of the covenant had never been recovered after disappearing from the pages of history at some point before or during the Babylonian conquest of the sixth century BCE. Many pious Jews felt that the Babylonian exile had never truly ended, partly because the very symbol of the present reign of God in their midst, there in the holy of holies, was gone.

So when Jesus came proclaiming that "the kingdom of God is at hand," it was an astonishing message. Many Christians tend to think of the "at hand" phrase in temporal terms (that the kingdom would be coming soon), and that's certainly implied in some cases. But there are also indications that Jesus may be speaking in local terms, not just temporal ones, when he says "the kingdom of God is at hand." The kingdom is at hand: that is, within reach. In essence, it is right there in front of you, or, as Jesus says in another place, "The kingdom of God is in your midst" (Luke 17:21). It is present and accessible, walking around in front of you in the person of Jesus Christ. The reign of God, which used to be manifest only in the holiest part of the temple, shut off from all but the high priest, was now present again, and it was right there in front of everyone. One of the many messages to be drawn from Jesus' sermons on the kingdom was that God's local, dwelling-in-the-midst-of-you reign was back, and now it was no longer restricted to the temple. It was loose in the world—no longer in a building, but in a carpenter-rabbi from Nazareth.

Jesus regularly referred to himself in temple terms—sometimes, even, as the temple itself. The clearest example of this is John 2:19–21, where Jesus calls his own body the temple: "Destroy this temple, and I will raise it again in three days." John tells us that the disciples later discerned that he had been talking about his own resurrection. But there's more to it than that; it wasn't just a clever turn of phrase to set up his disciples for an "Aha!" moment on Easter Sunday. It also appears to be a reference to a widely held expectation of the messianic office: it was thought that the Messiah would replace the current temple (which many

Jews thought was tarnished by a corrupt priesthood) with a new temple. The messianic prophecies to David, which look both to his son Solomon as temple-builder, as well as to a future Messiah, appear to be the seedbed for this expectation, and Ezekiel's vision of a new temple (which is clearly not the Second Temple) backs it up as well. The Messiah, the new Davidic king, would be a temple-builder. One can also find this expectation in other sources, such as *1 Enoch*, where a messianic figure, "the Lord of the sheep," sees the old temple structure carried off and erects a new one in its place.[2] This may be why, in Matthew's account of Jesus' trial before the Sanhedrin, the claim that Jesus was going to destroy and rebuild the temple was taken as a messianic claim. The high priest follows the introduction of that accusatory evidence with this demand: "Tell us if you are the Messiah, the Son of God" (Matt 26:63). They knew very well that a claim to destroy and rebuild the temple was an implicit claim to be the Messiah. The fact that Jesus associated this new messianic temple with his own body (John 2:21) may have been part of what led Paul to hold "the body of Christ" and "the temple of God" together as the same reality, and to find its living manifestation in the church.

Jesus' miracles also testified to his claims to royal priesthood. Even his first recorded miracle, changing the water into wine at the wedding of Cana, carries overtones of this idea. While the main point of the miracle was as an act of kindness to the hosts (and of acceding to his mother's request), we should not slide past the symbolism of the water and the wine. It is instructive to note that in Jesus' first miracle, he takes water for ceremonial washing—that is, water that was used to ensure a basic level of ritual purity in everyday activities—and turns it into wine, and it is wine that he later associates with his own sacrificial blood. Here Jesus takes a symbol of our attempt to try to stay clean in our relationship with God, and substitutes a symbol of the blood of his sacrifice, which alone can make us clean.

The turning of water to wine may also have another resonance with the Old Testament, and particularly with the Jews' expectations of the Messiah. One of the things that would mark the messianic reign was an abundance (or even a super-abundance) of the good gifts of nature: of wine and of grain for bread (Jer 31:12; Joel 2:19, 24; Zech 9:17), as well as of fish (Ezek 47:9–10). It should come as no surprise, then, that Jesus' "nature miracles" fulfill this expectation in a very direct way: creating

---

2. *1 En.* 90.28–29 (*OTP* 1:71).

an abundance of wine at Cana, multiplying bread and fish on at least two separate occasions, and providing overflowing catches of fish for his disciples.

Another major category of Jesus' miracles had to do with healing. Healing by the power of God was not unknown in Jewish society, but it was very rare, and no one could do it with the regularity or authority of Jesus. In the few other examples we have, both in the Bible and in ancient Jewish traditions, those rare healings are obtained by pouring out fervent prayers to God, but Jesus heals people by the sole authority of his own word. It was something only God could do, and it was also something that hearkened back to both the temple and to Eden.

Jesus' power to heal puts him in a special category in the biblical worldview: he was, like only a very few things associated with the temple, "most holy." Although not all biblical texts use the terms consistently, there are a few places where an interesting distinction is made between "most holy" and "holy." In many cases, "most holy" can simply refer to the absolute summit on the scale of holiness (as, for instance, in calling the holy of holies the "most holy place," as opposed to the "holy place" of the priestly area). But a few verses suggest that there were some "most holy" things which could flip the tables on the normal pattern of the clean/unclean laws of ancient Israel. Within the purity laws of Israel, contact with something unclean could defile an object or person that had before been clean, making the latter unclean as well. A whole host of ritual laws stood in place to allow people to purify themselves from these effects. Uncleanness would transfer and defile, but cleanness would not transfer from one object to another. Touching an unclean object defiled you, but touching a holy object did not make you clean. But there was one category, the most holy, that could do the whole process the other way around. If something that was most holy came into contact with another object, that object was then pronounced holy (Exod 29:36–37; 30:26–29; Lev 10:17). The most holy things—such as the furnishings inside the temple building, the altar, and the sin offering—could transfer holiness upon other things without being tarnished or defiled themselves. So in the Gospels, when Jesus breaks ritual purity laws in jaw-dropping fashion—as when he touches lepers to heal them (Matt 8:2–3)—it is a clear demonstration that he is "most holy," something like the most precious items of the temple, infused with the radiance of God's presence. Thus he can do what no one else can do, and transfer cleanness to the unclean without becoming unclean himself. His miracles of healing spoke the visual language of the temple's purity code, and transcended them all.

His healings were also tied to the story of Eden. When some Christians read about the penalty of humanity's sin in the garden—that is, death—they may tend to think of it in simple terms of mortality, an end-of-life event. But early Christianity saw death as a more complex phenomenon. The death that resulted from our fall was primarily about the spiritual death that results from our sins, such that we are now cut off from God, the source of all true life. And even when physical mortality was in view, they saw mortality more as a progressive reality than a single, end-of-life event. The death enacted by our fall included the moment of physical death, but also the whole process of what they called "corruption"—the gradual march of death through our physical members, apparent in a host of physical and spiritual maladies.[3] With this in mind, think again about Jesus' miracles of healing. The fact that he is taking away diseases and granting bodily wholeness is not just an act of wondrous kindness, as important as that is; it was also seen as an undoing of the mortal corruption at work in our bodies since the fall. When Jesus heals, he is rolling back the effects of our sin in the garden of Eden. In many cases, he also includes the spiritual element as well, enacting not just physical healings, but proclaiming the forgiveness of sins as part of that healing. This was not just an added extra meant to rile up the crowds (Luke 5:20–21), but an integral part of turning back the tide of Genesis 3.

Another major category of Jesus' miracles was exorcism, the casting out of demonic spirits. This was generally regarded as a priestly activity in the Judaism of Jesus' day; most priests memorized prayers for use in such situations. But as in the case of healings, Jesus is rather different: not only does he do exorcisms, he does them on his own authority. This, too, is an act that takes its context from the fall from paradise. It is a direct fulfillment of the messianic prophecy spoken to the serpent: "he will crush your head" (Gen 3:15). Jesus' acts of exorcism fulfill a prophecy given against the serpent at the moment of our expulsion, a sign that Satan's hold on us was being shattered through the one whom God had sent.

---

3. See Athanasius, *On the Incarnation* 8 (*NPNF*[2] 4:40).

Jesus' Passion Week: The Priest-King Stakes His Claim

One of the main objections that some ancient Jews had against Jesus' messianic claims was that he never became king and thus never brought about the expected messianic kingdom. If it was clear from prophecy that the Messiah was a kingly figure who would establish a worldwide, visible reign, then surely Jesus would be ruled out by the simple fact that he never did any of those things. One can see this line of thought, for instance, from Justin Martyr's Jewish interlocutor Trypho.[4] Justin's response does not argue that Jewish interpretations of the messianic kingship were wildly off-base. Rather, the main shape of the Christian argument is that these things are what Jesus is doing right now, and not only in a spiritual way, but in a quite literal way in the visible body of worldwide Christianity and its astonishing transformation of society around the world, a transformation which will be brought to completion upon Christ's return.

To the skeptical mind, here is another Christian argument that sounds a little like wishful thinking: an attempt to explain away some significant discordance between prophetic expectations and the actual reality of Jesus' life, by attributing his kingly reign to a category that cannot be examined and assessed by any normal means. But early Christian interpreters were not just desperately pulling answers out of a hat in order to find something that fit their circumstances. Their arguments were faithful to the Old Testament witness and very often made use of texts that their opponents had chosen to overlook, such as the traditions that pointed to a suffering Messiah (the most famous example being Isa 53), and that the messianic figure's worldwide reign would be marked by a heavenly, not an earthly, enthronement (Dan 7:13–14). Further, this delayed ascent to the throne seems to be what Jesus himself intentionally practiced: a period of service that climaxes in suffering, and then his vindication, triumph, and enthronement. Rather than seize the kingship at any point during his ministry, he only makes his open claim on that office when he embarks on the sweepingly symbolic acts of his final pilgrimage to Jerusalem, culminating in his resurrection and ascension.

Jesus' acts during the passion week were a far more outward claim to kingship than he had ever made before, almost as if he viewed these things as his coronation rites. Thus, while Jesus had been earlier anointed to the kingly office at his baptism, he appears not to have taken up the office until this point, as he reaches a sequence of events culminating in

---

4. Justin Martyr, *Dialogue with Trypho* 32 (*ANF* 1:210).

his ascension and enthronement in the presence of God. This long gap between anointing and reign is not unknown in the Bible; it is the pattern of David himself, who was first anointed as king by Samuel, then went through a long phase where he was not actively reigning in that office, but was instead walking a road of suffering service, until finally ascending to take the crown. Thus, to suggest that a messianic figure might have two very distinct phases of his work—one of suffering service, and another of reigning—is not a Christian invention; it is the pattern of David, whose kingship stood at the center of messianic expectations.

In regard to his priestly office, the events from Jesus' passion to his ascension stand as his definitive act of service. Here he makes atonement for fallen humanity, an atonement interwoven with the symbology of the temple festivals of Passover and the Day of Atonement, but which also hearkens back to our fall in the garden of Eden. Jesus becomes not only the sacrifice offered on our behalf, but the one who offers as well, who ascends into the presence of the Father to present the sacrifice there, and in so doing he does away with the consequences of our fall, as death itself is undone.

In the Synoptic Gospels, the events of the passion week begin with two public displays of Jesus' authority as king and priest. First is his entry into Jerusalem, riding a donkey in fulfillment of the messianic prophecies of Zechariah 9:9 and Genesis 49:10–11, both of which make explicitly royal connections. The crowds hail him in the manner of a triumphant Davidic king returning to the capital city. Not only so, but the cry they shout, "Blessed is he who comes in the name of the Lord!" might be derived from a greeting cry shouted by the crowds upon the appearance of the high priest, who bore the name of the Lord on his forehead, as he emerged from the temple to address the people (a plausible context for the appearance of that hail in the temple imagery of Ps 118:26–27).

This is followed shortly thereafter with Jesus' act of clearing the moneychangers out of the temple courts, an open display of both his kingly and priestly authority. It was kingly in that it followed in the traditions of other great temple reformers like King Josiah, and priestly in that he was doing the work that priests were supposed to do, namely, managing the activities that took place in the temple. It also served as a public rebuke of the current temple administration, thus speaking to the expectations of some Jews (like the Qumran community) that the Messiah would take on the corrupt priesthood of his day and replace it with a purer one. To press the point a little further, one could even say it was very much an Adamic

CHRIST'S MINISTRY: THE MESSIANIC PRIEST-KING   73

act. In the original temple-sanctuary of the garden of Eden, one of the tasks Adam was given was to "keep" the garden, a word that also carries implications of "guard" when used of priests in their temple sanctuary. Here Jesus guards the sanctuary against danger and disorder that has crept inside, undertaking for the temple what Adam had been charged to do for the garden of Eden.

There's an odd little story that Matthew and Mark both wedge into the narrative of Jesus' entry and clearing the temple, the last recorded miracle Jesus does before his death. On his way into the city on the second day of the week (having slept in nearby Bethany), Jesus sees a fig tree and goes to look for figs to eat. But finding it bare of fruit (unsurprisingly, since it was not the season for fruit), he curses the tree, saying, "May no one ever eat fruit from you again." The tree then withered up (Matt 21:18–19; Mark 11:12–14, 20–21). This strange story is usually interpreted with reference to the clearing of the temple courts, as a further rebuke of the corrupt temple administration. The structure of the Gospel passages invite us to take it as part of Jesus' condemnation of the temple system in his day, as if the tree itself were that system, and it had borne no good fruit. The story is immediately followed by Jesus teaching his disciples that if they have faith, they can command "this mountain" to throw itself into the sea, and it would happen. And, crucially, the mountain right in front of their eyes when he said those words would have been the Temple Mount itself.

But some early church fathers thought they also saw a secondary layer of symbolism in the cursing of the fig tree. In this event, they thought, Jesus was rolling back the effects of the fall, taking his triumphal entry right up to the gates of Eden and assaulting the symbol of our shame. While we are never told the identity of the tree of knowledge of good and evil, there is mention of another specific kind of tree in the garden: a fig tree. We know this because it was from fig leaves that Adam and Eve tried to stitch together garments after they had fallen into sin and realized their nakedness (Gen 3:7). It is not the tree by which we sinned, but it is the tree with which we tried to hide the shame of our sin. One of the clues marshalled in defense of this connection between Jesus' fig tree and Eden's is Mark's detail that Jesus looked for figs on the tree when it was not the season for figs. It seems like a wantonly cruel act to curse a fig tree for not having fruit when it could not possibly have had fruit, unless it was the symbolism of the leaves that Jesus was really after. By cursing the tree whose leaves exemplified the shame and guilt we felt from our sins, Jesus shows the liberty we have in him to leave our sins and failings behind us, and press on into the garden once again. Cyril of Jerusalem writes, "At the time of their sin, [Adam and Eve] clothed themselves with fig leaves; for this cause Jesus also made the fig tree the last of his signs. For when about to go to his passion, he curses the fig tree . . . saying, 'No more let anyone eat from you; let the doom be cancelled.'"[5]

The next major event, recorded in all the Gospels in one form or another, is the evening that Jesus spent with his disciples before his crucifixion, during which he shared with them his last supper (Matt 26:17–30; Mark 14:12–26; Luke 22:7–38) and gave them a final sermon centered around his "new commandment," that they should love one another (John 13–17). Though scholars have debated whether Jesus' last supper was a Passover meal and to what extent the theology of the feast may have influenced the development of the Christian Eucharist, traditional interpretations tie all three closely together: the Last Supper, Passover, and the ongoing practice of Christian communion. The early church saw it as significant that Jesus chose this particular feast as the scene of his passion and the institution of his memorial meal. Just as the Passover lambs were slaughtered in Moses' day to avert death from falling on the Israelites, so also Jesus' sacrifice for us turns away death, the consequence of our sins. As Paul proclaims in 1 Corinthians 5:7–8, "Christ, our Passover lamb, has been sacrificed. Therefore, let us keep the festival."

Another aspect of the Last Supper is that Jesus appears to be initiating his disciples into a priestly rite. Jesus has taken bread and wine and described them as the flesh and blood of his own body, which are given in his death as an offering for sins, and then he commands his followers to eat them. Rituals of eating were not unknown in Judaism; family Sabbath observances always included a meal, and Passover itself was a meal-based festival. But Jesus appears to be imbuing these elements with more than the customary Passover meaning; he is presenting the bread and wine as sin offerings. When he says, "This is the new covenant in my blood, poured out for you" (Luke 22:20), it is a direct echo of the language used in Leviticus for pouring out the blood of the sin offering. In fact, the phrase describing the pouring out of blood occurs in the context of sacrifices seven times in that book, and in each case it is a sin offering (Lev 4:7, 18, 25, 30, 34; 8:15; 9:9). If communion is a representation of a sin offering, then Jesus' command to eat of it places Christians—the

---

5. Cyril of Jerusalem, *Catechetical Lectures* 13.18 (NPNF[2] 7:87).

eaters—in the role of priests. The sin offering, as described in Leviticus, was not just a ritual of sacrifice and splashing blood about; it was also a ritual of eating. The meat of the sacrifice was to be eaten by the priests in the temple courts, and the fact that it was eaten there (rather than taken away to their family homes) suggests that the eating was itself part of the ritual (Lev 6:26–29). So by inviting his followers to partake of his sacrifice, he is instructing them to do part of the priestly worship: the eating of the sin offering.

It is also worth remembering that such offerings were one of the things designated as most holy. By the logic of temple theology, touching or receiving something most holy made the receiver holy as well. Therefore, if we are symbolically partaking of Jesus' sacrifice in communion, the implication is that we ourselves have become holy through receiving him, who is most holy, and thus communion becomes, among other things, an enacted theology of sanctification, a visible drama of the great truth that we are made holy through Christ.

If we want to follow this train of thought a bit further, there is a twist of which we should be aware. Jesus may be offering his disciples a position even higher than the normal priestly ritual accords. There was an exception listed in the Mosaic Law: the meat of any sin offering whose blood had been taken into the interior of the temple as an atoning sacrifice was not to be eaten, but burned up instead (Lev 6:30), as something devoted to the Lord. Hebrews portrays Jesus' sacrifice as just that sort, with the blood brought into the heavenly holy of holies (9:24–26). By having his disciples eat this sin offering, then, Jesus was inviting them even higher than the customary priestly ritual, essentially allowing them to participate in their union with God by partaking of the portion devoted solely unto him. From this angle, communion becomes a participation in the covenant feast of God himself.

There is, of course, one other significant hang-up here: Jesus upends one of the clearest taboos in the Law with his instructions. He commands his disciples to drink the wine that symbolized his blood, despite the fact that consuming blood was prohibited in the Mosaic Law (Gen 9:4; Lev 3:17; 7:26–27; 17:10–14; 19:26; Deut 12:16–24; 15:23). When Jesus suggested to the crowds earlier in his ministry that eating his flesh and drinking his blood was the way to eternal life, many of his own followers left in disgust (John 6:53–66). So why would he command them to breach this taboo? The answer might also be found in the Mosaic Law. The reason given for the prohibition on consuming blood was because "the life of every creature is its blood" (Lev 17:14; see also Deut 12:23). If the life of every creature is the blood, then to receive the blood is to receive the life. Jesus' act of instituting the cup of communion was the shattering of an ancient taboo, but because it was such a well-known taboo, the act became all the more powerful: this was the ritual symbol of receiving the very life of Jesus into ourselves, the sign of being joined to him.

Now, having brought the story of Jesus up to the verge of its climax, we turn our attention in the next chapter to the sequence of events which show Jesus completing his definitive priestly act and receiving the throne as the messianic king: his death, resurrection, and ascension.

6

Christ's Passion:
The Priest-King's Coronation Rites

ONE OF THE LOVELIEST symmetries that early Christians saw in the Gospels was the one between Jesus' passion and the days of creation. Specifically, the three days of Good Friday, Holy Saturday, and Resurrection Sunday were thought to align with Genesis 1–2 in a rather striking way. In these three days, we can see echoes of the sixth and seventh days of creation, followed by what patristic writers called "the eighth day"—that is, the day of resurrection, and the first day of the New Creation.

"New Creation" is a familiar idea to most Christians, because it appears in a much-memorized verse used to explain the process of transformation that happens when we come to faith: "Therefore if anyone is in Christ, *this person is* a new creation; the old things passed away; behold, new things have come" (2 Cor 5:17 NASB, see also Gal 6:15). We tend to read this verse with reference to ourselves as individuals—if we are in Christ, we are new creations. There is nothing untrue about that, but the grammar of the verse itself, coupled with early Christian sensibilities about New Creation, suggest that it could be read with a bigger picture in mind. The phrase in Greek leaves out the subject and verb before "New Creation" (not uncommon in Greek), so it literally reads, "If anyone is in Christ—New Creation." Now, we have to render it one way or another, with reference to an individual application or to God's cosmic plan of redemption, and it's worth noting that some translations are now tending to opt for the latter: "Therefore, if anyone is in Christ, the new creation has come . . ." (NIV), or for a more open-ended reading: ". . . there is a new creation . . ." (NRSV). Read in this way, the verse carries resonance with another passage that also mentions old things becoming new, the vision of the fulfillment of God's cosmic plan in Revelation 21:4–5: ". . . the old order of things has passed away. He who was seated on the throne said, 'I am making everything new!'"

This idea of New Creation is a biblically based way to approach the patristic vision of cosmic redemption in Christ. His crucifixion on the sixth day of the week (the same day as the creation of humans) was his act of remaking humanity by taking away the sin that had kept us separated from God. On the seventh day of creation, God rested, and on the seventh day of the passion week, Jesus rested in death. Then we come to the first day of the new week, the "Let there be light" moment of the resurrection. This was referred to as the eighth day, not because early Christians were advocating for the institution of an eight-day week, but because they wanted the connection with the creation week of Genesis 1 to be clear.

What Jesus had done was a mirror image of the work of creation, and now we are in a new "week" of creation, beginning with Christ's remaking of redeemed humanity through his incarnation, death, and resurrection. As we turn our minds to the story of those three days (as well as the ascension, which is inextricably linked to them), we do it with a view to the old story of the creation narratives, the desolation of God's cosmic temple, and the tragic condition of his rebel priesthood.

The Trial & Crucifixion

After celebrating his Last Supper with his disciples, Jesus went by night to the garden of Gethsemane. The traditional location for this garden, on the lower slopes of the Mount of Olives, is right in the shadow of the great Temple Mount. Indeed, Jesus' whole passion could be said to revolve around the temple, like a planet orbiting its sun. His arrest happens in the garden, where he can look straight over into the courts of the temple, with its blazing altar and east-facing doors. When he is crucified on Golgotha (whose traditional location is on the opposite side of the Temple Mount), he was likely looking up at the blank back wall of the holy of holies. So when he cries out, "My God, my God, why have you forsaken me?" (Matt 27:46; Mark 15:34), the temple, facing the other way, dominates his view, almost as a visible sign of his Father's back turned on him while he bears the weight of the world's sin.

One of the other symmetries having to do with these locations is with the very idea of a garden. Many early Christians thought that it was more than coincidence that Adam, upon his creation, was placed in a garden, and that the events of the new Adam's passion, from his arrest to his resurrection, both begin and end in a garden (John 18:1; 19:41). He is arrested in the garden of Gethsemane on the east side of the temple, and after his death he rises again in a garden near Golgotha, on the west side of the temple. Such things may, of course, be coincidences, but there is something winsome about the notion that this symmetry is a sign pointing back to God's great-creation temple, just as many of the signs in the Old Testament pointed forward to Christ.

The themes of Jesus' kingship and priesthood arise throughout these events. When we study the trial and crucifixion of Jesus, the language of royalty emerges from every scene, in a way that is markedly different from the rest of his life and ministry. Whereas before any references to his being a king were handled with intentional quietness (Jesus often slipping away by himself when crowds got it in their head to make him a king), now that claim lies out in the open. On the night of his arrest, Jesus declares that he can call on legions of angels (Matt 26:53), and the very power of his presence causes his enemies to fall to the ground (John 18:6), a scene which speaks both to Jesus' divine authority (as it immediately follows one of his "I Am" statements) and recalls King David's repeated expression of faith: that when his enemies came against him, they would stumble and fall (Pss 27:2; cf. 9:3; 17:13; 20:8; 35:7–8; 36:12; 57:6; 89:23).

At Jesus' trial before the Sanhedrin, he speaks of his royal claim in terms of the ascendant reign of the Son of Man from Daniel 7:13–14, enthroned at God's right hand: "From now on you will see the Son of Man sitting at the right hand of the Mighty One and coming on the clouds of heaven" (Matt 26:64; cf. Mark 14:62; Luke 22:69). When the Jewish authorities translate their charge against Jesus into terms the Romans will understand, they tell Pilate that he is claiming to be a king (along with a few other more spurious charges; see Luke 23:2). Pilate takes this as the main accusation against Jesus, and when pressed, Jesus essentially allows the charge to stand as Pilate has phrased it, though in John's Gospel he clarifies his kingship as being "not of this world" (John 18:33–37; cf. Matt 27:11; Mark 15:2; Luke 23:3). Unlike previously in his ministry, where he would quietly dodge such issues, now he embraces them. He appears to understand these events almost as his coronation ceremonies, leading up to the literal fulfillment of Daniel 7's prophecy in his ascension. In John, he even predicts his crucifixion as the moment of his great triumph, when "the prince of this world" will be driven out and Jesus will draw all people to himself (John 12:31–32; see Col 2:15). Thus the main charge against him stands, and becomes the basis for the humiliation that follows: the robe, the crown of thorns, the mocking adulation from his torturers, and the notice nailed to the cross above him, declaring that he is the King of the Jews.

Some of the priestly connections to the cross are open and visible, while others are rather more subtle. Christian tradition has always recognized that Jesus is presented in his passion both as the offering and the offerer, the priestly sacrifice and the priest himself. At his Last Supper, he speaks about his flesh and his blood in terms familiar from sacrificial rituals. This understanding of Christ as a sacrifice can be seen throughout the New Testament (Rom 3:25; 1 Cor 5:7; 1 John 2:2; 4:10), but the clearest references are in Hebrews 7–10, where Jesus is not only the sacrifice, but the high priest who offers the sacrifice of himself. In John's Gospel, Jesus is also portrayed as the offerer, making the point that he is laying his own life down, not that it is being taken from him (10:11–18).

There are also a few connections that do not lie quite so near the surface, but which require one to connect the dots. For instance, all four Gospels relate the detail that the soldiers at the cross cast lots for Jesus' garments, a quite literal fulfillment of Psalm 22:18. But John also adds an interesting note, telling us that one of those garments, Jesus' tunic, was "seamless, woven in one piece from top to bottom" (19:23). This seems like an odd detail to include unless it was considered significant. It may be the case that John was just attributing two parts to the prophecy of Psalm 22, but we should also note that a finely woven linen tunic was one of the main parts of the priestly wardrobe (Exod 39:27). Further, Josephus tells us that that priestly robe was seamless, just like the one Jesus wore, and Jewish tradition ascribed this manner of weaving to all the priestly garments.[1] Most importantly, when the sacrifice for all of Israel's sins was being presented on the Day of Atonement, the high priest would remove his normal priestly garments and bring the blood of the sacrifice into the holy of holies wearing only the tunic and its accompanying linen pieces (Lev 16:4, 23–24). There seems to be a thread of clues in John's text that Jesus, when he went to the cross, was wearing the same sort of

---

1. Josephus, *Antiquities* 3.161 (*Complete Works*, 105).

clothing that the high priest wore to bear the blood of the sacrifice on the Day of Atonement.

Although Christ was crucified during the Passover festival, Christians have long seen echoes of the Day of Atonement ritual in his death.[2] Hebrews borrows the imagery of the Day of Atonement and attributes it to Jesus' passion. Just as the high priest brought the blood of the sacrifice into the holy of holies itself, an act that was only done on the Day of Atonement, so Jesus also brought his own sacrifice into the heavenly holy of holies, which is the presence of God himself (Heb 9:11–14, 25). Even the location of Golgotha, standing outside the city walls, is imbued with symbolic symmetry vis-à-vis the Day of Atonement sin offerings in Hebrews 13:11–12, which notes that such offerings also had to be taken "outside the camp" to be disposed of.

One of the strange parts of the Day of Atonement ritual was that the tabernacle itself, and later the temple, also had to have atonement worked for them, because they were "among [the Israelites], in the midst of their uncleanness" (Lev 16:16). In the rules given for this ritual, the whole tabernacle required atonement, including the altar and the holy of holies, and thus the blood of the sacrifice is sprinkled not only on the ark of the covenant's lid, but in front of it as well, apparently to provide atonement for the place itself (16:15–19). Hebrews picks up on this intriguing practice and makes it part of Jesus' act, in whose sacrifice "the heavenly things" corresponding to the tabernacle's articles and objects are purified (9:21–23). But what could this mean? We have already seen how these elements were regarded as "most holy" because of God's presence, a level of holiness entirely removed from defilement. If the tabernacle was the place of the abiding presence of God, how could God's holiness dwell in something that was unclean and needed to be purified? And if that objection holds in the case of the tabernacle, how much more for the heavenly sanctuary itself? Why on earth would heaven need atoning purification worked for it? The terminology used suggests more than simply a ceremony of dedication, so in what sense do these things require atonement?

Here we may come back around to one of our opening points: the tabernacle and temple were understood to represent, in miniature form, the great cosmic temple of God's whole creation. But because of the sin of its rebel priests, it was now a broken temple, with God and his creation separated from one another. God's cosmic temple of creation thus

---

2. As, for instance, in *Epistle of Barnabas 7* (Holmes, *Apostolic Fathers*, 400–405).

requires "at-one-ment," the bringing together of these disjointed parts that have been laid desolate by our rebellion. They are in need, to borrow a phrase from Paul, of a ministry of reconciliation. Bringing these things together requires something that can overcome the death that results from our separation from God, and so it is by a symbol of death—the blood of a sacrifice—that the atonement of Christ was prefigured in the tabernacle, not only for us humans, but for the entire creation-temple as well. The Day of Atonement ritual was, in some sense, a renewal of creation, a ritual by which the relationship between the Creator and all his creatures could be brought back together again. In offering atonement for the tabernacle as well as for the people, it was a symbol of enacting at-one-ment between all the parts of God's broken creation. It was, in visible form, a prophecy of what God would do through Christ: "reconcile to himself all things, whether things on earth or things in heaven, by making peace through his blood, shed on the cross" (Col 1:20; see also Eph 1:10)

When we consider the crucifixion of Jesus in light of God's creation-temple, there are other symmetries that also come to the surface. The cross itself was prefigured in many places throughout the Old Testament, as in the pole with the serpent that brought the Israelites salvation from certain death (Num 21:4–9; John 3:14–15) and in the wood that made the bitter waters sweet (Exod 15 22–25). Two such symbols lay at the heart of the temple itself: Aaron's staff which had budded (Num 17:1–10) and the lampstand in the sanctuary. The lampstand was fashioned to look like an almond tree, and Aaron's staff had essentially budded into an almond tree, complete with flowers and fruit. Both of these symbols were taken by Christians to be signs of the tree of life (when looking back toward Eden) and of the cross (when looking forward to Christ), because the cross itself was thought to be the fulfillment of the tree of life.[3] Out of all the ways that one could execute a condemned prisoner, there is something fitting in the fact that the new Adam would be crucified, thus bringing by a "tree" our redemption from our ancestors' sin at the tree of knowledge, and our deliverance to the tree of life.

---

3. See Justin Martyr, *Dialogue with Trypho* 86 (*ANF* 1:242), and John of Damascus, *Exact Exposition* 4.11 (*Writings*, 352), both of which list many such Old Testament foreshadowings of the cross.

The Death of Christ

One of the most striking reasons for reading the passion narratives in parallel with the creation accounts is the haunting concordance of God's Sabbath rest with the death and entombment of Jesus. Why would an omnipotent God—who, by definition, never needs to rest—choose to devote a day to rest after creating the universe? This has been a fruitful question for theologians, both Jewish and Christian, since the book of Genesis was written down. Many of the possible answers have to do with God's relationship with us and the blessings we receive by having a day to dwell intentionally with him. As we saw earlier in this book, there is also a good case to be made that the idea of divine rest speaks directly to the nature of the cosmos as a temple, in which God would take up residence. But the Gospels provide us with yet another interpretation: the Sabbath-day rest of God prefigured the death and entombment of Jesus. After the sixth day of creation was done—the day of humanity's creation—God rested, and after the sixth day of Jesus' passion week was done—the day of humanity's remaking through his blood—Jesus himself rested in death.

Various Christian denominations have spent a great deal of time speculating about what exactly Jesus was up to during that day in which his body lay dead in the tomb. Was his spirit bursting open the gates of hell and leading prisoners out, or was he already spiritually in paradise, or perhaps in some kind of soul-sleep? These are interesting and important questions, but they sometimes distract us from considering the significance of his dead body lying in the tomb. Some early church fathers thought the latter question was very important. On the sixth day, Adam's body was formed from the ground, and on the sixth day the new Adam's body returned to the ground. Cyril of Jerusalem describes Jesus' entombment as signifying the shattering of the curse that was laid on the earth itself: just as part of the curse of Genesis 3 spoke of the ground producing thorns, so also Jesus took up the thorns and was placed down into the ground "so that the earth which had been cursed might receive the blessing instead of the curse."[4]

One of the traditional ways of thinking about the problem of humanity in our fallen condition is the triad of sin, Satan, and death: our rebellion, our enemy, and our separation from God, who is the only source of everlasting life. When we think of Jesus' passion, many Christians nowadays give a great deal of attention to the sin aspect, and that

---

4. Cyril of Jerusalem, *Catechetical Lectures* 13.18 (*NPNF*² 7:87).

attention is not necessarily misplaced, because sin is a core part of the problem. But if our theology makes us think in terms of sin as the *sole* problem, then we should at least consider the fact that other traditions of classical Christian theology have seen things somewhat differently. Many early Christians, particularly those in the Eastern traditions of the patristic age, gave a great deal of emphasis to Christ's triumph over Satan and his shattering of death, to the point where death (rather than sin) was understood as the fundamental problem of fallen humanity. Death was described as something with present power over us: a tyrant exercising dominion over its captives.[5] Indeed, some of the greatest church fathers, like Athanasius, the defender of the divinity of Christ, wrote their understanding of the gospel primarily as a rescue from the power of death.[6]

There is a temptation to conceptualize death as a future, end-of-life event: physical mortality, and then the day of judgment. But this is not the way Paul describes death in the New Testament, at least not in every case; he sometimes shows it as an active principle at work in us right now—"The mind governed by the flesh is death" (Rom 8:6; see also his use of "death" throughout Rom 7; cf. Eph 2:1–5; 1 John 3:14). Because of sin, ours and Adam's, we are separated from God, who is the source of both physical and spiritual life. Once we are in our fallen condition, our spiritual death becomes a tyrant, under whose reign sin continues to proceed, like a symptom from an underlying disease. To read death only in the sense of a future penalty for sin (as so many of us are wont to do), and not in the sense of a natural consequence of sin, which is present with us in our daily lives, makes us miss out on some of the grand symphony of the gospel. The parts of the orchestra playing themes of sin and forgiveness are there on center stage, but they are not the only parts. There is also a grand song of Christ shattering the tyrannical power of death on our behalf—not only death as the penalty for sin, but death as the present spiritual disease from which we are all dying inside.

Death is both an ongoing condition and a future event, an interpretation that helps explain the disparity between the warning of Genesis 2:17—"On the day that you eat of it [the fruit of the tree of knowledge], you will certainly die" (NASB)—and the fact that Adam and Eve did not die on the day they ate of it. (Recall from the last chapter that patristic writers often wrote about death as present "corruption" at work within us,

---

5. See John Chrysostom, *Homilies on First Corinthians* 39.3 (NPNF[1] 12:235).

6. Athanasius, *On the Incarnation* 20–22, 27–29, 44 (NPNF[2] 4:46–48, 50–52, 60–61).

not just an end-of-life event.) Once we see death not just as a future penalty for sin, but as a spiritual disease even now at work within us, holding us in its power, then we can understand why so many early Christians articulated the great reward of the gospel not so much as "forgiveness" (as true as that would be), but as "life," a trend that appears in some of the earliest texts.[7]

Sin was the cause of the rupture between God and his creation, and the result of that rupture was death, so in an act of immeasurable love, the incarnate son of God undertook death for us. By dying, Jesus Christ not only atoned for our sins and assured our forgiveness, he entered into the void of separation between ourselves and God, and pulled it all back together again. His dead body, lying in the tomb, was a sign of his humanity entering into death, but at the same time becoming what humanity had been before death came ("dust to dust"), so that it might rise again in newness of life. As Irenaeus wrote of death and burial: "[The body] is placed, as it were, in the crucible of earth, to be re-cast again."[8] Thus in his death, Jesus had brought humanity back to the moment of its creation from the dust, and now a new humanity would arise.

The Resurrection

As we turn from the Sabbath-rest of Holy Saturday to the dawn of Easter morning, we are stepping out of the seven days of creation and into the first day of the next week. Early church writers called this "the eighth day," since it signified several things. It marked the beginning of God's restoration of creation by his refashioning of humanity in Christ (thus, a new day of creation after the seventh day), as Barnabas 15 says: "I [God] will create the beginning of an eighth day, which is the beginning of another world."[9] The eighth day also marked the institution of a new covenant, since the old covenant had been marked by circumcision, a rite practiced on males on the eighth day of life.[10]

Jesus' resurrection from the dead was the decisive step in the New Creation of humanity; this much we can see in Romans 5:15–19 and 1

---

7. See 2 Clem. 20.5; Ignatius, *To the Ephesians* 1.1; Polycarp, *To the Philippians* 8.1 (Holmes, *Apostolic Fathers*, 164–65, 182–83, 288–91).

8. Irenaeus, *Fragments* 12 (*ANF* 1:570).

9. *Epistle of Barnabas* 15 (Holmes, *Apostolic Fathers*, 428–29).

10. See Cyprian, Epistle 58, 4 (*ANF* 5:354).

Corinthians 15:21–22. The resurrection released us from the death of Adam's sin and brought us to life in Christ. We have moved from an old humanity, headed by Adam and defined by his sin, to a new humanity, headed by Christ. To paint it in the imagery of Genesis 1–3: Jesus had taken us back to the tree by his cross, had borne on himself the consequence of our sin by his death, had been buried back into the earth from which our bodies came, and now, having taken humanity all the way back to the beginning, the moment of New Creation comes, and Jesus rises to new life as the new Adam, in whose humanity sin and death can have no claim.

When we consider Jesus' priestly office, and particularly the presentation of himself as an atoning sacrifice, the resurrection emerges as a necessary element of the drama. As mentioned above, Jesus was both the offering and the offerer. If we were to transpose Jesus' death on the cross into the language of temple sacrifice, then his death is clearly insufficient on its own—that would be equivalent to a sacrifice being slaughtered on the great altar, and nothing more. But the killing of the sacrifice is not the end of the rite. Even after the sacrifice has been made, one still needed a living high priest to carry the sacrificial blood into the holy of holies. By his resurrection to new life, Jesus can now serve as that living high priest, and take the next step of the sacrificial ritual, which is tied to his ascension.

Hebrews also notes that it is the resurrection which shows Jesus to be the high priest *par excellence*: with death having no power over him, he lives on eternally as our one mediator, whom no other priest would ever need to replace. His immortality, testified to by his resurrection, is one of the points of connection with the archetypal figure of Melchizedek, because the prophecy of Psalm 110:4 says (apparently addressing a messianic figure), "You are a priest forever, in the order of Melchizedek," and the inclusion of the word "forever" suggests that the priest being spoken of was immortal (Heb 7:15–25).[11] The resurrection is also a kingly event, and not least in that it represents Jesus' great triumph over all the enemies of humanity. Insofar as the role of a king in the ancient Near East was to ride out to war and defeat the enemies threatening his people, Jesus fulfills the role of king completely. Jesus does what good kings do, and conquers the enemies of his people. His resurrection from the dead

---

11. See John Chrysostom, *Homilies on Hebrews* 13.5 (NPNF[1] 14:429).

is the act that shatters the hold of death and Satan, and moves the new humanity beyond their grasp.

Further, the resurrection offers an intriguing symmetry with the life of David, the archetypal forerunner of Jesus in the royal office. David's life was marked by a desperate passion sequence of his own, in which the king was betrayed by his son, saw much of the country turn against him, and had to flee into the living death of exile. Yet in the midst of the crisis, the favor of God raises David back up again; his army triumphs and he is restored to the throne. It is a pattern that mirrors, in some broad respects, Jesus' story from Gethsemane to the empty tomb. Further, the resurrection appears to be a direct fulfillment of some of the prophecies in David's own songs, as in Psalm 16:10: "You will not abandon me to the realm of the dead, nor will you let your faithful one see decay" (see Acts 2:27). The story of Jesus' passion has so many resonances with the desolations and triumphs of David that the entire book of Psalms was often read as a book about Jesus, to such a degree that some early Christian interpreters took certain psalms as essentially being spoken by Christ regarding the experience of his passion.

There is one more story of the resurrection that commands our attention at this point. John's Gospel gives us an account of Jesus' first resurrection appearance, to Mary Magdalene in the garden outside the tomb. As already mentioned, we should note the parallelism between Adam's garden and this one, but John's story takes us even further. Mary at first does not recognize Jesus, and mistakes him for the gardener (John 20:15). We ought not to read too much into a small detail like this, but we will note in passing that the new Adam, on the first day of the New Creation, standing here in a garden, is presented as looking like a gardener—essentially the same role that Adam had as the caretaker of the garden of Eden. The priest-king of creation had returned to his office.

The Ascension

The ascension gets short shrift in much contemporary theology, at least when compared to the level of attention given to Jesus' death and resurrection. The average Christian layperson would likely struggle to give a fully orbed answer for why Jesus ascended and what it means. It is often just taken as a simple explanation for why Jesus is not here anymore. Skeptics might find this rather convenient, that the supposedly risen

Messiah should mysteriously vanish to the heavens without displaying himself to anyone outside his own family and friends. But that objection does not hold as much strength if we view the ascension in the same way the early church did. It was far from just a convenient explanation for why Jesus was not around anymore; it was actually taken to be the necessary next step in his messianic mission, without which the atonement he wrought would not have been complete. According to the New Testament, the cross and the empty tomb would not have been enough on their own; there was one more necessary part to follow. The ascension must be held together with the crucifixion and resurrection as three acts in a single drama.

Let's return for a moment to that story of Mary Magdalene meeting the risen Jesus in the garden. In the middle of a beautiful and heart-touching scene, Jesus says something that sounds a little odd, if not harsh: "Do not hold on to me" (John 20:17). While this has sometimes been translated as "do not touch me," it is probably better rendered in the sense of "holding onto" or "clinging to." Interpreters through the ages have scratched their heads over this saying, and Augustine even admitted that while he couldn't discern a certain meaning from it, "some sacred mystery must lie concealed in these words."[12] This puzzlement has not abated, despite the fact that Jesus himself offers an immediate explanation for his harsh-sounding command: "Do not hold on to me, for I have not yet ascended to the Father. Go instead to my brothers and tell them, 'I am ascending to my Father and your Father, to my God and your God.'" Jesus links his command with a reference to his ascension, and then tells Mary to get about the business of making it known. While we might not be able to plumb the depths of Jesus' saying with any degree of certainty, we can at least notice that he seems to regard his ascension as a necessary and important part of his work, and one that needs to be engaged in a timely manner. This story does not show the risen Christ simply strolling about the garden and enjoying the fact that everything has been accomplished; no, he is already on his way to the next part of the drama. There was one more step that had to be done.

What is it about the ascension that makes it so necessary an element to the story of Jesus' death and resurrection? If Jesus has already been sacrificed for my sins and defeated death on my behalf, what more remains? Some common presentations of the gospel, focused as they are

---

12. Augustine, *Homilies on the Gospel of John* 121.3 (*NPNF*[1] 7:438).

on the salvation of individuals by the forgiveness of sins, have a hard time seeing the necessity of the ascension. It is only when we consider the larger theme of the priest-king taking up his reign and undertaking the restoration of his creation-temple that we begin to see all the dimensions of this event.

Let's start by looking at the priestly aspect of Jesus' role. When we consider Jesus' death as a sacrifice for sins, many of us tend to think only of the cross. But to anyone with a passing familiarity with the Jewish temple system, it probably would have struck them as oddly incomplete to say, "Jesus was crucified as a sacrifice for our sins," and then leave it at that. The reason why it is incomplete is that it is only half of the equation. As everyone knew in ancient temple cultures, the sinner longing for atonement needs not one thing but two: the death of the sacrifice in their behalf, and a priest who can present the offering in the divine presence.

This was especially clear on the Day of Atonement. It was not enough just to kill the sacrifices on the great altar outside the temple doors; the ritual would not be complete. It was necessary for the high priest to then bear the blood of the sacrifices up the steps, through the cloud of incense inside (as mentioned in Lev 16:13), and pass beyond the curtain into the holy of holies, there to present the sacrificial blood in the presence of God. When we speak of the cross alone as the whole drama of atonement, we are essentially leaving the sacrifice unpresented on the altar. The book of Hebrews clearly says that we need not only a sacrifice, but an offerer able to present it. So not only was Jesus the sacrifice, he was the priest offering the sacrifice. Hebrews links the certainty of our atonement not to the cross alone, but to the fact that Jesus has entered the heavenly holy of holies to present the sacrifice of himself there in the presence of the Father (Heb 9:11–28).

Indeed, it might be more than coincidence that the physical details of the ascension evoke the imagery of the priest's ascent into the temple on the Day of Atonement. Luke shows Jesus performing the priestly act of lifting up his hands and blessing his followers just before he is taken up (24:50–51). This is exactly the same as what the high priest Aaron did in the middle of the first great sacrifice ritual at the tabernacle. After slaughtering the sacrifices on the altar, "Aaron lifted his hands toward the people and blessed them," and immediately afterwards, he and Moses entered into the tabernacle to complete the ritual (Lev 9:22–23). Notice the pattern: the sacrifice is slaughtered on the altar; the high priest blesses the people; and then goes up into the tabernacle, into the presence of the Lord. It is the exact same pattern one can see in Jesus' crucifixion, his priestly blessing on the Mount of Olives, and his ascension into the presence of the Father. Recall also that temple worship itself was considered to be a sort of ascension into the presence of God, beyond time and space. So on the Day of Atonement, when the high priest climbed the steps from the altar into the sanctuary and vanished from the sight of the crowds through a cloud of incense as he entered into the presence of God's throne room, it is a very similar scene to Jesus ascending into heaven and being hidden from view by a cloud (Acts 1:9).

Hebrews tells us that Jesus' second coming is also connected with this ritual. Just as the entry of the priest into the temple was not the end of the ritual (merely the completion of certain acts of atonement), so also there is still another act to come. After having entered the temple and presented the blood, the high priest would return, back through the cloud of incense in the same way the crowds had seen him vanish (see Acts 1:11), and (along with a few more ritual acts) would bestow the assurance of God's forgiveness upon the people. With that picture of the priestly rite in mind, hear how Hebrews 9:28 puts it at the end of its description of Jesus' entry into the heavenly tabernacle: "He will appear a second time, not to bear sin, but to bring salvation for those who are waiting for him." To anyone who had ever seen the Day of Atonement ritual, this would have been the image in their minds: the high priest has gone up into the divine presence through the cloud of incense, and he will descend again through that cloud to bring the ceremony to completion. Thus the gap between Jesus' ascension and second coming is not just a strange hiatus in the middle of his messianic work, not a period of absence that needs to be explained away: in light of the prophetic rituals of the Day of Atonement, this disappearance-and-return narrative is exactly what one would have expected of the messianic high priest.

Now for the royal aspect of Jesus' ascension, which was so important that it lay at the heart of many of the disciples' first proclamations of the gospel in the book of Acts. The ascension and enthronement of Jesus in heaven is mentioned repeatedly in those early sermons and testimonies (Acts 2:33; 3:21; 5:31; 7 56).[13] It was taken as a direct fulfillment of the prophecy of Daniel 7:13–14, in which "one like a son of man" came with the clouds of heaven into the presence of the Ancient of Days, where he was given the sovereign authority of an everlasting, worldwide

---

13. See also Polycarp, *To the Philippians* 2.1 (Holmes, *Apostolic Fathers*, 282–83).

kingdom. Every time the disciples mention the ascension, they do so not as something to be explained away, but as an expected and visible proof of Jesus' claims about himself: he was the true messianic king as predicted by Scripture. They refer to Jesus as standing at the right hand of God, and Peter even calls him "prince" (Acts 5:31), a royal title that echoes the messianic prophecies of Ezekiel 37:25 and 44:3. Jesus' ascension, then, was the ultimate proof of his royal office. It was his triumphant ascent to the throne, the crowning moment of his coronation ceremonies.

It comes as no surprise, then, that the rest of the New Testament portrays the church age not as an interlude or a static waiting period until the second coming, but as the current reign of Christ and the period of his active priestly service (Rom 8:34; 1 Cor 15:25; Eph 1:20; 2:6; Col 3:1; Heb 8:1–2; Rev 5:6). The ascension, considered together with the crucifixion and resurrection, was the completion of the atonement rites of the great high priest and the ultimate vindication and glorification of the one true king, who fulfills the royal promises of Israel and reigns over all things. In Jesus' ascension, we see the priest-king, having purified the sanctuary and brought the disrupted temple back together in himself, take up his reign and put all his enemies under his feet, until even death itself—its tyranny already broken by the resurrection—is finally done away with (1 Cor 15:25–26).

From his position as the divine messianic king, he also sends the Holy Spirit upon the new community of his followers (Acts 2:33), thus bestowing a breath of spiritual life into his new humanity, just as Adam, upon his creation from the dust, was brought to life by the breath of God (of which we will have more to say in the next chapter). The Holy Spirit's coming was promised many times in the Old Testament (Isa 32:15; 44:2–3; Ezek 36:26–27; 37:14; 39:29; Joel 2:28–29), and it had come to be part of the Jewish expectation of the Messiah's role. When the messianic reign began, it would be the period the prophets had spoken of, and one of the marks of that period was the sending of the Holy Spirit (thus Peter, in his Acts 2 sermon, refers to "the *promised* Holy Spirit"). John's Gospel seems to have this prophetic fulfillment in mind when it tells us that the Spirit had not yet been given during Jesus' ministry, because Jesus had not yet been glorified (John 7:37–39). In this way, Pentecost becomes a sign of the inauguration of the messianic reign, an indisputable testimony that the king was now on the throne. But as in the case of his priestly ministry, the royal reign still has one more act to come, when Christ returns again with his enemies put under his feet, and then God will be all in all, and the fullness of the messianic reign—"the times of refreshing" (Acts 3:19–20)—will come.

There is one final way that some early Christians thought about the significance of the ascension: it was the sign of Christ bringing heaven and earth into unity. As Maximus the Confessor wrote: "Christ, having completed for us his saving work and ascended to heaven with the body which he had taken to himself, accomplishes in his own self the union of heaven and earth."[14] Essentially, Jesus had taken humanity, by the vessel of his own human nature, back into the courts of heaven, thus returning the "microcosm of the cosmos" to the very presence of its Creator. Jesus, in offering himself as the final sacrifice, has offered humanity back to God. The temple of creation is thus brought back together in him, raised into communion with God, and unity restored between heaven and earth (Eph 1:10; Col 1:19).

---

14. Maximus the Confessor, *Commentary on the Lord's Prayer,* quoted in Clément, *Roots,* 55.

7

New Creation:
The Early Christian Perspective

IN HIS FIRST HYMN on the nativity, Ephrem the Syrian wrestled with the paradox of the incarnation of Christ: "This Lord of natures," he wrote, "today was transformed contrary to His nature."[1] Indeed, across the whole sweep of the Christian tradition, the mighty mystery of God-made-man has continued to astonish us and to challenge the limitations of our understanding. Nevertheless, we can seek to try to know it better, by tuning our ear to what the Spirit of God has taught the church throughout the ages. But for modern Christians who begin to turn to patristic writings on the incarnation, we may find that we are in for a bit of a twist. If you thought that the incarnation was a big deal for rather obvious reasons, you may come to find that other Christian generations have counted it an even bigger deal than you had ever imagined. Whether or not one comes to accept the patristic view of what the incarnation means for our salvation, it is worth taking the time to understand it.

Many Christians tend to think about the incarnation as a prerequisite for our atonement. It is one of the steps that has to be checked off for true atonement to happen: Jesus had to be fully God and fully man in order to both bear and forgive our sins. That insight is true (and we owe something of our ability to articulate it to the theologians of the patristic age), but much of early Christianity would say that there is still far more to the picture than just that. The incarnation was not simply a prerequisite to atonement; it was, in and of itself, the doorway to our union with

---

1. Ephrem the Syrian, *Hymns on the Nativity* 1.97 (*Hymns*, 74).

God. It was both a prerequisite to atonement and the path to humanity's original goal, its *telos*. The incarnation of Jesus Christ was part of a larger narrative about human nature and our upward call to grow into loving union with God, and it addressed our ability to be incorporated into the new and living reality of the body of Christ. In much contemporary theology, particularly in the West, the main show of what Jesus did for us is the cross, but for much of patristic theology, the simple fact of the incarnation often seized center stage.

At the base of it all is a philosophical perspective on human nature: rather than viewing humanity as a set of atomized individuals, some early Christian writers tended to view it as a single, united, communal reality. Human nature was something held in common among us all.[2] This view is sometimes accused of just being Plato's mystical spirituality in disguise, but it actually appears to be a biblical idea. When Paul said that we were all "in Adam" (1 Cor 15:22; Rom 5:12–19), the early church fathers and mothers interpreted this somewhat more literally than we often do today (something along the lines of the view taught in Hebrews 7:9–10, that Levi paid the tithe to Melchizedek via Abraham's tithe, because Levi was "still in the body of his ancestor" when it happened). C. S. Lewis, in his *Mere Christianity*, articulated the same view of the real unity of human nature, describing humanity as more like a growing tree than a series of discrete individuals.[3]

In this view, the incarnation of Jesus suddenly takes on wild new dimensions, over and above his qualifications to work atonement on our behalf. As Irenaeus wrote, "[Jesus] took up humanity into himself."[4] Gregory of Nyssa echoed the same refrain: "The Word, in taking flesh, was joined with humanity, and took our nature within himself . . . the stuff of our nature was entirely sanctified by Christ."[5] Simply being connected to Jesus was the basis of our salvation, the healing of our human nature. The stuff of which I am made—my human nature—may now exist in communion with the Trinitarian God through the union of Jesus' divine and human natures, because Jesus' human nature is linked to my own. In other words, if the eternal Son of God has united himself to human nature in a real human person, then the doorway to union with

---

2. See Gregory of Nyssa, Catechetical Oration 32 (PG 45:77-84); Athanasius, *On the Incarnation* 9 (NPNF² 4:40-41).

3. Lewis, *Mere Christianity*, 180.

4. Irenaeus, *Against Heresies* 3.16.6 (ANF 1:443).

5. Gregory of Nyssa, *Against Apollinarius* 2, quoted in Clément, *Roots*, 46.

God has been flung wide open for all of us. All that is necessary is to become united to Jesus' sinless human nature rather than Adam's tainted legacy—a movement made possible for us by Jesus' atoning sacrifice and his triumph over death—and thus I am drawn into communion, through Christ, with the very life of God. By being incorporated into Christ's new humanity, I am immediately and necessarily brought into communion with God, simply by virtue of the incarnation itself.[6] This may sound strange to some ears, but at its heart, it is merely an extension of the biblical logic of the mystical union described as "the body of Christ" and, quite simply, of being "in Christ," a phrase which forms the core of Paul's vision of redeemed humanity. If I truly am in Christ and part of the body of Christ in more than a merely metaphorical way (or, to use the reverse, if Christ is in me—Gal 2:20; Col 1:27), then it is in that communion that I am brought back into union with God.

The Protestant reformers also saw union with Christ as being at the heart of our redemption. Both Martin Luther and John Calvin thought it was the bedrock of the biblical view of salvation. Within some Protestant perspectives, the union of Christians in Christ is effectively accomplished by the indwelling presence of the Holy Spirit (following such passages as Rom 8:9–16). Since we are connected to the Spirit, who works in the church to truly make us the body of Christ, we are thus bound to Christ through the united life of the Trinity and the grace at work in the community of faith. Regardless of whichever angle you use to understand the concept, the fundamental truth remains: our identity as Christians is centered in our union with Christ our Lord. By his incarnation and by the continuing work of the indwelling Spirit, we find ourselves granted the heritage of our creation: the upward call to grow into loving union with our Creator.

New Humanity, New Creation

Whether by means of Christ taking humanity up into himself, or by the Holy Spirit's work of incorporating us into Christ (or both), a new humanity is being fashioned even now, not under the old headship of Adam, but under Christ. Not only does Paul talk about "New Creation" as the state of every Christian (2 Cor 5:17; Gal 6:15), all of Scripture is replete with images of this new humanity, from prophetic texts like Ezekiel's promise

---

6. See Gregory of Nazianzus, Oration 29, 19 (*On God and Christ*, 86-87).

of "a new heart and a new spirit" (36:26), to New Testament Epistles telling Christians to put on "the new self" (Eph 4:24; Col 3:10) and the well-known image of being "born again" (John 3:3; 1 Pet 1:3). John's Gospel even says that Jesus died in order to take all "the scattered children of God" and to "bring them together and make them one" (11:51–52). Paul also speaks in terms of "one new humanity" when he is addressing the bringing together of Jews and gentiles in the Christian community (Eph 2:15). In all these texts, we see the work of Christ described in terms of a new humanity being fashioned in those who come to him. And it truly is the work of Christ: just as the Son of God was the active divine agent of the first creation, the Word by which all things came to be (John 1:3; Col 1:16; Heb 1:2), so also it is by the Son of God that the New Creation springs forth.

It's worth taking a moment to think about Jesus' creation of a new humanity in himself, because it is a window into a truly beautiful insight. If we take the early church belief that the day of Jesus' resurrection was "the eighth day"—a day associated not only with resurrection, but a new covenant for a renewed creation—then we begin to get a picture of this emerging New Creation. The early Christian document Epistle of Barnabas suggests that the creation of a new humanity on resurrection Sunday was just the beginning of a much larger process. It says: "[God] made a second creation in the last days" (6.13) and "I will create the beginning of an eighth day, which is the beginning of another world" (15.8).[7] The New Testament testifies that the process of restoring creation does not begin and end with humanity alone; there are other acts to come. Romans 8:19–22 shows the whole creation groaning as if in the pains of childbirth and yearning toward a liberation that will one day come for it, a liberation connected with the renewed humanity itself: "For the creation waits in eager expectation for the children of God to be revealed" (v. 19). In Revelation, we are given a glimpse of the final consummation of the new heavens and the new earth, and in the center of that scene God proclaims, "I am making everything new!" (21:5).

So what is the emerging shape of this New Creation? The biblical texts do not add many details beyond the verses quoted above. But there does seem to be yet another lovely symmetry that we can discern in the plan of God, if only in its barest outline. Just as humanity stood in the middle of God's original creation—the spirit-and-matter being standing

---

7. *Epistle of Barnabas* 6.13, 15.8 (Holmes, *Apostolic Fathers*, 398–99, 428–29).

astride dual worlds of spirit and matter—so also humanity seems to stand in the center of God's plan of creation and re-creation. Consider this pattern: in Genesis 1 we can see the first six days of creation, which culminate with the making of Adam and Eve. Now compare that to the corresponding pattern of the New Creation. If the "eighth day" is the first day of a project of New Creation, on which humanity is made new in Christ, then we appear to have a mirror image in progress. In the first creation, the process ends with humanity; in the New Creation, it begins with humanity. The New Creation begins here in us, but will go on to extend through all of the created order, as the "week" of New Creation proceeds like a mirror image of the first. The first six days of creation began with the natural world, rising to humanity at the summit; and the New Creation begins at the re-creation of humanity at the summit and then will flow back down to include the natural world. How exactly that final process will work, or what it will look like, or when it will happen, are all unanswered questions; we are simply told that in the end it will be so, when our God makes all things new.

Pentecost and New Creation

Let's return for a moment to the narrative of the Gospels and Acts, because here we see the dynamics of New Creation at work in the church. We left the story in the last chapter at the ascension, and the following event—Pentecost—really should be viewed as an extension of the ascension (some early Christian communities apparently celebrated the ascension on Pentecost Sunday).[8]

One of the expectations for the messianic age was that the Spirit of God would be poured out in power, and so Jesus' ascension and enthronement is quite naturally followed by the sending of the Spirit. It was one of the things that was expected to accompany the reign of the messianic king. Jesus himself connects the two ideas in John 16:7: "Unless I go away, the Advocate will not come to you; but if I go, I will send him to you." Jesus is not saying here that it is impossible for two members of the Trinity to be present at the same time; such a reading might leave itself open to the heresy of modalism. He appears to be saying that the sending of the Spirit is a function of his going; that is, when he ascends to begin his messianic reign, enthroned in the heavenly places, he will send

---

8. See Tertullian, *On Baptism* 19 (*ANF* 3:678).

the Spirit as promised in the Old Testament (Ezek 37:1–14; 39:29; Joel 2:28–29; see Acts 2:14–18, 33).

There are some clues that by the time of Christianity's rise, the Jewish Festival of Weeks, on whose observance Pentecost falls, was associated with the renewal of the covenant. Both the Qumran community and the book of *Jubilees* appear to have held this idea, so it is fitting that the sign of the messianic new covenant—the pouring out of the promised Holy Spirit—should come on that particular day. At Pentecost, the new covenant promised by the prophets had finally come, with the Spirit being poured out from on high at the beginning of the messianic reign.

Pentecost also fits into the broader picture we have been painting, drawing out connections with both the temple and creation. The temple imagery is easy to see in this story. The visible manifestation of the Spirit's presence, shown in tongues of fire that came to rest on them (Acts 2:3), calls to mind the "pillar of fire" that showed the divine presence leading the people of Israel during their wilderness wanderings, which itself was another form of the "pillar of cloud" that would descend to rest upon the tabernacle (Num 14:14; Exod 33:9; 40:34). There was also an ancient Jewish tradition that associated tongues of fire with the heavenly temple, as seen in *1 Enoch*, where the main character approaches a building that houses the throne of God:

> I kept coming (into heaven) until I approached a wall which was built of white marble and surrounded by tongues of fire; and it began to frighten me. And I came into the tongues of fire and drew near to a great house which was built of white marble . . . And behold, there was an opening before me, and a second house which is greater than the former, and everything is built with tongues of fire . . I observed and saw inside it a lofty throne . . . and the Great Glory was sitting upon it.[9]

The visible symbols of the Spirit's outpouring were not something wild and new; they were direct fulfillments of temple traditions. The tongues of fire testified that the fledgling church had become the temple of God.

Luke, writing in Acts 2:2, also tells us about another part of the Pentecost experience: "a sound like the blowing of a violent wind." This symbol would have been likewise meaningful, attesting to the pouring out of the promised Spirit: in Greek, as in Hebrew, the word for "spirit" does double duty as a word for "wind" or "breath" (*pneuma*; Heb. *ruach*).

---

9. *1 En.* 14.9–10, 15, 20 (*OTP* 1:20–21).

In that sense, it is the most natural thing in the world for the Spirit to manifest in the sound of a rushing wind. In fact, the particular word used for wind in this verse is not actually *pneuma,* but a related term—*pnoē*—which usually has to do with a blast of breath. This should call to mind the moment of humanity's creation. The Septuagint version of the Old Testament uses *pnoē* for the breath that God breathed into Adam's body to bring him to life (Gen 2:7). Jesus draws on the same image when he breathes on his disciples and tells them to "receive the Holy Spirit" (John 20:22). The *pnoē* of Pentecost, then, would have called to mind the moment of humanity's creation and testified to the rise of a new humanity, fully alive in Christ.

The miracle of speaking in tongues at Pentecost also appears to echo the early chapters of Genesis. In Genesis 11, the postfall fragmentation of human society is illustrated in the story of Babel, where humanity's ancestral language is replaced with a babble of mutually incoherent tongues. Pentecost flips this story on its head: in the New Creation, the many languages of the nations are drawn back together again in the single message of the gospel of Jesus Christ. The effects of the fall are being undone in the new covenant-community of the church.

These symbols point us once again to the fact that God's plan was to bring about a New Creation, and in Jesus' death, resurrection, and ascension to enthronement, humanity was being re-created through him. This re-created humanity is not, however, just a return to what we were before; it is the inheritance of what we were meant to be, and in some respects far exceeding what Adam and Eve experienced. As Irenaeus commented on Genesis 2:7, whereas Adam received merely the breath of life, we have received the Spirit of adoption, the indwelling presence of God which makes us his own children and heirs.[10]

The Spirit's presence in the church was considered the definitive mark of the church's identity. The church was the temple in which the Spirit of God had come to dwell, and thus every ministry done in the church was done in the Spirit. There was no sense that the Spirit's work was limited to ecstatic manifestations; rather, the Spirit was the everyday power behind everything in the church, as clearly present in the most routine functions of prayer and good works as in moments of heart-raising worship and wondrous miracles. Thus Irenaeus says: "Where the church is, there is the Spirit of God; and where the Spirit of God is, there

---

10. Irenaeus, *Against Heresies* 5.12.2 (*ANF* 1:537–38); see also Rom 8:14–17.

is the church and every kind of grace."[11] This idea would grow into Christianity's earliest articulations of sacramentalism, in which every action and ritual undertaken in the context of the church's faith was seen as an avenue of God's empowering grace, because the church itself was the Spirit-filled sacrament of the body of Jesus Christ.

Back on the Growth Track, with Ever-Increasing Glory

But what does Spirit-filled life in the temple of the church look like? For individual Christians, this life carries with it a number of aspects in addition to the simple, glorious fact of our salvation. One such aspect, of course, is our identity and duty as God's royal priesthood, and the remainder of this book will be devoted to exploring that duty.

Another aspect is that of growth and development. Recall that one of the earliest patristic views on Adam and Eve's condition was that they were created in a state of moral infancy, called to grow into their relationship with God. It may not be coincidence that this is exactly how the New Testament portrays us upon our entry into the new, restored humanity in Christ. We too are moral and spiritual infants: having just been "born again" (John 3:3–5), we are now "like newborn babies," and we should "crave pure spiritual milk, so that by it [we] may grow up in [our] salvation" (1 Pet 2:2). We are called to grow into maturity, a maturity that develops in communion with the body of Christ and is characterized by increasing union with Jesus himself (Eph 4:13-15; cf. Col 1:28; Heb 5:12-14; Jas 1:4; 2 Pet 3:18). From this angle, the New Testament view corroborates the patristic sense of Adam and Eve's original calling as the royal priests of creation: not only to rule and to serve, but also to grow into ever greater union with God. In Christ and in his new humanity, we have been placed back on that growth track to the fulfillment of our ultimate identity.

This growth, it is clear, occurs within the living temple of God. In the Ephesians 4 passage referenced just above, the context of growing to maturity is not an individual road of self-actualization, but rather the interwoven fellowship and communion of the body of Christ. There is simply no place in biblical Christianity for a Christian life on one's own, apart from the living reality of the church. Christians who choose to go through life unattached to a local body of believers are essentially

---

11. Irenaeus, *Against Heresies* 3.24.1 (*ANF* 1:458).

orphaning themselves, to the detriment of their own growth and development. Or, to switch the metaphor back to the temple, it is like trying to serve as a priest without a temple to serve in, a hollow echo of the fullness of our vocation. The restoration of God's great creation-temple is underway, and we who are the church of Jesus Christ are the representation of that temple in miniature form. To think that we could be Christians outside of it is a notion that early Christians would have found absurd. Christianity is not a religion of individualism, it is a living, communal participation in God's New Creation, even now being manifested in the church.

The image of the temple of God as the context for Christian life is woven throughout the New Testament, and in every case (except perhaps 1 Cor 6:19–20), it is clear that it is being conceived of as a communal temple, not as a whole bunch of little individual temples. First Corinthians 3:16–17 says it plainly: "Don't you know that you yourselves are God's temple and that God's spirit dwells in your midst? If anyone destroys God's temple, God will destroy that person; for God's temple is sacred, and you together are that temple." (Here the NIV adds clarifying words, such as "together," to help us understand that the "you" being referred to is the whole group of the church, not individual persons; see also 2 Cor 6:16; Eph 2:19–22; 1 Pet 2:4–5.) Given this communal reality, we should be careful to remember that when we talk about the indwelling Holy Spirit, this terminology does not primarily refer to each of our individual hearts as little separate temples in which the Spirit dwells (though that is likely part of the picture); it much more often speaks to the reality of the Spirit's abiding presence in the community of the church. It is together with one another that we constitute the living temple of God, and it is there that the Spirit has descended and dwells, very much as in the holy of holies of old.

One of the ways the Bible describes the presence of God in the temple is with the word "glory." While this word could be used in many different ways in Scripture, it had a particular meaning when attached to the temple: it referred not only to the radiant majesty of God's presence in an aesthetic sense, but to the very reality of that presence. This idea of temple glory is sometimes labeled God's *shekinah* (a term we inherit from Jewish rabbinic sources), which speaks not only of the radiance of God's glory but the fact that his very presence dwelt in the temple (the word is related to the Hebrew root for "dwell"). It is a way of speaking about God's glory in a personal manner, as an aspect of his very being, and not merely as a phenomenological aspect like light or beauty or majesty. John's Gospel appears to use "glory" in this more refined sense of *shekinah* when he speaks about the incarnation of the Word of God, who "made his dwelling among us. We have seen his glory, the glory of the one and only Son" (1:14). Jesus was the dwelling-in-the-midst-of-us glory of God, like the *shekinah* in the temple. In fact, Jesus himself appears to draw on *shekinah* traditions to explain his identity. For instance, he puts himself in the place of *shekinah*'s role in an adaptation of a well-known rabbinic saying: that if two or three are gathered together with the Torah, there too would the *shekinah* be.[12]

Interestingly, the New Testament does not only attribute glory to God, but to us too. We are portrayed as sharers in God's glory (see, for example, Rom 8:17–21; Col 1:27; 2 Thess 2:14; 1 Pet 5:10). In 2 Corinthians 3:18, Paul underscores this view and ties it to the idea of the Christian life as a journey of growth: "We all, who with unveiled faces contemplate the Lord's glory, are being transformed into his image with ever-increasing glory, which comes from the Lord, who is the Spirit." So not only do we contemplate the Lord's glory, but we ourselves are progressive partakers in it as we are transformed into his image.

This is a vision of the Christian life that finds immediate resonance with the patristic theology of union with God, but which sounds oddly out of place to many Christians nowadays. How many of us describe our walk with Jesus as being an experience of transformation into ever-increasing glory? We sometimes tend to push our idea of participating in God's glory to a distant future date in heaven, and so we miss the fact that the New Testament plainly speaks about this part of our experience as a here-and-now reality. Right now, you are being transformed into the image of your Lord with ever-increasing glory. Right now, you are able to participate in the divine nature (2 Pet 1:4). There is certainly a sense that our glory will be further revealed and further experienced in the future (see Rom 8:18), but that is not to say that it is not already at work. When Paul speaks of the Christian being glorified, he puts it in the past tense, not the future (Rom 8:30). We, the royal priests who serve in the living temple, where the Holy Spirit dwells in glory, may receive that very glory, and participate in it here and now.

---

12. m. Avot 3:2, in Skarsaune, *In the Shadow*, 331; cf. Matt 18:20.

The Reign of the Priest-King and His Royal Priesthood

Glory is not the only present attribute of the Christian life that we mistakenly think of as being relegated to the distant future. Let's move our attention from the temple metaphor to the royal one, and here we can observe that the New Testament portrays us as participating in Christ's reign—at least in some small way—right now. While the fullness of our participation in his reign still awaits a future unveiling (2 Tim 2:12; 1 Cor 4:8), we cannot miss the fact that it is also true right now, if only in an incipient sense. One of the places this is visible is in Ephesians 2:6, where Paul, speaking in the past tense, uses enthronement language to describe the current position of those who are in Christ: "And God raised us up with Christ and seated us with him in the heavenly realms . . ." To give another example, Jesus makes his authority as the messianic king the foundation for sending us out as his emissaries in Matthew 28:17–20. The early church father Clement of Alexandria picked up on these themes, saying that Christians are "called to sovereignty" by our association with Christ the King.[13]

The full scope of our participation in Christ's reign will clearly only come in the future, but if we are to honor the whole witness of Scripture, then we need to understand what our present partaking of his reign signifies, and not to gloss over this empowering aspect of Christian identity. We would be in error if we merely spiritualize what the New Testament says about the present shape of Christ's messianic kingdom and our place in it. The writers of the patristic age did not think that Christ's kingdom was just a spiritual reality awaiting a future fulfillment; they thought that many of the kingdom promises were coming true in the daily experience of the church itself.[14] The opening line of John Chrysostom's divine liturgy shows this deep association between Christ's kingdom and the church: every time a worshiper entered a church service, the first thing they would hear was "Blessed is the kingdom of the Father and the Son, and the Holy Spirit!"

This rhetoric of the kingdom was not understood just as a metaphor or an ephemeral idea. In the ancient world, "kingdom" did not refer to a nebulous notion of sovereignty, but to an actual institution, visibly present in everyday life. Kingdom rhetoric likely would have called to mind an administration endowed with sovereign powers and appointed

---

13. Clement of Alexandria, *Comments on 1 Peter* (ANF 2:572).
14. See, for example, Lactantius, *Divine Institutes* 4.12 (ANF 7:110–11).

officials—even, as it were, boots on the ground. This is why the charge of Jesus as king was taken seriously at his trial. It was taken so seriously, in fact, that several generations later, when the Emperor Domitian heard rumors about Christianity and the kingship of Christ, he was concerned enough to reach all the way across his empire, having his agents scour the backwater farms of Galilee until they could find some relatives of Jesus to tell him whether this new kingdom was a threat to his own. These relatives (Jude's grandsons) assured the emperor that Jesus' kingdom was based upon his heavenly reign, not operating according to the same methods of power and coercion as worldly authorities, so it would pose Domitian no political threat before the day of judgment.[15] The fact that it was a heavenly reign, however, did not mean that it was merely a spiritual reign. The early church tended to view itself as an on-the-ground embassy of Christ's heavenly kingdom, exercising sovereign powers that were not beholden to the kingdoms of this world (to the point where leaders of the church could rebuke and refuse services even to emperors).

The kingdom is something very real, and very much a practical and active movement in the world today. Though "not of this world," as Jesus says at his trial before Pilate, it is on the move in the world even now. Local churches constitute the embassy outposts of the kingdom, and we are its officials, equipped with the full authority of sovereign ambassadors. We do not use the means and methods of earthly powers (i.e., the church should fight no wars and build no empires), but the kingdom grows in the midst of human nations like yeast in a lump of dough (Matt 13:33).

This idea of the kingdom as a present reality, with us as its officials, should come as no surprise based on the biblical theology we have already covered. If we humans were created to be reigning beings, endowed with dominion over the earth from the very beginning, then it stands to reason that we would take up that vocation again upon our entry into the new humanity in Christ. He has restored us to our office, which is truly priestly and truly royal, and we serve here and now in the administration of his reign through our service as members of the body of Christ. The question of what this all means, in terms of practical aspects of our daily lives, will be the subject of Part 2.

---

15. Eusebius, *Church History* 3.19–20 (NPNF² 1:148–49).

To Bring Unity to All Things

With all of these biblical and theological themes in mind, let's go back to take one more look at the seven points of the theological vision we have been studying, the story of God's great cosmic restoration in Christ:

1. All creation was intended to be a "temple" in which God dwells, in a loving journey of ever-greater unity with his creatures. This was to culminate in an eternal unity of heaven and earth as the temple of God's reign.

2. We human beings were made as the priests of this creation-temple, as well as the designated, authoritative, ruling ambassadors of God's reign within it.

3. Our fall into sin put us into a position in which we need individual salvation through the forgiveness of sin and the defeat of its consequences. But the fall also ruptured the unity of God's creation-temple. Because its priests have rebelled, creation is a desolated temple, and the intended union of heaven and earth has been severed.

4. The Old Testament system of temple worship intentionally echoed the pattern of the creation-temple and prepared the way for the restoration of humanity's offices through Christ.

5. Jesus Christ's incarnation, ministry, death, resurrection, and ascension are all essential pieces of his work in serving both as the true King and great High Priest, as well as the active divine agent of New Creation.

6. Jesus' redemptive work is not limited to the salvation of individual humans, but extends also to the communal and cosmic levels by creating a new humanity and restoring it to its role as royal priests of the New Creation.

7. This New Creation, which has begun with humans, but which will one day encompass all of creation, will ultimately culminate in the creation's intended goal: the union of heaven and earth.

Hopefully by now, the biblical and theological bases for this set of statements will be clear, along with the fact that they were recognized and supported by a broad swath of early Christian authorities. While this grand, overarching story of cosmic redemption does not replace the joyful proclamation of salvation for each individual person by the forgiveness of their sins, it is the proper context in which to truly relish that joy. My salvation is part of a drama as vast as the universe—and not just as a blip or a footnote, but as an integral, intentional part. My salvation grants me a chance to be who I was meant to be, a member of God's royal priesthood, and by my service to participate, even if only in a small way, in the glorious work that God undertakes even now: "to bring unity to all things in heaven and on earth under Christ" (Eph 1:10).

Part Two

Life in the Royal Priesthood

8

The Church: Worship in the Living Temple

WHETHER OR NOT YOU are willing to buy into the full scope of the early Christian vision of cosmic redemption through Jesus, at this point you have hopefully been convinced that the New Testament passages which describe our identity of royal priesthood are not just incidental, throw-away lines. Both our royal and our priestly identities carry with them traditions that go all the way back to the moment of creation and include vast depths of meaning in the legacy of ancient Israel. As such, it is worth taking some time to consider what this identity means on a practical level. If we truly are God's royal priests, what does that mean about how we should live?

I am not here to tell you that you have been doing things the wrong way or that you have been missing out on big parts of the Christian life. The Bible is very clear about what the life of a follower of Jesus should look like. What the royal priesthood angle does is add context, meaning, and encouragement to those dimensions we already have in place. As such, I will not be advocating a radical reworking of how we live as Christians and as the church. Rather, this practical exploration, guided by the wisdom and experience of the patristic era, should help us answer the questions "Why am I doing this?" and maybe even "How could I be doing this better?"

First off, we should underscore that being God's royal priests is not simply an identity or a status. It is also a calling, a vocation. To be sure, it is a very broad and general calling, since it includes all of redeemed humanity, but it is a calling nonetheless. And vocations come with duties. Many modern Christians are geared to think about the gospel in terms of the question, "What am I saved from?" (with the given answers being sin, hell, and so on). But there's another side to that coin, and it's the question, "What am I saved unto?" The answer, in this case, is not only heaven, but an eternal life of being drawn into union with God's holiness and serving faithfully in the roles for which he has made us (2 Tim 2:19; Eph 2:10). Eternal life begins not in a postmortem future, but right now (John 3:36; 6:47; 17:3). As marvelous as the story of our individual salvation might be, there is still another grand narrative running in parallel with it: the renewal of the reign of God throughout his creation-temple, until the final consummation when he makes all things new. And we have a part to play in that story.

God is sovereign, but within his kingdom, he has graciously appointed officials to share in the honor and duty of his reign. The kingdom of God is not just an abstract idea, not just a metaphorical gloss for a distant providence; it is an actual reign, and like all actual reigns, its authority is manifested partly through its officials. We who are Christians, we are those officials. We are called, appointed, and empowered to act as agents of Jesus' messianic reign, a reign that is still incipient, with its fullness yet to come, but very much inaugurated and on the move here and now. Just as Adam and Eve were created in God's image, invested with a portion of his authority and called to exercise his dominion over the created order, we also now bear that high vocation, restored to us through the work of Jesus Christ. And if we are officials of his reign, then we have duties to perform. Clement of Rome, a member of the postapostolic generation of Christian leaders, combined the free gift of salvation and the call to duty in a single, lovely image: through Christ, we "have come under the yoke of his grace."[1]

A few years ago, as I was researching the history of my local church, I came across a book that one of the former pastors had written in the nineteenth century. His name was Henry V. Dexter, and the book is called *The Shining Way*. When I flipped it open, I saw that it was a compendium of Scripture verses, collected around various themes. I have seen books like this my whole life; they constitute a whole genre. Usually now they are smaller, pocket-sized books used for little gifts or devotional purposes. But here is what jumped out at me right away: almost all such books I had ever seen were collections of *promises*. Scripture compendia were usually arranged around encouraging themes of God's promises: his

---

1. 1 Clem. 16.17 (Holmes, *Apostolic Fathers*, 68–69).

blessings and his assurances of grace and favor. But not Dexter's book—it was a compendium of *duties*. Every set of verses, stretching to chapters upon chapters, was arranged to show our duties toward God, toward our families, toward our neighbors, toward our nation, and so on.

This struck me as an indication that the popular Christian culture of our own age may have developed a bit of a blind spot, a spot which other ages—like the evangelicalism of the nineteenth century—could see very well. The fact that Dexter's book was a compendium of duties rather than of encouraging, inspiring verses was not just down to a peculiarity of his theological vision; rather, his book was popular enough to be rereleased in a school-based edition for national use (*The Bible Reader*). This consideration of duties was apparently a popular way for nineteenth-century Christians to study and absorb the word of God. That is something of a disjuncture from the common pattern today, when lists of duties are just not that popular anymore. And that may be part of the problem. Our culture has trained us to think of ourselves as consumers, recipients, islands of independent prerogatives, rather than as holding a high calling of duty and service answerable to a noble identity.

In these next few chapters, we will study the practical duties that come with being a royal priest of the living God. As you will see, most of these things are what Christians have always been doing, but now we may be able to answer with greater clarity why it is that we do what we do.

The Weekly Worship Service

Let's begin with the central feature of our communal life: the weekly worship service that constitutes the main rite of our faith. Particulars of the service vary from denomination to denomination, but in general, all Christians gather for a weekly service to sing praises, pray together, hear the teaching of Scripture, and (at least on some occasions) to share the eucharistic communion together. This service is the most basic act of being a Christian, and yet in our culture today, a wide swath of people who consider themselves Christians believe it to be optional. Several times over the course of my ministry, I have had conversations with people who claim to believe in Christ but resist all notion of setting foot in a church. "As long as I believe, that's the main thing, right? After all, I have faith in God, and I pray every day."

Part of the problem is that some Christians today have been trained to think only in terms of "What must I do to be saved?" The answer they have been given is that they must believe in Christ, and they are sometimes under the assumption that this belief amounts to a single act of intellectual assent. Unfortunately that's probably not what "belief" (or "faith") means in the biblical sense. Many scholars have made a convincing case that believing in Christ, as described in the New Testament, is a much larger, life-encompassing concept than just an act of simple assent. It is really about an embodied belief, an allegiance, an assent to Christ's lordship that is revealed not only in a few words we say, but in the way that we live. In Acts 16:30–31, the Philippian jailer asks Paul and Silas, "What must I do to be saved?," and the response is, "Believe in the Lord Jesus, and you will be saved." And then the story immediately shifts to the jailer's actions as a new believer: washing wounds, undergoing the ritual of baptism, and offering hospitality, after which the whole Christian community in Philippi is shown gathering together for mutual encouragement (vv. 33–34, 40). True belief is enacted belief, seen in what we do, and one of the main things we are called to do is to gather together as the community of King Jesus' servant-citizens.

Weekly church services are the main venue for our main responsibility as human beings. In our role as God's royal priesthood, we serve as worship leaders for all of creation, representing the chorus of nature's praise before the Father. We serve as intercessors, bringing the needs of the world before him. And we serve at the forefront of the eternal, angelic symphony of worship beyond all space and time. If we abscond those high and glorious duties, no one else may do them for us. There are no other creatures in all the universe endowed with the same grand vocation. We, and only we, may serve in this way, and since serving in the worship of God is not only a duty but a delight, it is something we ought to do with our whole hearts.

The old Christian word for a worship service, still used by many high-church traditions today, is *liturgy*. We often use that word now to refer to a specific style of worship which includes the recitation of written prayers. But in its classical sense, liturgy refers to the whole worship service. It is derived from a Greek word, *leitourgia*, the etymology of which breaks down to "the work of the people." Think about that for a moment: the early Christians labeled their weekly church gatherings as "work." Jesus himself is described in Hebrews 8:2 as a liturgist (often translated in this verse as "minister"), a word used in the ancient world for the labor of public servants. The service of worship, then, is the work of the people of God (it is not by accident that we call it a "service"). Christian worship is far more than a passive reception of God's blessings; it is the proper labor of the people of God. Together, as a community of faith, we fulfill our duties as royal priests, offering the sacrifices of praise and thanksgiving, and reigning with Christ through the authority of prayer.

All through Scripture, God has insisted on the devotion of one day every week to be set aside for just this sort of service. The repeated commands to keep the Sabbath form one of the core streams of the Old Testament law, and it was a stream that shaped much of the course of Christian practice as well. Now, after Jesus' resurrection from the dead, we have shifted our Sabbath practice over to Sunday, pointing toward the glory of the New Creation that God is building. And we, in our weekly worship and prayer, are part of that ongoing work, as the soul-shaking, world-altering message—salvation through Jesus into the new humanity—is celebrated and proclaimed anew. So if we choose not to be a part of that great work of proclamation and celebration, we should at least understand what we are discarding. We are being invited into the actual presence of the King of the universe, who has brought us from death to life, clothed us in the splendor of his glory, and endowed us with an awesome vocation as officials of his kingdom and priests of his New Creation. With all this in mind, we cannot pretend that participation in church services is unimportant. It is the most important event in the entire world on any given Sunday, and it happens every single week in your own hometown.

If the early Christian church was right, and humanity was designed to serve as royal priests of our Creator-God, then this work of offering him praise, prayer, and thanksgiving is hardwired into who we are. There is a certain kind of joy, almost inexpressibly poignant, about doing exactly what you were made to do. Many of us feel this joy when it comes to our own skill sets. If you are an athlete, there is delight in just having your body do the incredible feats that God's design and your hard work have shaped it to do. The same joy can be felt by actors at the end of a play, by writers in the grip of a creative burst, and by musicians lost in the wonder of performing their songs. Most of us, I think, at one time or another, have felt something like that: the satisfaction of knowing that we are well-fitted for a particular task, and the joy of simply doing it. When we worship, we are not just feeling the satisfaction of using one particular skill set among many; we are fulfilling the deepest meaning of our very beings. To be serving in the worship of God, loving him and being loved by him, invested with his authority and wielding that authority in our prayers—all of this speaks to the deepest truths of who we are as humans. I believe that nothing in all the world can match the experience of true worship, whether you feel it as an explosion of joy or the solemn calmness of resting in the love and grandeur of God. It is absolutely incomparable.

One Eternal Worship Service

Let me paint a picture for you, drawn from the early church's conception of Christian worship, to try to get at the heart of what makes church so incredible. We tend to think of church services as something that happens at particular times—usually Sunday mornings—in particular places, like a church building. But that's only a surface-level perception. In chapter 4, we saw that ancient Jewish traditions regarded the worship of the temple as being an ascent into the very presence of God. To step behind the curtain of the holy of holies was to step into the very throne room of God, into his eternal existence beyond the time-and-space limitations of the physical creation.

We who are Christians make that same ascent. A way has been made for us beyond the curtain through the body of our Lord, and so in a certain sense all of our Christian worship is done inside the temple, facing the open expanse of the throne room of God. Now, obviously, we are also still physically present in space and time, gathered on Sunday morning in our local church. But the idea behind Christian worship, from the very beginning, was that it followed a symbolic ascent up to God, joining our particular physical time and space with the eternal reality of God's presence.[2] First Clement speaks of Christian worship as happening "in the presence of God."[3] The heavenly throne room—that is, the presence of God in eternity—is not another "place" set some distance away from us in physical space; it is, rather, the fundamental setting of all reality, existing completely apart from the very categories that we think of as space and time.[4] This is why, in Revelation, the vision of John is not a transport to another planet or another dimension, it is an "unveiling" (*apokalypsis*) of omnipresent reality, of God's ever-present, sovereign rule and the eternal worship that goes on around his throne.

---

2. See Maximus the Confessor, *On the Ecclesiastical Mystagogy* 13 (75–76).
3. 1 Clem. 56.1 (Holmes, *Apostolic Fathers*, 118–19).
4. See John of Damascus, *Exact Exposition* 1.13 (*Writings*, 197–98).

THE CHURCH: WORSHIP IN THE LIVING TEMPLE 115

Once we spend some time thinking about all this, the idea loses its strangeness and seems exactly right. After all, Jesus himself promised that where two or more are gathered in his name, he is present there. It is not the case that Jesus has to rush down from the throne to physically enter our physical space with us every single time we gather, so it must be the case that, spiritually speaking, we are in his eternal presence when we are gathered and constituted as the body of Christ. We are mystically united to him, and he is at the right hand of the Father. Or consider it in terms of a geopolitical analogy: when we gather for church, we have entered the embassies of the kingdom of God, and just as embassies are considered the sovereign territory of their own nations, no matter how distant, so, too, the physical space of the church actually becomes the sovereign territory of the kingdom of God, and we are standing in the place of his reign, as it were, at the foot of his throne.

This may still sound like a bit of an odd idea, but it is rooted deeply in early Christian theology. Ancient liturgies intentionally used the hymn of angelic worship from Isaiah 6—the worship that goes on around God's throne—as an integral part of their own praises. John Chrysostom, the author of one of those liturgies, reflected on this in a sermon: "Above, the seraphim declaim the thrice-holy hymn; below, the multitude of people sends up the same. A common festival of the heavenly and the earthly is celebrated together."[5] Cyril of Jerusalem would tell his baptismal candidates that at their baptism service, "Each one of you is to be presented before God in the presence of myriads of angelic hosts."[6] Eastern Orthodox congregations still surround themselves with icon paintings of saints and angels, a visible reminder that when we worship, we are a part of the great choir of all creation, and that this cloud of witnesses is with us, a living part of the body of Christ, to whom we are united and with whom we worship.

To put it more plainly: the idea here is that there is really only one worship service, one eternal liturgy, which goes on everlastingly in the presence of God. When Christians gather to worship, there is a sense in which our worship constitutes something far greater than just a thousand little discrete events, happening at different places and different times around the globe; rather, we all join the one thunderous service of worship in the throne room of the Ancient of Days. Every Christian worship

---

5. John Chrysostom, Homily on Isaiah 6 (PG 56:97–107c).
6. Cyril of Jerusalem, Catechesis 3.3 (*Cyril of Jerusalem*, 90).

service is anchored in an event beyond space and time, beyond the scope of our physical creation. When we worship, we are entering communion with something that exists in timeless eternity, and so we, too, in our union with God, participate as part of that grand chorus of all the angels and saints, gathered together from every place and every time. Scripture bears out this vision: in Hebrews 12:22–23, which admonishes Christians to live holy lives, it is suggested that the heavenly community of faith in which we participate is a present reality in our lives: "You have come to Mount Zion, to the city of the living God, to the heavenly Jerusalem. You have come to thousands upon thousands of angels in joyful assembly, to the church of the firstborn, whose names are written in heaven. You have come to God, the Judge of all . . ." And in Revelation 5:8–14, the worship of the Lamb upon the throne is not limited to heavenly participation, but explicitly includes worship from "all creatures in heaven and on earth" (v. 13).

One of the ways this idea assists us in worship is that it allows us to be conscious of the vast, beautiful scope of the worship of all the heavens and earth going on around us every time we join together. Even if we happen to be just a handful of worshipers in a little country church that is struggling to keep its doors open, what happens when we gather to worship is the most astonishing thing in the universe. We are part of the endless round of worship around the throne of God, crying out with angels and archangels, and bringing our gifts to God, just like the elders casting down their crowns before him. We are a part of that very scene every single Sunday. The next time you are in church, try imagining that scene as you worship, because it's not just a nice picture—it's what is really going on. In church, we stand in the position of Elisha's servant, who only needs to have his eyes opened to see that he is surrounded by hosts upon hosts of angels (2 Kgs 6:17).

Since I pastor a church in a rural area, many of my contacts are with small congregations. It is not uncommon for these small churches to feel like they are failures. In our celebrity-driven church culture, they are constantly confronted with the sense that if they are not growing into megachurches, they must be doing something wrong. Sometimes, despite their intentional efforts at prayer and outreach and mission, they still feel like the fruit of their labors fails to match their hopes. To such congregations, I try to underscore the simple fact that while evangelism, mission, and growth are obviously important, they should not underestimate the staggering importance of just being the body of Christ. Whether or not a revival is breaking out, the fact that they are there, an embassy of God's kingdom standing in their own hometown, and that every single Sunday they are worshiping with angels and saints around the throne of God, is not something to be taken lightly. If they are honestly and sincerely offering worship up to God, they cannot possibly be a failure, because they are the body of Christ, and Christ is not a failure. He is glorious, and so are they.

There is one other corollary to this idea that might be worth mentioning, because it may be a fruitful field for dialogue amongst the broken pieces of the body of Christ. One of the consistent Protestant accusations against Roman Catholic eucharistic doctrine is that it presents the elements of communion as the very sacrifice of Christ himself, offered to God over and over and over again, every time they worship. This would seem to violate the clear teaching of Hebrews 9:25—10:14, that Jesus' sacrifice was a once-for-all event, not something that is offered over and over again. However, even though differences will remain in the way we understand the elements of communion, a renewed understanding of church services as participations in a single, eternal event should do away with the misunderstanding that Christ's sacrifice is being offered over and over again. In a very real sense, every single time the elements of communion are presented, they can be conceived—at least in part—as a participation in the one presentation of Christ's own sacrifice, which he himself offers as part of the heavenly worship in the presence of God.

The Mouth of All Creation

There is an added dimension of our worship that we usually miss. Our worship of God is not just something that happens between us, the worshipers, and God, the divine recipient of our praises. In our position as the royal priests of creation, we are also bearing the worship of creation before the throne of God. We looked at this idea in chapter 3, when we studied the patristic notion of humanity constituting a "microcosm of the cosmos," situated as the only creature in all of God's creation with a foot in both the material and spiritual worlds. We stand in the center of creation, enabled to be in relationship with God in a way that other physical creatures cannot, and thus we act as mediators (one of the fundamental dimensions of priestly service) between God and his created order. We bear the bounty of creation in gratitude back to him; we even (as it were) voice its praises before the throne; and we also represent and administer some of God's own authority toward created things (thus fulfilling our original commission in Genesis 1).

There are at least two main ways in which we act as mediators for the rest of physical creation in the context of our worship. The first is in our giving, which has been a feature of human worship going all the way back to the very first ritual of worship in history (the altars of Cain and Abel): we bring God the offerings of the natural world. In the earliest rituals, these offerings were direct products of the created order: animals, crops, and products made from agriculture, like bread and wine. Nowadays, offerings are usually monetary gifts, but money itself is a symbolic representation of the value of physical goods, so the principle remains the same. In our worship, we bear a tithe of God's own creation back to God, thus symbolically reestablishing the unity of God's creation-temple. Even the practice of communion was sometimes portrayed in the earliest sources as a sacrifice of gratitude, drawn from crops of grain and fruit, by which we "offer to God the first-fruits of his own created things."[7]

The second way in which we act as mediators for the rest of creation is in our songs of praise. It is striking to examine the many ways in which the biblical psalms, the hymnbook of ancient Israel, gave voice to aspects of the created order: mountains, oceans, forests, and the like. See, for example, Psalms 96:11–13, 98:7–9, and 148, in which the singers act as worship leaders for creation, calling forth its praises. Modern readers usually take these lines as symbolic statements, a beautiful bit of poetic license. No doubt God takes pleasure in the wonder of his good creations, but seeing as mountains and oceans have no personhood and no consciousness, it is difficult to conceive of these passages as literal descriptions of the mountains breaking into song. Yet there is another possibility: what if ancient Jewish and Christian tradition understood the worship of the psalm itself to be rendering the voice of these created things, mediated through human priests who could translate the wonder of their being into words to bring to the Most High? What if the rest of physical creation was rather like a mute man, who cannot bring a song by himself, and needs the help of a singer—the human priests who stand at the center of creation—to give voice to his praises?

As it happens, this is precisely the way that some early Christian sources speak about our role vis-à-vis the worship of creation. In the

---

7. Irenaeus, *Against Heresies* 4.17.5 (ANF 484); see also 4.18.1; *Didache* 9.4.

Apostolic Constitutions, we have some early Christian prayers (which may themselves hail from older Jewish prayers) in which our worship is described as being "on behalf of everything."[8] One of these prayers runs through a list of the mute worship offered by created things, and then sums up those things as being borne by our praises: "[The dome of] heaven knows the one who raised it . . . The chorus of stars amazes, pointing to the one who numbered (them) . . . Living creatures (point to) the one who produced (them) . . . Wherefore also all men ought, from their very breasts, to send up to you through Christ the hymn on behalf of all."[9] In the *Odes of Solomon,* an early Christian hymnbook, one of the songs describes Christian worshipers as inheriting this special task from God: "For he gave a mouth to his creation" (that is, humans are the designated voice for the created order in the presence of God).[10] In Cyril of Jerusalem's talks to new believers who were entering the church, he described common practices in weekly worship services, which included calling to mind all the other creatures in an exhortation to join in the worship of God:

> After this we call to mind heaven, the earth, the sea, the sun and the moon, the stars, every creature both rational and irrational, visible and invisible, the angels, the archangels, the dominions, the principalities, the thrones, and the many-faced cherubim, saying in effect with David, "Bless the Lord with me."[11]

In essence, the idea here is that part of our role as God's royal priesthood is to be mediators, appointed to bear the worship of the whole world before the throne of God. A mountain, a forest, or an ocean cannot actually give voice to praises for their Maker (at least not with anything approaching our level of conscious intentionality); but we, who behold their majesty and grandeur, can translate the wonder of their being and the joy of their existence into words of praise that we bear back to the Creator on their behalf.

We need not begin writing hymns as if mountains were in fact singing them, but we ought at least to retain the practice of the psalms, and act as worship leaders who call on all creation to magnify the Lord. Even

---

8. *Apostolic Constitutions* 7.36.6; cf. 7.38.8 (*OTP* 2:683, 686).

9. *Apostolic Constitutions* 7.35.5–6 (*OTP* 2:681); see also Justin Martyr, *First Apology* 13; Augustine, *Confessions* 5.1.

10. *Odes of Solomon* 7.22–25 (*OTP* 2:741).

11. Cyril of Jerusalem, *Mystagogic Catecheses* 5.6 (*Cyril of Jerusalem*, 183).

beyond the words of the songs that we sing, one of the most fundamental ways we do this is in giving thanks: observing the beauty and wonder of the natural world, and then turning it into litanies of thanksgiving to God. If we take a moment to reflect upon it, these acts of incorporating nature's praises into our worship are probably things we already do—many of our hymns glorify God for the splendor of natural beauty, and many of our prayers offer thanksgiving for the goodness of his created works—but we may not have realized just how central such things are to our calling as God's royal priesthood.

Dwelling with God

In the next chapter, we will look at some of the specific actions of the Christian worship service and how they are rooted in our royal-priestly heritage. But before we get to that, there is one last broad aspect of our weekly worship to examine. The Sabbath was established as a day of rest, and even though Christians shifted their worship to "the Lord's Day," that is, Sunday, some of the biblical mandate for the Sabbath was still applied. Early Christians were generally not legalistic in keeping rules that prohibited work during Sabbath observance; they regarded those things as part of the old law that had been completed in Christ, but it was thought good to rest if you were able to do so.[12] Nevertheless, there remained a sense that the spirit of the law behind the Sabbath regulations was still very much alive in the life of the church.[13] This "spiritual" keeping of Sabbath was applied not only to weekly worship, but to one's whole life of abiding in Christ—a "perpetual Sabbath."[14]

Thus in early Christian practice, honoring the idea of a day of rest was not so much about ceasing one's labors as it was about intentionally dwelling with God. Recall from chapter 2 that the original meaning of God resting on the seventh day of creation may have had to do with him taking up residence in his creation-temple. Later in Israelite history, the temple was described as God's "resting place" (2 Chr 6:41). In this sense, God's "rest" was about his act of dwelling in the midst of his creation, putting himself in the middle of his people.

---

12. See Barsanuphius and John, *Letters of Barsanuphius and John* 751 (*Letters from the Desert*, 190).

13. See Ignatius, *To the Magnesians* (longer version) 9 (*ANF* 1:62–63).

14. Justin Martyr, *Dialogue with Trypho* 12 (*ANF* 1:200).

Hebrews 3–4 appears to interpret the idea of God's rest in a similar way, applying it to the whole reception of God's promises for life in the promised land—a promise that the exodus generation did not inherit because of their lack of trust. Now, through Christ, those promises are fulfilled, and the chance is open once again to "enter God's rest" (4:9–11). God's rest is not just a state of God's action or inaction, it is here imagined as a sort of place that we can enter. The Odes of Solomon describe it in the same way: in one particularly beautiful song, the worshiper says, "I love the Beloved and I myself love him, and where his rest is, there also am I."[15] Further, this way of describing it—*entering* God's rest—drives away any notion of a merely passive experience. It is not just a matter of halting from one's labors. It is the language of someone moving in, an intentional act. In Christ, we do this by trusting his work of salvation and thereby entering the place of union where God has come to dwell with us. For ancient Israel, that intended place of union was to be the promised land; for us, it is Christ himself, to whom we are united and brought into the very dwelling-place of God, where we may "approach God's throne of grace with confidence" (Heb 4:16). The true Sabbath-rest is to enter the place of our union with God and to dwell with him there. This call to dwell with God resounds throughout Scripture, and especially in the writings of John, where we are told to abide in God and in his love. In this way, the themes of Sabbath-rest, which speak to our weekly day of worship, also open the window once again for us to consider that great goal of all things: to be drawn ever further into our experience of union with God.

Maximus the Confessor, who often wrote his theology in a philosophical key, describes the rest of our union with God in terms that almost foreshadow the Newtonian laws of motion: we have been brought from nonbeing to being and are thus in motion, always yearning toward our *telos*, the goal of our creation, and we must remain in motion until we come to possession of that to which our desire drives us—then, and only then, do we find rest.[16] There is tremendous wisdom here: we humans are always moving, always driven by desires inside us, some of which we cannot even understand or articulate. We have the sense that our souls are always questing, yearning forward to something that will finally give us the satisfaction, the completion we long for—something that will bring our quest to the peacefulness of rest. That one goal of our desires is God

---

15. *Odes of Solomon* 3.7; cf. 26.3 (*OTP* 2:735, 758).
16. Maximus the Confessor, *Ambiguum* 7.1 (*On the Cosmic Mystery*, 46).

himself, and any lesser pleasure will act like saltwater to one who is dying of thirst; our thirst continues to drive us on. It is only in Christ, the dwelling-place of our souls, in coming to union with him and abiding in his love, that we finally come to rest.

This movement of entrance into God's rest is something that should characterize every moment of our lives, but especially our intentional act of going to church. When we join in our weekly worship, it is far more than a duty, far more than just a way to receive some encouragement at the start of a new week. No, here we are coming home, here we are entering the promised land, here we are drawing near to the One who drew near to us, and we will find rest for our souls.

9

The Service: Rites of the Royal Priesthood

IN THE LAST CHAPTER, we looked at some broad aspects of the meaning of our weekly worship service. Now we will begin to consider some of the specific actions that make up that service: what they mean, why we do them, and how we can best honor God through their practice. The truth is, the basic parameters of Christian worship have not changed much in 2,000 years. Many people may not think so, but it's true. We get hung up on surface elements like the style of worship, and so a Pentecostal praise service and an Orthodox liturgy look like they are just about as different as could be imagined. But behind all the surface differences, we are actually all doing the same things, and they are the same things that the earliest Christians did too. Justin Martyr gives us a helpful rundown of what a church service looked like in the second century:[17]

1. Gathering together in a common place
2. Reading Scripture (Justin charmingly refers to the New Testament documents as "the memoirs of the apostles")
3. A sermon/homily (given by the "president" of the assembly)
4. Prayers (this category likely includes songs as well, since in ancient Christian liturgies the praying was the singing, and vice versa; many services were done in chant)
5. Greeting one another/passing the peace (here Justin shows them continuing to use the apostolic tradition of the "holy kiss")
6. Communion/Eucharist (together with more prayers)

17. Justin Martyr, *First Apology* 65–67 (ANF 1:185–86).

7. Giving offerings and alms

8. Baptism (while baptisms were not done every week, Justin sets his description in the context of a convert who has been baptized and is being brought into a church service)

The outward forms may change from culture to culture and century to century, but those eight aspects are generally still the same basic elements of Christian worship that all churches hold to, even 2,000 years later. But what is it about these elements that make them so significant and so characteristic of Christian worship? As we will see, the customary actions of our weekly gatherings are deeply tied to our identity as God's royal priesthood. By gathering together, presenting ourselves as living sacrifices, and representing the worship of all creation, we serve as a sign of what God is doing in his New Creation, reconciling all things to himself.

Worship as Sacrifice

Early Christian churches tended to conceive of their whole service of worship as a sort of sacrifice. We must not jump to thinking, however, that the language of sacrifice automatically implies that they were doing works to try to atone for their sins or expunge their guilt; far from it. The sacrificial laws themselves tell us that there were many other kinds of sacrifices, including those that simply served as gifts of love and fellowship between the worshiper and God. So when we say that early Christians conceived of their worship as sacrifice, this is not an accusation of a salvation-by-works theology; rather, they saw their worship as being directly in line with biblical references to a "sacrifice of thanksgiving" (Lev 22:29 NASB) and a "sacrifice of praise" (Heb 13:15). Church services were a response to God's invitation to offer those very sacrifices in place of blood sacrifices in Psalm 50, and a fulfillment of the prophecy of Malachi 1:11, which says that pure offerings will be brought to God in every place among the nations.[18] One can find this language of Christian worship as sacrifice throughout the New Testament: our praises are called sacrifices (Heb 13:15), as are our giving and our good deeds (Phil 4:18; Heb 13:16), as well as our faith in general (Phil 2:17), and the presentation of our bodies as "living sacrifices" (Rom 12:1).

---

18. See *Didache* 14.1–3 (Holmes, *Apostolic Fathers*, 366–67).

Even if they know these verses well, though, many Christians nowadays tend not to conceive of them in the same way that early Christians would have. Early Christians, living in temple-based religious cultures, would have seen that these verses not only call us to perform certain acts of worship, but give us the standing of a whole new vocation. When Romans 12:1 says that the offering of our bodies is our "true and proper worship," Paul uses a word which carries not only the sense of "worship," but a distinct connotation of *service*; i.e., the ministry of serving in a role of offering worship up to God. These verses thus imply that we are priests, and that these forms of worship are our calling and our duty (see 1 Pet 2:5). We ought not to spiritualize our concept of worship to the point where the image of sacrifice becomes only a figure of speech. Worship was seen as a practical thing, the fulfillment of a necessary and important function. Christian worship is not an optional event on a Sunday morning; it is a calling to take up the functions of the most important human office in the universe.

Justin Martyr articulates this early Christian understanding: "We are now of the true priestly family of God, as he himself testifies when he says that in every place among the Gentiles pure and pleasing sacrifices are offered up to him [Mal 1:11]. But God receives sacrifices from no one, except through his priests." Justin then goes on to list prayers, thanksgivings, and communion as some of the forms of Christian sacrifice.[19] Other patristic writers agree: Cyril of Jerusalem refers to the weekly communion-centered worship service as "the spiritual sacrifice, the worship without blood," and John Chrysostom speaks of giving alms, praying for others, and living a life of virtue as those sacrifices "whereof each one is himself the priest."[20]

In this sense, the weekly worship of the body of Christ takes on a new dimension. It is not just a gathering for edification or the setting apart of one day each week to give to God; it is also the place where we gather up the priestly work in which we have labored on the other six days and bring it into the presence of God to offer it up to him. We continue to have access to the presence of God anywhere and at any time (see John 4:21–24), but the weekly gathering of the church is nonetheless indispensable because of its role as a symbolic ascent into his presence, so that we may present to him, together as one priestly body, the fruits of

19. Justin Martyr, *Dialogue with Trypho* 116–17 (ANF 1:257–58).

20. Cyril of Jerusalem, *Mystagogic Catecheses* 5.8 (*Cyril of Jerusalem*, 183–84); John Chrysostom, *Homilies on Hebrews* 11.5–7 (NPNF[1] 14:420).

our service. In this way, Sunday worship is not disjointed from the rest of the week, not just one day out of seven where we step away from our normal lives to focus on God; rather, it is the place and time set aside for us to bear the priestly work of our everyday lives into the heavenly throne room as a sacrificial offering. Sunday worship is the apex of our weekly work, not standing as something separate, but built on the very foundation of our life and labor on all the other days.

What does this mean? It means that everything you do throughout the week is aimed at Sunday worship. On Monday through Saturday, you are gathering up the harvest from the fields of your daily life, and you symbolically bear it with you when you walk into church on Sunday. All your prayers, your good deeds, your generosity, your work of performing justice and mercy for your neighbors, your acts of laboring for the common good of your community in your career or your volunteer hours, your time spent in helping to plant seeds of righteousness in the lives of your children, your spouse, your friends, or yourself—all of these things are the bounty of goodness that we bring with us to church, there to present ourselves as living sacrifices.

Sunday, then, is "the day of joy" (as many early patristic writers liked to call it), a celebration of Christ's resurrection on the Jewish festival day of firstfruits, which we honor every week by bringing the firstfruits of our week's labors to offer them up to God. Sunday worship is the joyful culmination of a week of service in the ministry of God's kingdom, a celebration of what he has done through our priestly work. The call for us is to strive to bring him good and pleasing offerings. Just like worshipers in Old Testament Israel would be proud to bring the very best of their flock to the temple, a spotless offering that represented the height of what their daily labors could produce, so too are we called to live in such a way that we can take joy in what we bring to offer up to God: the fruit of a life lived for his glory.

Spiritual Sacrifices

There are many ways that we bring our spiritual sacrifices to God in our worship services. In the sections that follow, we will examine several of the rituals of regular Christian worship, following the general flow of Justin Martyr's description: Scripture and sermon, prayers and songs, communion, giving, and baptism.

Scripture and Sermon

Let's begin with a brief look at the ministry of the word. This was a priestly activity in ancient Israel (2 Chr 15:3; Neh 8:1–8; Jer 18:18), and there has long been speculation that the class of scribes, the experts in the Law so often mentioned in the Gospels, may in fact be off-duty priests (most of whom, because of their numbers, only rarely got to serve in the temple in Jerusalem). By the time of Jesus and the disciples, there was a massive shift in Jewish piety underway, in which the Torah—their Scriptures—would gradually take the central place in religious life that previously had been dominated by the sacrifices in the temple. This shift was made irrevocable by the destruction of the temple in CE 70, but it was already in motion beforehand: in synagogues and rabbinical schools across the Jewish diaspora, it was the Torah that was becoming the absolute center of faith and practice. It was from participation in the Scriptures that wisdom, understanding, and the blessings of God were conveyed to the people.

If we Christians are God's royal priesthood in more than just a metaphorical sense, then we can expect that our office inherits some of the prerogatives shown in the Israelite priesthood. This would imply that all of us have the Bible as our heritage—to hear it, read it, study it, and apply it, both for ourselves and under the instruction of the local church. Jesus, our great High Priest, lived a life that was shaped by the influence of Scripture: not as anything that had power over him or restrained him, but as the appropriate structure for a truly human life. We Christians emulate his example and allow the ministry of the word, through the blessing and guidance of the Holy Spirit, to shape and mold us after God's will.

The reading of Scripture has ties not only to Jewish practice and priestly service, but to our original mandate in the garden of Eden. Humanity was not simply created and set loose without any knowledge or instruction from its Maker; rather, it was the context of God's proclamations and commands that gave Adam and Eve's service its proper shape. Their lives were centered around what God had told them: they were to be fruitful, to tend the garden, and to eat of any tree except the tree of knowledge. It was the word of the Lord that gave them the appropriate structure for living and serving in their appointed roles. The same is true of us: our lives are shaped by the words God has spoken to us in the Bible, and it is his teachings and commandments that give us the appropriate structure for life and service. The renewal of creation presses on by being who we were meant to be: creatures shaped by the word.

Prayer and Song

Another means of offering our sacrifices in worship is through the prayers of the weekly church service. Tertullian describes prayer as the essential service of our priestly ministry: "We are . . . the true priests who, praying in spirit, sacrifice in spirit: prayer, a [sacrifice] proper and acceptable to God."[21] Specifically, prayers of thanksgiving were seen as a means of bearing the bounty of God's creation back to him in praise, as these are specifically mentioned in Psalm 50 as being the kind of sacrifices God desires (vv. 14, 23).

But we would be wrong to suppose that prayer was just one element out of many in a worship service. Rather, many early Christians tended to view the whole worship service as prayer. Prayer is the great common theme of nearly every gathering of the first Christian church in the book of Acts (1:14; 2:42; 3:1; 4:24-31; 6:4; 12:12). Ignatius, writing in the postapostolic generation, can describe worship services simply as "Eucharist and prayer."[22] Almost everything that was done or said in the church service (apart from the sermon) was directed to God in the form of prayers, and those prayers were awash with terms of thanksgiving. We will have a great deal more to examine with regard to prayer in chapter 14, but for now we can simply observe that the whole scope of Christian worship was, in a sense, prayer. Conscious of the fact that worship was taking place in the presence of God himself, everything in the service was oriented entirely toward him.

Singing was another means of bearing spiritual sacrifices to God. Songs have always been a part of Christian worship, even from the time of Jesus and his disciples (Matt 26 30). We inherited our customs of singing from the Jewish temple, where music was a central feature. One of the main functions of the whole class of Levites was to serve as worship leaders, and the beauty and power of Israel's psalms attest to the place of song in their religious life. Singing has a special poignancy about it, an ability to join heart and mind together in speaking forth the praises of God, in a way that merely reading a text cannot match. It takes rational

---

21. Tertullian, *On Prayer* 28 (*ANF* 3 690).
22. Ignatius, *To the Smyrnaeans* 6.2 (Holmes, *Apostolic Fathers*, 254-55).

THE SERVICE: RITES OF THE ROYAL PRIESTHOOD 129

thoughts in the form of lines of text and transforms them into works of art; it is a truly holistic form of worship, engaging both body and soul.

Of all the forms of worship which are pliable to local cultures and practices, singing is near the top of the list. That being the case, most of the singing from early Christian communities would probably have struck us as very strange. In many such communities the majority of the service was sung (or, we might say, chanted), and so it would be hard to distinguish prayers and songs as separate categories. As Augustine said, "When brethren are assembled in church, when is it not time for sacred singing, except of course while reading or discourse is going on?"[23] In some traditions even the Scripture readings were chanted, and in the Syrian churches represented by the great hymn-writer Ephrem, the songs themselves took on the didactic character of sermons. What can we draw from this? Perhaps one of the lessons is that we ought not to worry so much about the outward form of our music in worship. Instead of focusing so much attention on the style of our singing, we ought to place our focus on the Recipient of our spiritual sacrifices. In our songs, we directly celebrate the presence of the present God, who is "enthroned on the praises" of his people (Ps 22:3 NRSV). True Christian worshipers, who worship "in spirit and in truth" (John 4:23–24), should be adaptable to any style of music or singing so long as our hearts are pointed Godward.

Communion

There are at least two parallels to the ritual of communion in the sacrificial rites of the Israelite priesthood. One is the bread of the presence, which was one of the main features of the tabernacle and temple furnishings. It stood on a table within the sanctuary (that is, the area immediately outside the holy of holies), and it was to be always present there (Exod 25:30). Part of the priests' role was to eat this bread, and then it was replaced with new bread on a regular basis, so that even as it was eaten, it would still be always present before the Lord (Lev 24:5–9; 1 Sam 21:6; Mark 2:26). Also present on this table were the jars for drink offerings (Num 4:7). For such a vast building, there really was not a lot of furniture in the sanctuary of the temple: the altar of incense, the lampstand, and the table for the bread of the presence. It is striking, then, that bread and wine were among the very few items that sat in the holy place (and, even

---

23. Augustine, Letter 55.18.34 (*NPNF*[1] 1:315).

more strikingly, bread that symbolized the abiding presence of God with his people). It is no surprise that when early Christians looked back at the temple, they saw the communion of Christ enshrined within it.

The other parallel between the temple and communion is the practice of sin offerings. The imagery of communion is multifaceted, and while some of those aspects tend towards viewing it as a symbolic memorial meal (the connection with a Passover supper, for instance), others speak more to the idea of a sin offering and priestly participation. When Jesus celebrates his last supper with his disciples, he describes the elements of his body ("given for you" [Luke 22:19]) and blood ("poured out for you" [Luke 22:20]) in ways that point to the practice of sacrificing sin offerings in the temple ("for the forgiveness of sins" [Matt 26:28]).

If Jesus simply wanted his disciples to understand that his death on the cross was a sin offering, he could have just told them that. He was their rabbi, certainly not limited in his teaching ability, and his normal pattern of communication with them was through the spoken word, not by inducting them into symbolic rituals. But in the case of communion, he goes a step further than merely giving a verbal teaching about his sacrifice, and makes them eat and drink the portions of his offering. He is inviting them into the ritual as participants and recipients. Paul, in addressing the controversy of whether to eat meat that may have been part of pagan rituals, notes this connection between eating and participation: "Consider the people of Israel: Do not those who eat the sacrifices participate in the altar?" (1 Cor 10:18). It is possible Paul is referring to a general participation of the worshipers (some sacrifices, like peace offerings, included the worshipers themselves eating of the sacrifice), but ritual eating of sacrifices was more often a priestly act.

In both cases, then—the bread of the presence and the sin offering—the connections between communion and the temple rituals underscore our identity as God's priesthood. One of the functions of priests was to bear to God the offerings and sacrifices, the bounty of the created order, on behalf of the people. But another function was to act as recipients of those offerings as divinely appointed mediators, and this was primarily done by eating. Not all sacrifices and offerings were eaten; some were entirely burned up or poured out, but in many cases, it was the priests' duty to eat the offerings. In a certain sense, this was simply practical, a way to provide the priests with food, but much of the time it was clearly conceived as part of the religious ritual.

What might this say of our practice of communion in worship? One of the things it ought to do is serve as an enactment of the truth that we are sustained by Christ himself. Communion signifies many things in the life of the church: a thanksgiving (the literal meaning of "Eucharist"), a remembrance of the cross, an anticipation of the messianic feast to come, and an act of union between Christ and the members of his body. But another dimension, startlingly obvious from the symbology of the act itself, is that we are to feed ourselves on Christ: he is the bread of life, and in him alone are we sustained.

In John 6:26–58, Jesus gives a long teaching on his identity as "the bread of life," and it is here that he first introduces the imagery of eating his body and drinking his blood. (Here the context is not directly tied to communion, but to the historical analogy of manna). In this discourse, Jesus is trying to convince his hearers, who expect his messianic ministry to hearken back to the glory days of Moses and the manna, that what they really need is eternal life (that is, the life of the eternal age, the life of relationship joined to God in eternity). They cannot get that by eating manna; all those who ate manna died. The only way to obtain eternal life is to eat not manna, but the bread of life, and Jesus is that bread. Peter, at the end of the discourse, appears to have gotten the message: what he needs is eternal life, and Jesus is the only way to get it (John 6:68).

The *Didache*, an early Christian handbook, also makes the connection between the symbology of communion and the reception of eternal life, by way of a eucharistic prayer: "You, almighty Master, created all things for your name's sake, and gave food and drink for humans to enjoy, so that they might give you thanks; but to us you have graciously given spiritual food and drink, and eternal life through your servant."[24] Notice that this passage hearkens back to creation, recognizing God's gracious giving of food and drink to all humanity from the very beginning. Just as God provided Adam and Eve with food after their creation, so Christ gives us food to receive in the New Creation. It should not surprise us to find a parallel between our worship practices and the practice of Eden's paradise. God makes eating a central feature of our first creation (Gen 1:29; 2:16), and so our participation in the New Creation is also centered around an act of eating. In communion, we enact our reception of the goodness of God's provision for us, the true food for our souls: Jesus Christ himself.

---

24. *Didache* 10.3 (Holmes, *Apostolic Fathers*, 358–59).

Communion speaks to this imagery: eating the body of Christ and drinking his blood. Believing in Jesus, receiving him by faith, is the only way to eternal life (John 6:29). Thus communion, whether conceived of as a symbol or an actual participation, stands as an enactment of the principle at the heart of the gospel: it is by receiving Jesus, by joining ourselves to him, by accepting his sacrifice into our very beings, that we receive eternal life. It is a living drama of the gospel itself, standing in the center of our worship.

Giving

Monetary giving has been part of Christian worship from the very beginning, and it appears to be descended from the offering of gifts in the temple system, which went to support the ministries of the temple, the livelihood of the priests and Levites, and the distribution for the poor. It appears prominently in Paul's writings as one of the main means of Christian service. Patristic writers often encouraged this practice too, though they stressed the voluntary nature of giving, not necessarily being bound by the law of tithes. This was not, however, seen as an excuse to give less than a tenth, but rather as a gracious invitation to view all of one's possessions as belonging to the Lord, and to be ready to give up any or all of it.[25] In this way, giving is not only an act of assistance to the work of the church and the needs of others, but a symbolic, joyful declaration of one's liberation from slavery to worldly concerns.

In writing about monetary gifts, the fathers and mothers of the early church stressed the giving of alms for the poor. It was seen as one of the essential acts of Christian service, to be done willingly and joyfully. It was, in fact, a participation in God's own character and joy: "Give to everyone who asks you, for truly such is God's delight in giving."[26] To give was to be like the Giver. Further, giving is beneficial to all: not only does giving assist the poor, for whom God's concern is evident throughout Scripture, but it also helps preserve the rich from dangerous attachments to their wealth. There was even a notion in some circles that God had given rich people and poor people to one another in the fellowship of the church so that the rich people could give money to assist the poor people's evident physical needs, and the poor people could offer prayers

---

25. See Irenaeus, *Against Heresies* 4.18.2 (ANF 1:485).
26. Clement of Alexandria, *Who Is the Rich Man?* 31 (ANF 2:600).

to assist the rich people's evident spiritual needs (a hint of this reciprocity can be seen in 2 Cor 9:13–14).

Baptism

Baptism, like communion, is a fruitful and multifaceted symbol of many aspects of our faith. It signifies repentance, as John's baptism did, but far more than just repentance: it is the physical symbol of our new life in Christ. In a certain sense, it is the way for our bodies to say yes to God's offer of salvation, just as our spirits say yes to it by faith. Some of the most important aspects of baptism are its visual language of new birth, being born again "of water and the Spirit" (John 3:5), and of sharing in Christ's death, burial, and resurrection by the symbolic action of going under the water (Rom 6:3–4). Even among patristic traditions that did not always practice immersion, the connection with burial was still considered primary; it was a longstanding custom to do three acts of dunking or pouring, which corresponded not only to the Trinity, but to Christ's three days in the tomb.[27]

In chapter 5, we saw how the baptism of Christ carries echoes of the creation narratives. The same is generally true of all Christian baptism, and especially as it was practiced in early Christianity. One minor note of connection is the presence of water. Baptism can be seen as an echo of the experience of passing through the primeval waters of Genesis 1:2 in our movement to the New Creation.[28] Many early baptism services had the baptisand strip down naked to undergo the ritual (such baptisms were done in small groups of a single gender), which was taken as a return to the state of Adam and Eve, a direct allusion to the experience of Eden.[29] The most striking echo of Genesis in Christian baptism, however, comes in the baptismal renunciations. At the beginning of the baptism service, the believer is asked to renounce Satan and all his works. In essence, we are going back, each one of us, to that meeting between Eve and the serpent, and repudiating the devil there. Cyril explains to the newly baptized, "So when you renounce Satan . . . you annul the old treaty made with hell, and there opens before you God's paradise which he planted

---

27. See John of Damascus, *Exact Exposition* 4.9 (*Writings*, 344).
28. See Tertullian, *On Baptism* 3 (*ANF* 3:670).
29. Cyril of Jerusalem, *Mystagogic Catecheses* 2.2 (*Cyril of Jerusalem*, 173).

in the east . . ."[30] The service of Christian baptism was seen as a drama of renouncing the fall and going back to the garden through the salvation wrought by Christ, there to be remade again.

Baptism was also, at the same time, a complex symbol of priestly initiation. Just as we saw echoes of creation and of priestly ordination in Jesus' baptism, the same things stand true of ours. Ordination to the Jewish priesthood included a full ceremonial washing, an anointing with oil, and the robing of the new priest in his priestly garments. Early Christian baptisms included these exact same three elements. First there was the washing, which was the baptism itself. In Jewish tradition at the time of Jesus, this ritual washing was to be done with living water—not water in a stagnant pool, but water that moved and brought life: streams, rivers, or ritual mikvehs built so that the water would move through in a natural way. (Here, indeed, we may have another shared theme with Eden: recall the prominence of rivers in both Eden and the biblical temple visions.) It was this kind of water that was thought to bring ritual purity, sweeping away one's uncleanness. Thus Jesus' saying in John 7:38—that rivers of living water would pour from him and from his followers' hearts—was a promise of the purifying, sanctifying work of the Holy Spirit within us and through us, as prophesied in Zechariah 14:8 and Ezekiel 47:1–12. Early Christian customs followed this Jewish practice: the *Didache* advised that, if possible, Christians should be baptized in running water.[31]

After the baptism, early Christians would undergo a chrismation, an anointing with oil. While not specifically instructed to do this in the New Testament, the practice was based on the language of Christian anointing in texts like 2 Corinthians 1:21 and 1 John 2:27. It was conceived of as the ritual that showed the believer's receiving of the Holy Spirit, perhaps as hinted at in Ephesians 1:13: "When you believed, you were marked in him with a seal, the promised Holy Spirit." This ritual of baptism and chrismation follows the experience of Jesus' passion: the movements of baptism correspond to Jesus' death, burial, and resurrection, and the chrismation to the Holy Spirit poured out at Pentecost. Beyond all these things, though, it is worth noting that this act, just like the immersion of baptism, was part of the priestly ordination ritual. Tertullian makes this connection directly: "After that, we come up from the washing and are anointed with the blessed unction, following that ancient practice by

---

30. Cyril of Jerusalem, *Mystagogic Catecheses* 1.9 (*Cyril of Jerusalem*, 171–72).
31. *Didache* 7.1-2 (Holmes, *Apostolic Fathers*, 354–55).

which, ever since Aaron was anointed by Moses, there was a custom of anointing them for priesthood with oil."[32]

A third element of the priestly ordination ritual was being robed in priestly garments. This was also part of the early Christian rite of baptism. After coming up out of the water, the baptisand would be clothed in a white garment. This was a multifaceted symbol, showing how we "clothe [ourselves] with the Lord Jesus Christ" (Rom 13:14; cf. Gal 3:27) as well as how we have put off the old self and put on the new (Eph 4:22–24). It is an enacted drama of entering the new humanity in Christ: just as Adam and Eve were clothed in garments related to their fall (first the fig leaves by which they tried to hide their shame, then God's provision of animal skins, a symbol of death), so we, on entering the new life, are clothed with symbols of purity in Christ's new humanity. In parallel with the idea of a priestly ordination, the white garment appears to serve as an echo of the priest's linen tunic, the very piece worn by the high priest to enter God's presence in the holy of holies.

To sum up: in baptism (as practiced in early Christianity), we follow three simultaneous symbolic journeys. First, the journey of our Lord in his passion: going down into death, being buried under the waters, rising in new life, and ascending out of the waters again, after which the symbol of the Holy Spirit is poured out. Because we walk the road of our Messiah-King and are united to him in faith, we share his journey from death to enthronement. Second, the new Adam takes us back to the moment of our first creation. We renounce Satan, turning away from him in the power of Christ's victory, and then pass through the waters to our re-creation and new birth as part of the new humanity. Third, we undergo a ritual of priestly ordination in the ceremonial washing, anointing, and robing. In Christ, we are restored to the priestly office that we were designed to fill, and we enter a new life of serving and reigning as the royal priests of the New Creation.

---

32. Tertullian, *On Baptism* 7 (*ANF* 3:672).

10

Holiness: The Call of the Priestly Life

"What is God's will for my life?" This question arises regularly in the course of pastoral ministry, as honest-hearted Christians seek out what steps the Lord would have them take. Particularly among younger Christians, who face big choices in careers, homes, and families, the question becomes an insistent refrain. When I am asked this question, I usually try to start my answer with an unexpected curveball: that whatever else God may be leading you to do, his exact will for your life is clearly laid out in the Bible itself. Yes, that's right: his exact will for your life is laid out in the pages of the New Testament, right under your nose. Now, it may not help you figure out who you should marry or what job you ought to have, but those things are really of secondary importance when compared with the scope of God's grand call on your life: *to be holy*. Paul declares that holiness has been God's fundamental plan for us from before the creation of the world (Eph 1:4), even going so far as to portray the Christian life as a two-pronged experience of salvation and holiness: "He saved us and called us to a holy life" (2 Tim 1:9; see also 1 Thess 4:7).

In many Christian circles, the process of growing in holiness is given the term "sanctification," and is thought to progress either by a gradual upward trajectory or by stages (different denominations hold different views on the matter). Unfortunately, the growth aspect of our life in Christ is sometimes treated as little more than an afterthought to the justification we received in the forgiveness of our sins. Sanctification is presented as something that ought to be happening in our lives, but the rationales offered are often untethered to any larger view of the Christian life. In many cases, the reasoning for pressing on in one's journey of sanctification is given in terms of individual rewards or consequences: you work toward holiness in order to have deeper experiences of closeness with God, or so you don't backslide, or so you don't lose some of your potential rewards in heaven. While all of those things are true in a certain sense, they miss the larger picture.

Imagine if we talked this way about marriage (and perhaps some of us do, to our own detriment): putting so much emphasis on the wedding day and the fact of the marriage itself that we pay very little attention to the daily work of growing in relationship with our spouse. The marriage is simply a fact about us that is taken for granted (like our justification), and while we admit that it would probably be good to work intentionally on the marriage relationship, it slides to the bottom of our daily priority list because, quite frankly, the main thing is the marriage itself, and we've already got that. Working on the relationship might make it a little more pleasant, and it's something that we vaguely believe we ought to be doing, but it doesn't take on the air of a present and urgent necessity in our lives.

What happens to marriages governed by that kind of attitude? They tend to break under the strain, one way or another. You cannot treat marriage as just an accomplished fact, because it's more than just a rubber stamp on the story of your life; it is an invitation to a daily journey, a calling that is meant to continue shaping your identity for the rest of your life. This is also true of the upward call of our Christian journey. Being saved through the forgiveness of sins is not just a rubber stamp on one's life, but an entry into a journey that will shape you into who you were meant to be within God's gracious design.

Here's another example: picture the Christian journey as a scenic train tour across North America, riding from New York to Vancouver. This tour is designed as a vacation package to display the wonders of the natural landscape and local culture along every mile of the way, from the verdure of eastern forests to the grand sweep of the prairies to the stark majesty of the Rocky Mountains. Now, you could, if you chose, buy a ticket just as a way to get from New York to Vancouver, and spend the whole time sleeping in your train car and never looking out the window. You would still get to Vancouver. But you would have missed the whole point of the thing if you did it that way. This sort of windows-shut ride in silence is essentially what we're offering when we present the gospel as a simple matter of getting saved so you can go to heaven. Such a gospel is the truth, but perhaps not the whole truth. As grand as that message is, it still manages to impoverish the full wonder of what we are called to be as Christians.

Holiness is our glorious patrimony, a legacy of joy written in letters of Christlikeness throughout every moment of our lives. As Benedict of Nursia wrote in his monastic rule, "As we progress in this way of life and in faith, we shall run on the path of God's commandments, our hearts overflowing with the inexpressible delight of love."[1] Far from being something straight-laced or narrow, holiness carries within it the very breadth of the character of God, who proclaims throughout his Scriptures, "Be holy, because I am holy." With this call as our refrain, we should not be surprised to find holiness woven into the very fabric of our calling as God's royal priesthood.

Two Aspects of Our Holiness

One of the basic qualities of the royal priesthood is that it is holy. Peter, in applying to Christians the idea of royal priesthood from Exodus 19:6, includes the fact that we are called holy (1 Pet 2:5, 9). Many Christians, however, struggle to understand all that holiness means to us. It is not a word that fits the context of our culture, used nowhere else in our daily lives, so people struggle to define and apply it. Is it simply the opposite of sin, and if so, how is it different from the more easily grasped idea of *goodness*? Further, why is it that the Bible applies this term in two very different ways to the lives of believers? On the one hand, we are constantly being called holy, as if it is an identity that is already firmly established, but on the other hand, we are also constantly being called to live holy lives, as if it's something we need to attain.

Let's take this second question first: Why does the Bible speak of holiness as something that is already true of us, but also something that may not yet be true of us? The New Testament regularly calls Christians holy—so frequently, in fact, that it becomes one of the most common forms of address: when writing to groups of Christians, Paul often calls them "saints," or, more literally, "holy ones" (see, for example, 2 Cor 1:1; Eph 1:1; Phil 1:1; Col 1:1). We are also told in various places that Christ has already made us holy by his once-for-all sacrifice (Heb 10:10; cf. 1 Cor 1:30; Eph 5:26; Col 1:22). But on the other hand, the New Testament also clearly portrays holiness as something that is still in progress, and

---

1. Benedict of Nursia, Prologue, 49 (*Rule of St. Benedict*, 19).

which we must strive to attain: "Make every effort . . . to be holy; without holiness no one will see the Lord" (Heb 12:14; cf. Rom 6:19; 2 Tim 2:21; 2 Pet 3:11). So how can both dimensions be true? Is holiness something we already have, or something we are still working on getting?

The answer, of course, is that both aspects are true, but each one looks at the issue from a different perspective. In earlier stages of my faith, I often struggled with the idea of holiness, because it is so often interpreted as moral perfection. And since I am well aware that I am not morally perfect, I have a hard time thinking of myself as holy. If I were holy in any sense, I thought it was just because Jesus' holiness covered for my lack of holiness. In some streams of Protestant theology, this idea is referred to as a "legal fiction," in which Jesus' righteousness is imputed to us, thus rendering us justified before God and declared holy in Christ. So even though I was not actually holy, I was reckoned to be so on account of Jesus. There is a great deal of truth to this view, but it fails to cover the whole scope of what Scripture says about my holiness. It still leaves me a little bit unable to talk about myself as being holy, because in this view it is a holiness that's foreign to me, as it belongs to Jesus. But if we struggle to say the same things about ourselves that the Bible says about us, then it probably means we have missed part of the picture. There remains a very real sense in New Testament theology that I am holy not just because of moral perfection (whether mine or Christ's), but as a fundamental aspect of my identity.

Holiness, Perfection, and Our Restored Identity

But what is holiness, if not just moral perfection? After all, doesn't Matthew's Gospel use "perfect" as a word-for-word translation of "holy?" For instance, where God says in Leviticus 11:45, "Be holy, because I am holy" (cf. Lev 19:2; 1 Pet 1:16), Jesus takes that idea and turns it into "Be perfect, therefore, as your heavenly Father is perfect" (Matt 5:48). But this rhetoric of perfection has more to it than merely moral implications: the Greek word *teleios* has overtones of maturity, completeness, and fulfillment. It is the word used about someone who is fully being what they are meant to be, the person who is inhabiting their *telos*. The Father, of course, is perfect, in this and every sense. He completely fulfills his character. He is who he is, and can never be less than that. We, as Christians, are likewise called to live into our identity, to grow and mature by God's grace into who we were meant to be.

To see this sense of perfection illustrated in a profound way, one can look at the book of Hebrews, where Jesus is spoken of in terms that make many Christians scratch their heads: he is described as having been "made perfect" through what he suffered (Heb 2:10; 5:8–9; 7:28). Now, if Jesus has always been sinless, our perfect Savior from before the world began, then in what sense could he have been "made perfect" by his sufferings? It seems blasphemous to suggest that he was lacking something, or that something about him had to be improved upon. Quite so, because in fact this is not at all what Hebrews is saying. The word used for "made perfect" relates to the completion and fulfillment of an identity. Specifically, Hebrews uses it to refer to Jesus' high priestly calling (7:28), and it just so happens that the ancient Greek version of the Old Testament uses the exact same word to speak of the completion of the consecration rites for Aaron as high priest (Lev 8:33 LXX). When Hebrews says that Jesus was made perfect, it is saying that he has been brought, fully and completely, into his vocational calling as our high priest: the consecration rites have been completed in the cross. For Aaron to be dedicated as priest, he was dabbed with blood on his ear lobe, his thumb, and his big toe (Lev 8:23); and on the cross, Jesus completes this ritual with his own blood, which streams from the wounds on his head, his hands, and his feet. Jesus is "made perfect" by completing the consecration to his priestly vocation.

Hebrews does not just apply this terminology to Jesus, though. It also applies the same word to us, and connects it directly to the idea of our progress in holiness: "For by one sacrifice [Christ] has made perfect forever those who are being made holy" (Heb 10:14). That is to say, by the sacrifice of Jesus, in which our sins are atoned for and by which we enter into the New Creation, we have been brought to the fullness of our *telos*: we are established in our identity as priests in his priesthood, as kings and queens in his reign, consecrated completely for his service. The early church father Clement picks up this language as well, speaking about how Christians have been made perfect in love, which he links both to God's original calling on our lives and to our ultimate destiny as participants in Christ's kingdom.[2]

---

2. 1 Clem. 49.5; 50.3 (Holmes, *Apostolic Fathers*, 110–13).

So, in addition to the simple idea of practical goodness and moral rectitude, we can add to our view of holiness this sense of perfection, of a fulfilled calling. Yes, we are holy because the holiness of Christ is given to us (1 Cor 1:30), but it is not the case that this holiness is something completely foreign to us; we are also holy because God has brought us into a new category of being. We are consecrated into a new identity, which is very much our own: the royal priesthood, the fulfillment of who we were made to be from the very beginning. Just like Old Testament priests, who were holy not only because of how they lived but because of who they were (Exod 28:36–37), so also with us: we are now living in the category of God's holy ones, an identity which is our very own birthright. We ought not to struggle to call ourselves holy or saints, even with the knowledge that we are not yet morally perfect in a practical sense. We are God's holy saints because of our identity, restored to us in Christ. Thus one can conceive of the two aspects of holiness in terms of vocation: you have stepped into a new job, and now you are being asked to learn how to do it. You have been brought into the nobility, and you ought to learn how to live nobly, but you are called a noble simply because of who you are.

In the Old Testament, holiness-as-identity was also expressed in terms of separation from the world. The priesthood was holy because it was a group of people called out, separated from the rest of Israel, and commissioned to serve the Lord in a particular way. This was also true of Israel as a whole: it was called a holy nation because God had called them out from all other nations and made them his own (Lev 20:26; Deut 7:6; 14:2, 21; 26:19; 28:9–10). This extends to us as Christians as well: because we are "a chosen people" of God (1 Pet 2:9), we are, by definition, holy. Here the two aspects of holiness are easily seen working in tandem. We are holy because we belong to God's holy community, called out of the world into a new reality; and we are called to live into that identity in a practical sense. We are called to be, day in and day out, who we really are. We fulfill our vocation, at least in part, by manifesting our separateness from the world in the way we live our lives, as a people devoted to the Lord.

Holiness truly is, then, a dual reality. Just as portrayed in the New Testament, it is something already established (in our fundamental identity in Christ) and, at the same time, something that is still in progress (in the practice of our daily lives). To give another analogy, you can think about it like the process of acculturation to a new country. You have been brought over into the kingdom of God, and now you are a citizen of that kingdom. But, like any new citizen, you must learn how to live in this country, how to take its language, its customs, its whole way of being, and then make them your own. You are holy because you are a full citizen in the holy kingdom, and now you should learn how to live like a citizen.

Holiness Granted, Holiness Gained

Even if holiness is now part of our identity, how exactly do we grow in it? Is it by God's work or ours that we manifest greater holiness in our daily lives? The answer, once again, is both, but God's work is the more fundamental of the two. God's work—the operations of his grace within our lives, through the Spirit—is the necessary cause of all our holiness. Even after we are in his royal priesthood, a holy citizen of his holy kingdom, our growth in holiness can never be simply a product of our own efforts. It is not any sort of merit that we gain by sheer grit and determination, attributable to our own powers and skills; it is simply the natural process of our growth and development towards Christian maturity from our starting point as spiritual infants. One does not look at an adult and say, "My goodness! I remember when she was just a little baby! What remarkable efforts she must have put in to grow into an adult body!" No, that growth is simply due to the gracious work of the Creator. The baby must do certain things, of course—most importantly, to take its proper nutrition and to avoid things that would endanger its healthy growth—but they cannot claim their maturation into adulthood as any merit of their own efforts. It is all down to the grace and goodness of God.

This part of the equation is clearly seen in Scripture. Even with all the repeated admonitions to Israel to work at being holy by keeping the commandments, there is still this dominant refrain that rings over it all: "I am the Lord, who makes you holy" (Exod 31:13; Lev 20:8; 21:15, 23; 22:9, 16; 22:32). It is God's action that really counts. He is the one who is truly holy, and our holiness is based on his. Hebrews 12:10 even suggests that by growing in holiness, we participate in God's own holiness: "God disciplines us for our good, in order that we may share in his holiness." Once again, then, we should make note that union with God is shown as the goal of the Christian life and calling.

We do, however, have our part to play, too. The actual growth in holiness comes from the operation of God's grace in our lives, but we should help to prepare the way for its work in our hearts. This is why there is such a repeated insistence on our efforts in the Bible's teaching on holiness. We are not simply inert sponges that can soak up holiness; we need to learn its ways and put them into practice. Remember, though: this is not a matter of whether or not we are saved, so any accusation of works-based righteousness would entirely miss the point here. The question here is about how the Christian grows to maturity, and in that question, our works have an important role to play.

Growth in holiness is a gift of God alone, but we must still receive it. To use the analogy of an infant growing to maturity once again, we must make sure that we are being properly nourished by the teaching of God's word, by the practice of prayer, and by our union with the life of the body of Christ. In addition to receiving the proper nourishment, we must also make sure that we are living into our calling to be separate from the world—not in the sense of moving into isolated enclaves, but of steering clear of the many temptations around us, recognizing that those temptations, and the sins to which they lead, can prevent our growth in holiness in the same way that a child playing with a buzz saw is in danger of not attaining the fullness of his bodily growth.

Our participation in growing in God's gift of holiness—which patristic writers liked to refer to as *synergeia,* from which we get our word "synergy"—is well illustrated in an example from John Cassian, who describes the work of the Christian in attaining the virtues of a holy life as being similar to the work of a farmer. Farmers obviously have a role to play in growing crops; if they want a good harvest, they must work hard to prepare the ground for their plants to flourish: plowing the soil, clearing rocks and weeds, adding fertilizer, and so on. But they have no power, in and of themselves, to bring forth a crop. There is nothing that farmers can do that will directly make each seed germinate and sprout; only the power of nature, as granted by its Creator, can do that. The truly effective work of making crops grow can only come from the creative power of God. The farmers can and should prepare the soil, but they cannot force the seed to sprout. Nor can they control any number of other things, like whether there is adequate sun and rain for a crop to grow. Even the farmers' own strength in doing the work of preparation and care ultimately comes not from themselves, but from God: "[Their] own will and strength would have been powerless unless divine compassion had supplied the means for the completion of them."[3] So, again: the necessary cause of all our growth is from God alone, yet we have a role to play in participating with the operations of his grace. We are called to prepare the soil of our hearts, that the seed of his grace might grow bountifully there.

The Arena of the Heart

This call to holiness is intimately tied to the priestly and royal aspects of our identity. The priestly aspect is easy to see: holiness was something of a job requirement for Old Testament priests. If the ritual cleansings for ordinary worshipers to approach the temple were necessary parts of their devotional practice, it was certainly more so for those who worked in the temple itself. The same principle extends to us. Just as priests would have been unable to effectively perform their labors unless they were ritually clean, so we also become ineffective priests if we are living unholy lives (2 Pet 1:3–8; cf. Heb 12:14).

But how does the call to holiness relate to the royal part of our identity? According to patristic writers, it is one of the ways that we carry out our obedience to God's original command for us: to rule the earth and subdue it (Gen 1:26, 28). We were made from the dust of the earth, and so, in a sense, God's mission for humanity—to administer his reign over earthly creation—begins with us and in us. We are called to rule our unruly hearts, to subdue them to the reign of Christ, and in this way we take the first step in fulfilling our original commission as human beings. We were called to subdue the earth, and that task begins in the earthly reality of our own daily lives.

At the very least, the fact that we were made to reign should leave us unwilling to accept rebellion within our own hearts. Basil articulates this idea with his characteristic sharp-edged eloquence: "O human, you are a ruling being. And why do you serve the passions as a slave? Why do you throw away your own dignity and become a slave of sin? . . . You were appointed ruler of creation, and you have renounced the nobility of your own nature."[4] Our commission to rule, then, begins with us. Reinstated to our reign through the greater reign of the new Adam, we exercise our

---

3. Cassian, *Conferences* 13.3 (NPNF[2] 11:423).

4. Basil, On the Origin of Humanity, Discourse 1.8 (*On the Human Condition*, 37); cf. *The Shepherd of Hermas* 47.3 (Holmes, *Apostolic Fathers*, 550–51).

royal powers by claiming the battlefield at our heart's very door: the arena of ourselves.

We must also remember that this battlefield is not just an exercise of our commission as human beings, but that we take up that calling within the reign of Christ, who is even now engaged in the work of putting all his enemies under his feet (1 Cor 15:25). By marshaling our efforts in the work of holiness, striving against the hold of sin in our own hearts, we participate in the great march of Christ against his enemies. Gregory of Nazianzus refers to Christ's reign of conquest in 1 Corinthians 15 in connection with our battle against interior sins, contrasting the state of someone ruled by their sinful desires—"an insubordinate rebel with passions which deny God"—with one who has been brought under submission to the reign of Christ, in whose life "all things . . . obediently acknowledge him."[5] These passions of the human heart, which so often lead to sin, are among the enemies against which the whole reign of Jesus marches here and now, and we are called to take up the standard and march with him upon the battlefields of our hearts.

This martial imagery was very much at home with the way early Christians considered their interior lives (though other metaphors were commonly used too). Take Tertullian for example, who encouraged imprisoned Christians by reminding them that they were "called to the warfare of the living God."[6] Some Eastern Christian communities even conceived of baptism as a rite of enrollment in the army of Christ, in which we take up arms (spiritually speaking, of course) against demonic powers and against our own sinful passions.

One of these martial metaphors for the call of holiness was that of the arena. Some patristic writers—all of whom rejected the actual practice of gladiatorial games—nonetheless used that analogy to describe the process of growing in holiness. We are called to enter the arena of our own hearts, to subdue the wild beasts (the passions), to defeat the enemies (our sins), and so bring our own little battlefield into submission to Christ. This rhetoric appears early in our sources, in the postapostolic generation itself. Clement, writing about the struggle against jealousy and strife in the body of Christ, says, "We write these things, dear friends, not only to admonish you but also to remind ourselves. For we are in the

---

5. Gregory of Nazianzus, Oration 30, 5 (*On God and Christ*, 96).
6. Tertullian, *To the Martyrs* 3 (*ANF* 3:694).

same arena, and the same contest awaits us."⁷ Jerome, writing some three centuries later, uses the same idea and presents the call to holiness as an invitation and a challenge: "It is for you to choose whether you will enter the arena and win the crown."⁸

While patristic writers liked to highlight the element of valiant struggle in the arena, we should remember that Paul also employed the arena metaphor, but used it as a reminder of the humiliation of bearing the cross before the world (1 Cor 4:9). In Paul's use of the imagery, the arena represents the mocking spectacle and accusations of the world against the bearers of Christ's gospel, something to be borne with great humility and longsuffering. While the metaphor is put to work here for rather different purposes than in patristic sources, it affords us an opportunity to rein in any possible excesses of the martial symbolism. This view of Christian holiness as an arena is no call to take pride in our own strength, but rather to lean on the strength of Christ, in the patient self-abasement by which he shattered the power of our sins on the cross, and to follow him in humble obedience. One cannot expect glory and the roar of the crowd in battling one's sins; it will far more often be a road of patient, persevering toil, marked less by our own feats of strength and more by embracing the broken humility through which the grace of God can be poured into our lives.

The patristic writers were of one mind in believing that this arena was a necessary first step of Christian life and duty. Other ministries might follow or accompany it, other ways to spread the blessing of the reign of Christ onto a needy world, but the Christian's first responsibility was to learn to submit their own heart to the reign of Christ on a daily basis. Nowadays, such a strong focus on striving for personal holiness might come under criticism for being too self-centered, as if it is just an exercise in spiritual navel-gazing. After all, with so many desperate needs in the world around us, how could it be proper to give so much time and attention to personal holiness, when we could be preaching the gospel and feeding the hungry and striving for justice in our society? Isn't a fixation of personal holiness, rather than justice, a mark of Pharisaism? This is a critique worth bearing in mind, because it is true that in some circumstances, even a drive for personal holiness can become a self-centered exploit; anything taken to an extreme has the danger of becoming

---

7. 1 Clem. 7.1 (Holmes, *Apostolic Fathers*, 52–53).

8. Jerome, Letter 130, 14 (*NPNF*² 6:268); cf. Ambrose, Letter 63, 72 (*NPNF*² 10:467).

disordered. However, a quick glance around our world today would testify that we ought to be sounding the drum louder for the call to personal holiness. There are far too many Christians who have rushed headlong into outward-facing ministries while the battlefields of their own hearts are still very much enemy-occupied territory, and their passions and sins eventually find them out, often in devastatingly public fashion. It would have been better for them to spend more time in the arena.

How Holiness Works

The pursuit of holiness is nothing less than our unhindered "Yes!" to God and his plan to re-create all things through Christ. Holiness is the healing of our very nature, the restoration of our path toward union with God through participation in his character. The analogy of healing was central to the way patristic writers thought about the Christian life. Their program for holiness was not something narrow and stern; it was an invitation to come and be healed through the ministry of Christ. They had a wide range of ways of conceiving the problem of human fallenness, and we will consider two of those models here, in order to gain a mental picture of how growth in holiness actually operates to bring healing to our twisted nature. In both models, the problem is essentially that sin has changed the direction of our hearts: instead of having full possession of our thoughts and desires, thus able to direct them to God in holy contemplation and worship, we are instead in the position of having those thoughts and desires roaming feral about the world. Instead of seeking to move toward the delight of greater union with God, we have been reduced to trying to gather up as many stray pleasures as we can to try to satisfy ourselves.

From Pride to Love

The first model of fallenness centers on the sin of pride. It is widely known that early Christian writers warned of the dangers of the seven deadly sins (though in fact, the original Eastern Christian teaching was of eight deadly *logismoi*, roughly translated as "thoughts," which was later reduced to seven in the Western tradition). Pride was one of these deadly sins, but patristic writers suggest, with something approaching a broad consensus, that pride is in a category of its own, sitting at the center of all our problems. Pride was *the* sin, the fundamental act of choosing a self-centered existence rather than a God-centered one. It was the original sin of Satan and his demons in their angelic rebellion against God, and so Satan's temptation to Eve ran along the same lines: instead of choosing God's way, listen to your own desires and center your choices on them. It is the sin of dethroning God and putting ourselves in his place. Every one of the other deadly sins is, at root, a manifestation of this self-centered choice. We continue to choose ourselves, to let our disordered desires reign, rather than submit to the reign of God's good commandments. Even when we are saved by God's grace, the earthly patterns of our minds remain hardwired in the state in which we have used them for so long. We continue to be predisposed to choose ourselves rather than God, every single day. There needs to be a rewiring done in our hearts and in our minds.

So what does the journey of practical holiness do? It is our way of submitting to the Spirit's work, of giving ourselves over to his rewiring through a long program of getting back into shape, spiritually speaking. If you are obese and you convert to vegetarianism, that doesn't make you instantly healthy in and of itself. There remains a long process of diet and exercise in front of you, by which you can gradually restore good health to your body. This happens to be the very analogy Paul uses—physical exercise is useful for some things, but training in godliness is useful for everything in your Christian life (1 Tim 4:7–10).

By training, by habitual exercise in spiritual disciplines, we learn, little by little, to disempower the reign of our self-centered desires, and to put God's commandments back in their proper place of leadership in our lives. Like the process of undoing any deep-rooted habit, this transformation takes a great deal of time and hard work, but it is made possible by the grace available to us in Christ and the sustaining presence of the Spirit. Without the grace of being united to Christ, this journey would not even be possible; our self-centeredness is so deeply rooted in sin that, apart from Jesus, it is a cancer without a cure. In him, however, we are now able to join in the pilgrimage of his new humanity, as he remakes us from the inside out. Like any pilgrimage, it only really works if you are willing to walk the road to its destination. Even as we recognize the difficulty of this pilgrimage, though, we must also remember that it is a journey of joy—not of judgment and self-recrimination, but of the deep healing of our souls.

As we grow in this way, gradually learning to replace sins of self-centered indulgence with the virtues of godly restraint, we ultimately become able to experience and participate in more and more of the attributes of God. Maximus the Confessor tells us that to grow in virtue is to grow in our participation in God himself, because the virtues find their substance in his divine, eternal attributes: "Every person who participates in virtue as a matter of habit participates in God, the substance of the virtues."[9] Thus the journey of holiness leads us to a deeper experience and realization of the goal for which we were made: the journey of loving union with God our Maker.

The single virtue that takes center stage here, often seen as the highest of them all, is *agapē* love (or, in older terminology, charity). This virtue is the bottom line of Paul's paean on "the most excellent way" (1 Cor 12:31; 13:13), as well as the summit of Peter's list of the journey of growing in godliness (2 Pet 1:5–7). It is often used to speak of God's love for us, but Scripture is clear that we are called to practice it too, as our journey of holiness in the Spirit makes us able to do so. We tend to call it unconditional love nowadays, but older English writers used to call it disinterested love. Disinterested makes it sound like a boring, grudging sort of love, but that's not actually what the term means: disinterested love is that kind of love that does not bear the person's own interests in mind. It is not self-centered, it is not looking out for its own good or what it can get out of this relationship for itself: it takes no concern for its own interests. In this way, you can see how the virtue of love is the ultimate achievement of the journey of holiness. It has taken pride, our fundamental act of self-centeredness, and replaced it with a God-centered capacity to reach out without any self-centeredness at all, taking no account of our own interests, but simply loving God and the world in a free and unhindered way. To get there, though, we need the training whereby we undercut the reign of our hardwired, self-centered passions, and little by little learn to replace them with virtues, that God's reign in us might be all in all.

---

9. Maximus the Confessor, *Ambiguum* 7.2 (*On the Cosmic Mystery*, 58); cf. 2 Pet 1:4.

From Darkness to Light

The second model that allows us to understand our fallen nature is based on the intertwined biblical metaphors of sight and light. One of the great strengths of this model is that it gives us a way of conceptualizing why and how our nature became twisted by sin, as well as why it remains so even now. In this model, the essential problem of our sinful fallenness is that we have become blind, and so on our own we cannot attain the great goal for which we were made: seeing God, and being transformed by the sight. For many Christians today, this set of sight-based images is unfamiliar to the way we think about the overarching narrative of God's plan, even though they saturate the pages of Scripture.

The highest variety of the experience of God as shown in the Old Testament was to see God, something so high and holy that it was taken to be deadly for unholy humans. Only in the rarest instances is someone described as having seen God, such as at the covenant feast of Israel at Mount Sinai (Exod 24:10–11). Most of the time, it was simply stated that no one could see God and live (Exod 19:21; 33:20; cf. Gen 32:30). Nevertheless, this hope of seeing God, of taking in the light of his face, was central to the devotion of ancient Israel, enshrined in the highest anthems ("In your light we see light," Ps 36:9) and the holiest prayers ("[May] the Lord make his face shine on you," Num 6:25; see also Pss 4:6; 31:16; 67:1; 80:3, 7, 19; 119:135).

The New Testament also speaks of the great goal of Christian life with this set of images. Hebrews tells us that without holiness, "no one will see the Lord" (12:14). The ultimate expression of Christians' heavenly experience of relationship with God, the climax of what John says on the matter, is that "they will see his face" (Rev 22:4). This experience is not something to which we have yet gained full access (1 John 4:12, 20), but in seeing Jesus, we have nonetheless been granted freedom from our spiritual blindness (2 Cor 4:4). In a certain sense, since Jesus is the visible image of God, we have seen God in an anticipatory way (1 John 1:1–3), which will be brought to fullness when Jesus comes again, a vision so glorious that it not only strikes wonder in our hearts but actually transfigures us in Christlikeness (1 John 3:2). The end of our road of holiness, our journey of being made like Christ, is the vision of the Son of God in all his radiant glory. This is why medieval Christian writers so often wrote about the highest experience of heaven as being "the beatific vision."

But what do these images of sight have to do with the day-to-day work of practical holiness? In the Greek-speaking traditions of early Christianity, the effects of the fall were sometimes attributed to a sort of spiritual blindness on our part. The part of humans they called the *nous*, which is most often translated as "mind," could be taken to refer to the apperceptive faculty of the human soul—that is, the part of the soul that *sees* (a roughly approximate idea is the feature we sometimes call "the mind's eye"). Our minds instinctively operate by a sort of inner visualization, which seems so natural to us that we may be unaware of how all-encompassing and extraordinary this faculty is. Anyone who tries focused contemplation or meditation will become immediately aware of how instinctual this visualizing is, and how hard it is to convince one's wandering mind to stop doing it, even for a short time. The *nous*, in patristic thought, was made with one great purpose in mind: to behold God, and not only with our physical eyes—to throw open all the shutters of the soul so that his light could penetrate deep within us.

But as part of the ongoing corruption of death that entered humanity because of sin, this visual faculty of the mind was darkened or clouded (Rom 1:21). Cut off from spiritual life in union with God, it became blind to spiritual reality, and so it was turned to other things instead. Human desires fixated not on God, but on created things, seen by physical sight or in the mind's eye (Rom 1:22–25). Instead of the radiant light of the Godhead, the vision of which was meant to fill us with light, we turned our eyes to the darkness of all that was not God (see 1 John 1:5–7). This biblical imagery of light and darkness became one of the dominant themes across a broad swath of Eastern Christian theology, permeating the patristic writings on how to live a holy life.[10]

To return for a moment to the story of the fall, it is worth noting that Eve's act of giving in to temptation began as an act of sight: "The woman saw that the fruit of the tree was good for food and pleasing to the eye" (Gen 3:6). As soon as she and Adam had eaten, Genesis tells us that "their eyes were opened" (3:7), which is likely a reference to the knowledge this tree was meant to impart, but it also suggests a dramatic change in the way they saw the world. According to this model of fallenness as blindness, this is the point where Adam and Eve's spiritual sight was cut off by sin, and now they saw merely with their physical eyes. And this idea is not just in the creation narrative; the connection between sight and

---

10. See, for example, the Pseudo-Macarian homilies, especially the first and fourth (*Fifty Spiritual Homilies*, 37–44, 50–62).

fallenness can be found throughout the Bible. Deuteronomy 29:3–4 says to the Israelites that though they have seen God's marvelous works with their physical eyes, "[yet] to this day the Lord has not given you a mind that understands or eyes that see or ears that hear." The complaint about Israel's blindness becomes a common arc throughout the prophets and into the New Testament: that though they are seeing, they cannot really see (Isa 6:9–10; Ezek 12:1; Matt 13:13–16; Acts 28:23–31; Rom 11:8; 2 Cor 4:3–4).

This set of symbols is a possible window into understanding what Jesus is talking about in his enigmatic saying in Matthew 6:22–23 (bracketed material added): "The eye is the lamp of the body. If your eyes are healthy [the word is "simple," "whole," or "good"], your whole body will be full of light. But if your eyes are unhealthy ["bad" or "evil"], your whole body will be full of darkness. If then the light within you is darkness, how great is that darkness!" Now, given the patristic model of conceiving of sinful fallenness as a sort of blindness, in which our mind's eye has been cut off from perceiving the transfiguring light of God so that our desires are led to the darkness of everything that is not God, then Jesus' statement makes perfect sense, to the point where it is simply a summation of this well-known theological imagery. Essentially, what you look at with your eyes and your mind conveys either light or darkness to you; indeed, it makes you a recipient of and a participant in either light (that is, God) or darkness (everything that is not the light of God). We tend to say "you are what you eat," but this ancient Christian interpretation says, "you are what you look at"—you take it into yourself just like food, and it transforms you. The idea that the sight we take into us transforms us is also found in John's saying: "We shall be like him, for we shall see him as he is" (1 John 3:2). Paul, too, makes use of this imagery in 2 Corinthians 3:13–18, where he contrasts the blindness of Israel, their minds veiled from understanding their own Scriptures, to the Christian's reception of transforming light by seeing God's glory unveiled in Jesus.

How does the progress of practical holiness help in this situation? The essential idea is this: our sight has been restored in Christ, but we still need to train our minds into the habit of keeping our gaze on God rather than on our dissipated desires, attached to all these other things we see or imagine in the world around us. And it is not just a matter of outward things; some of the fiercest desires we have are our attachments to a particular idea about ourselves, always in front of our mind's eye like an idol.

The work of holiness, guided and empowered by the Holy Spirit, is the process of pulling back our disordered, rampant desires from all the other things they have become attached to, and giving them over to God, to his goodness and his blessings. Through our mind's eye, our hearts are drawn to so many other things besides God, and these habits have become deeply ingrained through sin. We have spiritual sight now through Christ, but we need to learn how to use it properly, to focus on the right things, that we may be filled with God's light in ever-increasing glory. Like the man Jesus healed of blindness in Mark 8, our healing is a two-part act: restoration of sight, and then later seeing clearly, as we allow him to draw back our disordered desires from all the other things we look at, and to submit our gaze to him alone.

11

Desire: How to Train Yourself to Be Godly

THERE IS A SIGNIFICANT difference between the patristic model of growing in holiness and the widespread model held among many Christians today. It is not uncommon nowadays to treat the spiritual disciplines advised in Scripture as a hodgepodge of good advice. They are things we know we ought to be doing, but we're not always sure why. Does fasting have an integral role to play in the structure of Christian life, or is it the optional add-on it is often usually taken to be? Where exactly should it fit in, and what goal are we trying to reach by using it? We talk vaguely about "growing" in our Christian lives, but often without much of a sense for the spiritual mechanisms for how that growth happens, nor what the end goal of that growth is in our present lives.

Not so the patristic model, which was keenly interested in both the end goal and the spiritual mechanisms by which growth happens. They viewed the active disciplines of the Christian life as something like an established course of treatment which would help us on our journey to healing, and the reasons behind each step of that treatment were well understood and often discussed. In other words, early Christians developed not only a theology of sanctification, but a methodology of sanctification. Growing in holiness was a journey with a clear road map, and there were steps along the way that could be learned and put into practice.

Their methodology was also fairly all-encompassing of the biblical commands. If the New Testament advised it, there were Christians who were going to try to follow that advice to the fullest, whether it was a matter of fasting, selling one's possessions to give away to the poor, submitting to one another in a radical lifestyle of self-emptying obedience, or confessing their sins publicly and openly to each other. Even Paul's simple admonition to "work with your hands" (1 Thess 4:11) was taken up and applied as a spiritual discipline. The patristic view of the life of active holiness was nothing less than a holistic attempt to keep all the commands of Scripture.

Some people get nervous about the threat of legalism when we talk about a system of disciplines built on following commands. Others find the thought simply unappealing, picturing desert ascetics performing torturous acts of bodily mortification. Neither of those objections really has any staying power in this case. Early Christianity's ethic of spiritual growth was not about following rules for the sake of rules. Those same desert ascetics would be the first to remind us that we are not under law, but under grace. Following the commands of Scripture, including the most difficult ones, was not undertaken as an act of grudging obedience; it was done because the things commanded of us are the very things that will bring us healing and rest. The commands of Christ are not burdensome (1 John 5:3). Quite the contrary, they open up for us the adventure of living in true freedom, a freedom to which we would have no access were it not for the way we follow the road of godly discipline.

The goal of holiness was always kept firmly in view: it was our road to deeper union with God through participation in his character by grace; and this divine union was taken to be the great *telos* of all humanity. If union with God was the ultimate goal, there were also proximate goals to keep in mind: for example, holiness enabled us to serve effectively in our authentic vocation. In living holy lives, our service as God's priests would be purified and sustained, and the prayers and spiritual warfare by which we enact our royal prerogative in God's kingdom would be empowered. Without growing in ever-greater holiness, we would miss out on the adventure of becoming who we were meant to be.

Many Christians today, if they are urged to walk in holiness at all, are often presented with a negatively oriented view of the process: if you want to grow in holiness, *stop sinning!* Becoming holy is a matter of cutting out the bad stuff, or so say innumerable sermons on the subject. Such an interpretation is not completely wrong (we should, after all, stop sinning), but it is a little incomplete, in at least two respects. First, as a methodology, one might suspect it of being a bit too simplistic. A journey of a single step to achieve one's goal—especially a goal as lofty as holiness—is probably missing something.

Second, there is a mistake about the nature of holiness in this assumption that the road of sanctification is mainly a matter of ceasing from sinful acts. Holiness is not an empty void, not just the base level of existence that is left over when sins have been subtracted away. We cannot continue to tell young people just to avoid giving in to sinful temptations, as if avoiding sinful acts was the whole of holiness. It is no wonder that that approach so often fails, and fails so miserably. If it succeeds in some cases, it tends to make narrow, closed-off Christians who have locked up the specter of their desires behind impenetrable walls, and know nothing of the open-horizoned, brimming-with-true-desire life of an authentic saint of God. Holiness is far more than just the absence of sinful actions; it is something that is actively positive, real, and substantial. It is something which must be built, one brick at a time.

So when we talk about the process of growing in holiness, it is important to underscore not only the negative aspect (the renunciation of sinful acts), but the positive as well: building habits of virtue in place of our old habits of sin. Christian maturity is more than the absence of evil; it is substantial and vigorously alive. It is not automatically obtained simply by removing sins, and it is not something that happens by accident. It involves a long course of practical actions to retrain and renew our hearts and minds (Rom 12:2), and as those actions become habits, they manifest themselves as virtues. Virtue is, to some, an old-fashioned-sounding word, but it is hard to find a better one to describe the very real way in which our participation in God's holiness reveals itself in active and growing character attributes in our daily lives.

The practice of building virtue involves concerted effort on our part. The New Testament is not speaking figuratively when it tells us to "make every effort" in our Christian growth (Luke 13:24; Heb 4:11; 12:14; 2 Pet 1:5, 10; 3:14). But we must always remember that our efforts rest entirely on the flood of God's grace coursing through our lives. In a very real sense, the call to build virtue, though it may sound taxing and strenuous, is just a matter of learning to rest in God's efficacious grace. As we will see in this chapter and the next, most of the active disciplines of the Christian life consist, at their heart, of simply turning to God. They are means by which we abide in Christ and allow his life to manifest itself in us. They are the act of the sick person turning to the one who is offering healing, of laying ourselves down upon the strength of the one who offers us rest. There are many virtues of the Christian life, and there is no single, exhaustive list of them in Scripture. We can begin to get a sense for what these virtues are in certain texts, like Paul's fruits of the Spirit (Gal 5:22–23) and Peter's ladder of ascending godliness (2 Pet 1:5–7). But at their core, they are all simply ways of describing our growing union with God, our participation in his unified character.

We already ought to know all this, and it is troubling how often we forget. We sometimes treat our attempts at holiness like we are training for a triathlon by doing nothing but cutting fast food burgers out of our diet. Obviously, you ought to cut out fast food burgers if you want to have any hope of reaching your top potential, but that's not all you should do. You need to exercise! Physical fitness is not just what is left over after you stop eating junk food, and holiness is far more than the absence of sin. It is nothing less than a participation in the very character of God. Just like we train ourselves to be physically fit, we must also train ourselves to walk in holiness, as Paul says: "Train yourself to be godly. For physical training is of some value, but godliness has value for all things, holding promise for both the present life and the life to come" (1 Tim 4:7–8). And in case it is not clear enough there, Paul immediately follows up this rhetoric of athletic training by saying, "This is why we labor and strive . . ." (v. 10, with the word for "strive" also often used in the context of athletic competitions). We are called to a rigorous course of training in our growth in godliness (see 1 Cor 9:25–27).

But what did this course of training look like? While many monastic writers referred to this training as *askēsis*, from which we get the term "ascetic," the broader way it was described was simply *praxis* (from which we get "practice"). Asceticism conjures up in many minds a vision of hoary, raw-boned desert hermits, desperately trying to deny all pleasure and desire, but the word itself simply refers to exercise and discipline, and it could be used of anyone (see 4 Macc 13:21). Further, far from denying desire, the call of the ascetic was to harness desire toward its proper end: the infinite delight of seeing God and being transformed in the radiance of his glory.

But *praxis* probably remains the more accessible term for many of us. It was one of two broad categories of spiritual development in Maximus the Confessor's system of thought: *praxis* (which we might think of as the outward actions of various spiritual disciplines), then *theōria* (a habit of prayer best rendered as "contemplation"), and then the ultimate goal, union with God. This matches the classic Christian journey of growth that has been observed and detailed in the experiences of many believers, from the early church to our own day: the journey of moving through overlapping stages of purgation, illumination, and union. (The next few chapters follow the broad outline of that arc of Christian growth, with an examination of practical holiness, prayer, and union.) Whether or not one agrees with this schematic of Christian growth, it is instructive to compare and contrast this idea—of a pilgrimage with recognizable stages that leads to the ultimate goal of Christian life—to the common habit nowadays of talking about Christian growth in a rather nebulous way, wherein, very often, neither a practical path nor a clearly conceived goal is ever mentioned.

Maximus's vision of the journey of Christian growth adds one further twist on the idea: he suggests that Christians are called to signify and point the way toward the coming restoration of all things. Recall that humanity is "a microcosm of the cosmos," as described in chapter 3. Since Christians have entered the new humanity and are now part of God's restoration of the cosmos, we visibly display God's intention for his whole created order by our progress of transformation with ever-increasing glory (2 Cor 3:18). Not only are we part of God's transformation of the cosmos in our re-creation through Christ, we are, in each of our own lives, a visible demonstration of his plan for the whole universe. So we, illuminated by the grace of the Spirit and increasingly transformed into Christlikeness, anticipate in our daily lives the transformation of the cosmos into the new heavens and new earth, where God will be all in all.

Rewiring Our Desire

The early Christian understanding of sin was rooted in a biblically based psychology of human desire. Because the mechanisms by which sin takes hold were fairly well understood, the patristic age was able to produce a fully articulated model of human healing through God's grace, poured out in the context of our *praxis*. The leading ethicists of the patristic period understood that our problem lay much deeper than sinful acts, and was rooted instead at the level of our desires.

Some Christians nowadays try to attack sinful actions themselves as the root issue, rather than working on the steps that lead up to the sin. We tell ourselves that we will be fine if we can just stop doing whatever sinful habit has taken root in our hearts, whether it's uncontrolled eating, or looking at pornography, or lashing out when we lose our temper, or shopping for yet more items that far exceed our actual needs. Our general impulse is to focus attention on the problem behavior, and just to try, by sheer willpower, to stop. We will sometimes even memorize Bible verses that also tell us to stop, and we'll pray that God would empower us to stop. The only problem is that this "just stop doing it" approach to dealing with sin rarely works, and most of us have learned that the hard way. We need to back up a few steps and look at the heart of the problem.

In the previous chapter, we saw that the patristic understanding of holiness was a matter of learning how to take our unregulated, disordered desires, roaming about after a thousand lesser things, and give them back to God. It is a matter of turning our gaze from the world's darkness to God's light, so that we might be filled with light ourselves. This understanding is based in the way the Bible talks about sin. Listen to how James describes the process of how sin works: "Each person is tempted when they are dragged away by their own evil desire and enticed. Then, after desire has conceived, it gives birth to sin; and sin, when it is full-grown, gives birth to death" (Jas 1:14–15). The roots of our sin lie not in the outward acts themselves, but in disordered and rampant desires.

To address the problem of sin in our lives, it is not enough just to aim at the sinful action itself; we need to go back and sort out the problem of our desire. The word James uses focuses specifically on the kind of desire that is brimming with self-centered craving (it's often just translated as "lust")—a desire that is already running feral around the world, seeking pleasures to try to fill our wounds with anything that might salve the pain. But we don't need any of those things we run after; what we need is the healing of the wounds. We need to be able to address the fact that our desires are now wired wrong because they have grown used to operating in the darkness of being separated from the light of God. To address only the sin and not the desire is like accepting chemotherapy as our sole defense against cancer, without even bothering to reduce our risks beforehand by exercising and choosing healthy foods.

The ethical teachers of the patristic church focused on desire. Instead of saying that we just ought to stop doing sinful acts, they sought out and developed a course of action that would help to train themselves from following their sinful desire, and thus (it was hoped) breaking the link before desire could conceive and give birth to sin. If you have in mind those gaunt desert hermits again, you might be tempted to think that their answer was just to try to shut desire down, to dry it up at the source. But you would be wrong. The fundamental thing that has gone awry is not that we have desires, but that our desires are disordered. The desert fathers and mothers saw desire not as a weed to be uprooted, but more like a wild-growing hedge that needed some serious trimming and shaping to become what it had been planted to be. What was needed was a way to recapture authentic human desire and restore it, by the gracious work of the Spirit, to its correct orientation toward God. Then desire, far from being quashed, could be filled to overflowing with absolute goodness and delight.

Let's do a quick overview of the stages of this process, filling out the picture from the basic framework of James 1. The first stage of our interaction with the world—whether that's an event or an object in front of our physical eyes, or one that comes before our mind's eye—is the movement of natural human desire and emotion. We will simply call this "natural desire," as a way to describe the inherent tendencies with which God made us. We were made to see beauty, goodness, and truth, and to delight in those things. Thus when we see the natural beauty of a sunset, our heart moves with joy. The same reaction applies to the way we can appreciate the flavor of a delicious meal or the compelling beauty of another human form—these are basic, natural desires that are inherent to our created nature, crafted by God and pronounced "very good."

In our original nature, these things were present in a holy and wholesome way. If not for the fall, it would be possible for a man to observe the physical beauty of a woman's body and render God the glory for the beauty he beheld in purity and joy. It would be possible for a man to taste the flavors of a pizza and rejoice in the goodness of God's creation without feeling the urge to cram as many pieces down his throat as he could. But because of the fall, because we are cut off from the spiritual light of God that purifies and transforms us, darkness has flooded our nature. And in that condition, these natural desires flip very quickly—immediately, in fact—into the kind of "evil desire" of which James speaks. Instead of a desire that begets joy and gratitude, a response of giving from an overflowing soul, now our desires beget the mad cravings of lust and gluttony, a response of taking the desired object for our own imagined pleasure. But, of course, it's all counterfeit pleasure—in taking it for ourselves, we lose the joy of it, and are left bitterly unsatisfied in the end. Unlike the joy of beholding the goodness of God, these counterfeit pleasures never last. At this point, we are all the way down the track that James describes: sinful desire has been conceived, and when we act on it, sin is born. The progression looks something like this:

> Natural desire → Sinful desire → Sin

Whereas we often try to break the chain at the second arrow, cutting this track before an act of sin is outwardly committed, the ethical teaching of the patristic age would advise us to focus on the first arrow. We need to rewire our patterns of thought, such that natural desire (which should not be avoided or uprooted, since it is part of God's good creation) does not lead inexorably to sinful desire. If we do not set our focus there, then we have already lost the greater part of the battle. Sin is still in our hearts, whether we act on it or not, and sin's roots will run very deep if we let them spread.

This transformation of desire, the cutting of the first arrow, can only be done by the empowerment of the Spirit; the movement from natural desire to sinful desire is automatic without the grace of God. But since we do have the grace of God at work in our lives, now we have the possibility of healing from these destructive patterns. Behold the awesome goodness of our God: not only does he expunge the guilt of our sins, freely offering his own Son as our atonement, he then also pours forth his mercy on us, that we may find true healing for our deepest wounds. And by doing so, he brings us back to the "very goodness" of our original creation, including our desires. We were made to be desiring beings, yearning toward the goodness, truth, and beauty of God, and delighting in the reflection of his goodness, truth, and beauty in the things that he has made. Gregory of Nazianzus writes about us being "tormented by desire" for the things of God in the fullness of the kingdom yet to come.[1]

So how do we go about the process of rewiring our desires? There are two big steps to the process, and both cut into the diagram above and reroute that first arrow in another direction. The first step is *praxis* (or *askēsis*, depending on which term you prefer to use): a series of practical, day-to-day habits that teach us to say no to sinful desire. They seek to draw the habitual course of our minds away from the idolatrous objects of our desire, and to direct them back to God.[2]

Not only do these spiritual disciplines actively draw our attention back to God, they also prime us to be ready for action whenever temptation might arise. The training they provide comes into effect when that automatic arrow tries to lead us from natural desire to sinful desire, and

---

1. Gregory of Nazianzus, *Dogmatic Poems* 8, quoted in Clément, *Roots*, 79.
2. See Pseudo-Macarius, *Fifty Spiritual Homilies* 31.1 (194).

by the empowering grace of God it equips us to refuse that movement. You can think about the disciplines as being like a manual lever on a train-track junction: by pulling that lever, you can switch the tracks so that the train of your natural desire doesn't go to sinful desire anymore, but can be rerouted to a new destination.

And this is where the second step comes in. We are not just left with aborted desire, forced to keep cutting off every wisp of pleasure in the pursuit of a desiccated life. The train of desire does not stop; it just keeps rolling. So at this point, having learned how to say no to our movement towards sinful desire, we offer our desire up to God instead. There is a fundamental movement of turning in the Christian spiritual life: turning away from our sins, passions, and the attachments of our disordered desires, and turning to God instead. This turning lies at the root of our spirituality in the very idea of repentance, whereby we, in our daily lives, continually reconfirm our decision to turn from our sins and follow Jesus.

Spiritual discipline teaches us habits that enable this turning. We are trained in ways that can cancel the first arrow of the diagram above, and then replace it with an arrow that points to our desires' properly ordered end, God himself. Thus the new paradigm looks something like this:

> Natural desire → (habits of *praxis*) → Desire turned to God

Let's think about this second step for a moment, because it may sound unfamiliar. The path to healing runs through the practice of learning to offer our desires up to God. In my case, even though having known this patristic method for some time, I am still startled when I see it in action, because it is such a resounding, tables-turning movement of grace's triumph over sinful desire. I can recall one time hearing about how my young nephew, who was hungry and hoping for something to eat on a car ride, asked his father if he had brought any snacks along. The father apologized, and said he had nothing to give just then; the boy would have to wait until they got home. Now, in this situation, most kids would either start complaining, or (in what we usually think is the best-case scenario) maintain a patient silence on the matter until they get home and have their snack. But my nephew said, "That's okay, Dad. I'll just offer my hunger up to God." On hearing that story, not only was I impressed by his attitude, but I was immediately struck with the conviction that I had still not learned how to do that when I was hungry. Yet this is precisely what patristic *praxis* would have us do.

There's a wonderful irony here. Christians so often talk about "fighting sin," "struggling against sin," and so on, making use of our martial metaphors, and of course there is value to that kind of rhetoric. We do wage war against our ingrained patterns of sinful desire. But there is also a sense in which the battle is won not so much by fighting our desires as by setting our desire free from the bondage to which it has been enslaved. It is a movement of joyful liberation more than it is the eradication of an enemy. Some people fancy that Christianity leaves one repressed, bound to the exacting standards of a moralistic, legalistic God, and that freedom is found only when one is master of oneself. The opposite is actually true: it is only in Christianity that true freedom is found, because in anything else there is no escape from our slavery to our own sin. We are bound in the prison of our untamable desire, locked in the cycle of always yearning and never finding the joy of infinite satisfaction, until by the grace of Christ we can send that desire racing—faithful, glorious, and free—to where it has always longed to go.

Yes, we are called to set our desires free. Our whole lives—including our desires—are to be offered up to God as part of our living sacrifice. John Climacus writes, "The man who decides to struggle against his flesh and to overcome it by his own efforts is fighting in vain . . . Offer up to the Lord the weakness of your nature."[3] The fundamental movement of human desire is a turning toward God, lifting ourselves up to him in confession, thanksgiving, petition, or praise. When our desires are rightly ordered, we can lift them immediately to him as acts of thanksgiving; until then, we offer even the weakness of our broken desires in humble longing before him. Later in the same passage, Climacus recounts a startling example of turning one's desires toward God:

> I was told once about an astonishing level of chastity attained by someone. There was a man who, having looked on a body of great beauty, at once gave praise to its Creator, and after one look was stirred to love God and weep copiously . . . And if such a man feels and behaves in similar fashion on similar occasions, then he has already risen to immortality before the general resurrection.[4]

What a striking difference between this practice and the way we usually counsel ourselves regarding how to handle lust! Now, not

---

3. Climacus, *Ladder* 15 (173).
4. Climacus, *Ladder* 15 (179).

everyone can do what the man in this story did; it is the fruit of a very long course of Christian *praxis*, such that, in his case, looking at someone with a beautiful body led him immediately and instinctively to an act of Godward praise. In most of our cases, underdeveloped as we still are in the practice of turning away from sinful desire, the link from seeing something desirable to lusting after it remains almost instinctual. But even so, this example ought to make us think twice before we instruct young people (or really, any of us who live in this sex-saturated society) to act as if they are creatures with no such desires at all. Much modern Christian instruction on how to deal with lust begins by essentially saying that we ought to pretend we are creatures without desire, and never to admit that there is pleasure in seeing the beauty of the "very goodness" of the human body God has made. In view of the patristic model, that sort of teaching is profoundly unhelpful, and may lie at the heart of why we wrestle with so much sexual sin in the church today.

Our desire is a gift from God, and rather than assuming that it constitutes a source of shame, we ought to let the Holy Spirit transform it back into a fountainhead of Godward gratitude. We are not called to paper over our desires with a veneer of play-acted holiness, but to embrace them in the context of Christian *praxis*, in a way that eventually enables us to harness our natural desire directly into thanksgiving and praise. As Maximus the Confessor wrote, "The soul is made perfect when its powers of passion have been completely directed towards God."[5]

On Passions and Virtues: Walking the Long Road to Healing

It sounds wonderful, doesn't it? To be able to learn how to say no to sinful desire, to turn that desire toward God instead, and thus be immersed in the glorious participation of his unending love? And it is wonderful. But it is also a long road to get there.

Our sinful desire is not just something that pops up now and then, like something out of a whack-a-mole game which we can easily tap back down each time. Because of the way sin has hijacked our nature, the state of sinful desire has become so ingrained in us as to constitute almost a second nature, a counterfeit nature, which is exceedingly difficult to

---

5. Maximus the Confessor, *Centuries on Charity* 3.98, quoted in Clément, *Roots*, 177.

unravel. It has the sort of aspect that we associate with a compulsive behavior, or even an addiction: our minds and hearts are predisposed to jump toward sinful desire, even when we are longing to turn ourselves back to God. When sin takes on this shape, as it does in all of us, it is no longer a matter of discrete, sinful actions, but a disease that has metastasized to every part of our lives.

Sinful desires, in this compulsive and habitual state wherein we all experience them, are sometimes referred to as "passions" in patristic literature. In order to obtain consistent victory over the passions, we need far more than just a philosophy of resisting each discrete temptation, because the problem runs much deeper than the whack-a-mole of temptation. We need healing, a course of treatment that addresses the disease itself.

And this is the wonderful news: we have a course of treatment that does just that, and it is all about the grace of God. It is his power, and his alone, that heals us. Like the analogy of the farmer and the seed from the previous chapter, there are things that we ought to do to help clear the way, but the actual growth must come from God's work on our behalf. He has already taken away the guilt of our sins, has already delivered us from spiritual death and brought us back to life, and now he offers a further grace out of the bounty of his love: a pilgrimage of healing. The power of sin has already been broken for us by Christ's death and resurrection, and now we may clear out the rubble of its shattered reign. The author of the Pseudo-Macarian homilies makes this clear:

> To uproot sin and the evil that is so imbedded in our sinning can be done only by divine power, for it is impossible and outside man's competence to uproot sin. To struggle, yes, to continue to fight, to inflict blows and to receive setbacks is in your power. To uproot, however, belongs to God alone.[6]

In the next two chapters, we will be looking at specific steps that Christians in the patristic era undertook to advance on their course of treatment: practices like fasting, submission, confession, and a host of others that made up the warp and woof of everyday Christian life. But before we begin that examination, there are a couple important considerations to keep in mind.

First, we must understand that this is a long journey, and for most people the end goal will only be experienced incrementally in this

---

6. Pseudo-Macarius, *Fifty Spiritual Homilies* 3.4 (48).

lifetime. But God lavishes his mercy on those who walk these roads, and anyone who has taken even the first step on the path of building godly virtue can testify that the inherent delight of righteousness and the joy of gaining liberation from sin, even if only experienced incrementally, are rewards that far surpass the cost of our exertion.

So take courage and walk that road, but do it with patience, perseverance, and grace. Patience for your growth, because such things take time; perseverance through your struggles, because they will come upon you; and grace for yourself, because you will stumble and fall repeatedly along the way. Christ has unlimited grace for you, and if this is a path of growing in Christlikeness, then you ought to be like Christ and give yourself some grace. Do not let yourself feel defeated by your continued struggles against the passions, nor even your continued failures. There is only one thing to do when we stumble, and that is to get up, keep going, and trust in the good work of God on our behalf. "Therefore, do not become despondent. When you fall, arise . . . Simply do not become neglectful. Take courage in the fact that the Lord who established you in this work will also direct it."[7]

The truth is, struggles are simply a hallmark of the journey. "War against us is proof we are making war," Climacus writes. "Do not be surprised if you fall every day, and do not surrender."[8] In fact, it is probably better to have to toil along this road than to have a smooth and easy ascent, because our persevering labor over the difficult terrain of the passions is the very fire of God's kiln and the rough side of his sander; it is what he uses to do the real work of teaching us humility and utter dependence on him, and from those qualities all the other virtues grow. "Endure passions and afflictions thankfully," says Barsanuphius, "for they are a discipline from God . . . So do not be afraid of temptations, but rejoice that they are leading you to progress."[9] Climacus agrees with this assessment, and even goes so far as to contrast those people who seem naturally inclined to the acquisition of virtue with those who "have to fight hard against their own natures to acquire [virtues] . . . suffering occasional defeat on the way." The bottom line he comes to is this: "It seems to me that the very fact of having to struggle . . . puts them into a higher

---

7. Barsanuphius and John, *Letters of Barsanuphius and John* 330 (*Letters from the Desert*, 122).

8. Climacus, *Ladder* 4, 5 (115, 130).

9. Barsanuphius and John, *Letters of Barsanuphius and John* 244, 496 (*Letters from the Desert*, 110, 145).

category than the first kind."[10] It's a long journey, and you will fall repeatedly along the way. Don't lose heart.

A second thing to keep in mind is this: the process will look different for every Christian. Although this course of treatment has broad parameters that should fit everyone's experience and ability, the exact way it is lived out, and the virtues it grows in a person's life, will match all the glorious uniqueness of our individuality. Your journey of *praxis* will probably not look like that of the desert father Antony, and even if it did, you would emerge from the process with a different balance of the virtues than Antony did, for the simple reason that you are not Antony, and he is not you. We are called to let Christ be formed in us (Gal 4:19), and it must be precisely that: *in us,* not in someone else, and not as a transformation into someone who is not us. God is such an artist that he makes each saint a masterpiece of startling uniqueness, each of them fully themselves in Christ.

John Cassian speaks of growth in the virtues in a way reminiscent of Paul's teaching about the variety and distribution of spiritual gifts: not everyone has the same balance of virtues, and no one can have all of them to the fullest extent. "Straight away [eager beginners] want to take up a discipline like [the great exemplar of some virtue], and because of human frailty their efforts are necessarily in vain. It is quite impossible for one and the same man to shine outstandingly with all the virtues."[11] The point here is not that you are doomed to failure, but rather that God has designed you to shine gloriously in one or two great virtues, and to learn the other virtues as a faithful disciple, even if not as a master. The great heroes of the Christian faith are not remembered for being paragons of all the virtues, but are held up as shining examples of one or two particular aspects in which the radiance of their characters glowed with Christlikeness: Antony for his disciplined perseverance against temptation, Francis for his joy, George Mueller for his faith. One of the wonderful adventures on the road to holiness is discovering those areas of life in which you were made to blaze as a beacon of God's glory, and to let him bring you to the fullness of life at just that point.

The counsel of the patristic age was this: within the broad outline of Christian *praxis,* find a way forward that matches who you are. You cannot be Benedict or Macrina or Maximus, but you can be yourself, and

10. Climacus, *Ladder* 26 (234).
11. Cassian, *Conferences* 14.6 (158).

you should be. God gave those men and women to the church at their particular time because it needed them at that time; the church at this time needs you. As you grow in discernment, you will find ways to craft a rule of life that fits what you are able to do, that matches the measure of your progress and the context of your community of faith, and that hones the particular virtues which God designed you to display. There is no one-size-fits-all approach to Christian discipleship; there is only the road of following our Savior into healing and holiness, and each of us must take that pilgrimage and make it the journey of our own heart.

12

Disciplines: The Practice of Christian Training (Part 1)

Now we turn our attention once again to practical matters: How exactly does one grow in holiness? All such growth is enabled and empowered by God's grace alone, but it still leaves the question of what we are called to do in order to participate in that work. For the church of the patristic age, this was one of their favorite subjects: the brass tacks, down-to-earth business of learning to live as a citizen of God's kingdom. There were two major ways in which growth in holiness was thought to happen: first, by training one's habits through spiritual disciplines, and second, through participation in the life of the church. These two channels of holiness—personal spiritual discipline and communal church life—are mutually interdependent and catalyze each other in marvelous ways.

In chapter 9, I briefly presented a sketch of how Sunday worship is intimately connected to the rest of our week. If we conceive of worship as sacrifice—specifically, the act of bearing our sacrifices into the presence of God—then the work of our week becomes the harvesttime for gathering up the things we will offer before God. Every Sunday, we should be coming joyfully to the assembly of God's priests, with our hearts full of labors done for his glory and for our neighbors' good, there to present them before the throne. I want us to keep this idea of sacrifice and weekly worship in our minds as we consider the task of spiritual disciplines, the steps of *praxis* on which patristic writers focused so much attention.

One of the subtle temptations of spiritual disciplines is to see them as an individual task, centered around one's own life and growth in holiness. And while such disciplines are done by individuals, they are done in the context of the wider body of Christ. Any attempts at Christian *praxis* which are wholly removed from that context tend to be dangerous endeavors, leading not to humility and love as the summit of our spiritual growth, but to self-centered pride in one's own labors. There's a winsome little story in the sayings of the desert fathers that captures this contrast between individual labors and the vibrancy of being connected to the life of the church:

> They used to tell of a certain monk . . . that although he kept frequent vigil and prayed, he was neglectful about joining with the congregation in prayer. And one night there appeared to his gaze a glorious pillar of brilliant light, rising from the place where the congregation had gathered; and it reached to the heavens. Then he saw a small spark, which [flew separately] about the pillar, and sometimes it shone brightly, but sometimes it was extinguished. And while he was wondering about the vision, it was explained to him by God, who said, "The pillar which you see is the prayers of the many who are gathered together . . . And the spark is the prayers of those . . . who despise the appointed services of the congregation. So now, if you would live, perform that which is customary to perform with the congregation, and only then, if you . . . are able to pray separately, do so."[1]

It is only in connection with the life of the church—the church as the living sacrament of Jesus Christ—that our spiritual disciplines become the vibrant, transformative agents of real growth in holiness. In this chapter and the next, while we focus our attention on individual disciplines, we will also observe the ways these disciplines connect to the life of the church. There are many ways in which this is true, not least the reciprocal dynamic in which the spiritual nourishment of fellowship with the body encourages true individual growth, and in which any member's growth in holiness aids and encourages all the members' growth. But one particular aspect that we will focus on here is the paradigm of sacrifice. As we perform our labors throughout the week and then come together to offer them to God, something wondrous happens: the disciplines of renunciation which we have undertaken for the sake of the kingdom are transfigured and returned to us in lavish celebrations of grace.

I have called them disciplines of renunciation, because in large part this is the dynamic of growing in Christian holiness: letting go of some of those outward things to which we have become attached so that we can

---

1. Athanasius et al., *Paradise of the Holy Fathers*, saying 135 (2:30-31).

learn to direct our desires to God. Even the broadest, pleasantest practices, like Scripture reading and prayer, entail an element of renunciation in the form of giving up time and attention that would be easier to devote to other things in our lives. But when one comes to disciplines like fasting, submission, and simplicity, the stark tenor of renunciation comes out clearly. The road of Christian formation is a road of *kenosis*—the voluntary self-emptying that Paul ascribes to the manner of Christ's humble servanthood, and which he advises us to take up as our attitude as well (Phil 2:5–8). There is a great deal of voluntary renunciation and humble self-emptying that comes with walking this road, exactly as one might expect from a call to deny yourself and take up your cross (Mark 8:34).

But we should not get the notion that this is the whole story, that Christian growth is just a grueling road of giving things up, like a perverse retwisting of Narnia to be always Lent and never Easter. In Paul's description of Christ's *kenosis,* the second half of the story (after voluntary self-emptying) is exaltation (Phil 2:9–11). If we think again about Jesus' call to take up our crosses, we all know very well that the next act after the cross is the triumph of the resurrection. This is the same pattern we find in our weekly work of Christian discipline: self-emptying renunciation is met by the overabundant blessings of new life in the worship and fellowship of the church (and, ultimately, in the new heavens and the new earth).

This works something like the familiar story of Abraham's call to sacrifice his son Isaac, as told in Genesis 22. This call, naturally, was not something Abraham wanted to do—it was the most painful form of renunciation imaginable. But he was willing to answer that call in faith, and God graciously intervened at the last moment, not only giving him back his son, but the blessing of a ram to serve as the sacrifice. This dynamic—bringing the sacrifice of our *kenosis* to God, and receiving matching and abundant blessings in response—is one of the many ways that our individual spiritual disciplines are linked to the life of the church. Our renunciation in fasting is returned to us in feasting (in my tradition, potluck suppers); our confession is returned to us in reconciliation with our brothers and sisters; and our poverty and simplicity are returned to us in the hospitality and generosity of the body of Christ. The seed that we sow to die in the field, with its outer husk to be shattered, issues forth in new life and a hundredfold return of what we have given up (John 12:24–25; Matt 19:29). What we give up for Christ here, in the disciplines that train us to turn our desires back to God, results in a bountiful harvest in the body of Christ and in the life to come.

A Framework for Ascetic Disciplines

There are many different ways to categorize and describe the various disciplines by which Christians are trained to set their affections on God. There is no exhaustive list, and neither is there a rule that each person has to undertake all the disciplines mentioned (at least not in their fullest form). In fact, many church fathers and mothers noted that other sources of deprivation—like sickness or suffering—can act in the place of ascetic disciplines if they are received in the proper way. Paul himself makes this connection, noting that "suffering produces perseverance; perseverance, character; and character, hope" (Rom 5:3). Suffering itself can sometimes act just as powerfully as fasting or submission to shape a person's growth. The list of disciplines that appears below, then, is not intended to be a full or final expression of what each person's *praxis* ought to look like, since each person's circumstances are different. A cancer patient may gain more growth through the road they walk than a desert father through all his ascetic labors. The following list is simply an outline of some of those disciplines that patristic writers found to be helpful in bringing us to the healing of our passions.

As a framework for helping us understand how these disciplines work, I have set each discipline in opposition to one of the "seven deadly sins" as described by Gregory the Great. This does not mean that each discipline is only effective against that particular sin (fasting, for instance, has far more applications than just as a defense against gluttony). In general, each of the disciplines is effective to some degree against all of the passions, since each provides a training ground for practicing the skills of detaching our desires from self-centered ends. But I have chosen to set them in these one-on-one matchups as a way of reminding us that these are positive acts. Asceticism is too often seen as a negative practice—a denial of the world or a repudiation of the body—when in fact it is the practice of gaining healing from our wounds and building active virtues in the place of our sinful habits. It is a positive process, set against the negative effects of sin. It is an act whereby we prepare the way for the empowering, creative, grace-laden work of the Spirit to spur even greater growth in our lives.

There is one more point to keep in mind, on which we touched at the end of the previous chapter: the application of these training methods to each Christian's life is a matter of careful discernment and prayer. Some will be tempted to dive in and try each discipline to the fullest possible extent. Despite what you might expect, the desert fathers and mothers advise strongly against such a move. They consistently counsel moderation, and they stress that the precise outworking of these disciplines in one Christian's life will not exactly match the corresponding outworking in another Christian's life. One desert elder, John, advises us to "Keep to the middle way . . . For this is the way of the fathers: neither to be wasteful nor to be crushed in one's discipline."[2]

In the following pages, we will look at three sets of disciplines which aid us in overcoming the first three of the seven deadly sins, and in the next chapter we will examine the final four sets, along with a look at the overarching place of prayer and Scripture in the process of Christian growth. Ascetic disciplines are one part of the patristic methodology toward holiness, but only one part, and they are held together by a passionate commitment to prayer and to the ministry of the word.

Against Pride: The Practice of Submission

Pride, as we have seen, is in some ways the foundational sin—the self-oriented frame of our desires, centering our lives upon ourselves as our first impulse, and thus leading us into all manner of other sins. This is not simply a matter of whether a particular person is stuck up or vain; it is the default setting of every fallen human soul. When we feed any other sinful desire, whether it be lust or greed or wrath, we are essentially allowing the tyranny of the fallen self to have its sway in the usurped kingdom of our hearts, and that is the very definition of pride. It is the attempted replacement of God with ourselves.

All of us do this. It is so pervasive in fallen human nature that even our pursuit of virtue can fall beneath its grip, whenever we begin to make our own feelings or the sense of our own accomplishment the measure of our progress. John Chrysostom tells us that if you were to imagine a race in which virtue, saddled with pride, was matched against sin, saddled

---

2. Barsanuphius and John, *Letters of Barsanuphius and John* 212 (*Letters from the Desert*, 104).

with humility, then sin with humility would win every time.³ Pride is so fundamentally destructive that it can even sour the goodness of the virtues, and it turns each person into an enemy of themselves.⁴

How do we begin to retrain our souls away from the grip of such an all-pervasive monster? For many writers of the patristic age, the answer was simple to explain (but not simple to do): put yourself in a constant state of submission to one another. The term most often used for this practice in patristic texts was "obedience," which became one of the foundational monastic vows, but its practice was recommended for all Christians. In many cases, it involved binding oneself in absolute obedience to a spiritual authority figure—to an elder hermit, the abbot or abbess of a monastery, a member of the clergy, or simply a spiritual father of some sort. The believer would consult with this spiritual authority on many matters of their Christian growth and daily discernment, and would simply follow what the authority figure said. They would follow this counsel even if it was something they would have opted not to do on their own; obedience required them to lay all such self-will to the side. In one famous case, John Kolobos a hermit who was just starting his life as a desert monk, was instructed by his elder, Abba Pambo, to plant a dead stick in the sand and water it, even though to do so required a daily, miles-long hike to the nearest river. This strikes us as a wildly pointless act, but Pambo meant it to be a training ground in the disempowerment of the fallen, prideful self (and in this case, John Kolobos's obedience was so pure-hearted and perseverant that God eventually honored it by miraculously making the stick take root and blossom, or so the story goes).

For many Christians, especially those enmeshed in individualistic cultures like my own, this kind of submission strikes one as bizarre, if not downright distasteful. It involves a radical *kenosis* of the self, a surrender of what we see as our own rights and prerogatives, and in so doing it cuts starkly against the grain of our taste for independence and autonomy. We are quick to see the problems of a system like that. What if the authority figure judges the matter incorrectly, and you end up wasting your time doing something meaningless instead of something fulfilling? Is it really sensible to surrender your own choices like this, when you will one day have to answer for the choices you made? Isn't it a system that seems prone to abuse? All these questions are valid, to one degree or another.

---

3. John Chrysostom, *On the Incomprehensibility of God* 5, quoted in Clément, *Roots*, 154.

4. See Climacus, *Ladder* 23 (207–13).

As far as abuse goes, the believer was never required to follow sinful commands; in fact, quite the opposite: one's obedience to God always trumped any other authority. But in most cases, the choice to follow radical humility was seen as a greater work than any other movement of self-will one could come up with, no matter how proper or fulfilling the latter might seem.

This kind of obedience, as a full disempowerment of the fallen self, was most often practiced in monastic communities; lay Christians would not usually have been under quite so stringent an arrangement. This practice was voluntary for laity, and in the case of most it would be something along the lines of spiritual mentorship. But I have chosen to present the starkest form of the practice, because I think the contrast with our own tendencies is illuminating. Perhaps our reaction against this practice reveals that we are still a little too inclined to hold onto the sovereignty of the self. We live in an age where, in many church communities, submission in the life of the body of Christ is hard to find. Church discipline is rendered ineffective because those who would be subject to discipline just uproot and join themselves to another fellowship, all while sowing havoc and discord throughout the body. Rather than submit to the decisions of a local church's governing body when those decisions go against their preferred position, some Christians prefer to stir up trouble. Even among Christians who are not inclined to that kind of toxic behavior, the root of this passion still strikes deep in our hearts: How many of us, when a church decision goes against what we would want, have as our first response to bow our hearts and open our hands in humble obedience, and to thank God for the leaders set over us and for the Spirit's guidance in our congregation?

Yet this is precisely the attitude that the New Testament calls us to have. We are asked to submit to our leaders in the church (Heb 13:17), and, in an even broader sense, to practice submission toward all fellow Christians (Eph 5:21). The patristic practice of radical obedience could have its dangers, certainly, and there will be situations in which wisdom and a right conscience might require one to take a stand against bad leadership; but overall, submission as a spiritual discipline tends to engender humility and deep relationships of trust within the body of Christ. Mentorships spring up as something natural rather than forced, and we learn not to be held under the sway of our own passions, the innate self-centeredness that would always like to have things go our way. Sometimes it is the best of God's gifts to be asked to walk a road other than the one we prefer to walk, and to learn the grace of submission. One desert father penned a beautiful paean to the power of humble obedience: "It is . . . the mother of all virtue, the entry into the kingdom; it raises us from earth to heaven; obedience lives in the same place as the angels; it is the food of the saints who by its nourishment grow to fullness of life."[5]

How can a twenty-first-century Christian practice this spiritual discipline? There are a range of practical options available. One could follow the recommended course in patristic literature, which is to seek out a spiritual mentor and practice submission to their guidance. A more radical option would be to bind oneself to a monastic community as a lay oblate and submit to the practices that form their rule of life. But the simplest is this, and it is what the New Testament seems to advise: to think through the people in your life under whose authority you live, whether in your work (Eph 6:5–8; 1 Pet 2 18–25), at home (Eph 5:21—6:4; 1 Pet 3:1–7), at church (Eph 5:21; Heb 13:17; 1 Pet 5:5–6), or in society at large (Rom 13:1–7; 1 Pet 2:13–17), and to take up the practice of intentionally refining your attitude toward them into one of humble submission.

This is not something that will happen naturally or easily; it requires some work. It is often difficult to refine one's attitude in the moment of interaction. The best practice is to use the classic Christian form of prayer called examen: every night, take a few minutes to review the events of the day, asking the Holy Spirit to convict you of those places where you stumbled and to grant you strength and grace for the day to come. In this way, as you review your reactions to those in authority over you, doing this in a regular and prayerful way, you are making space for the Holy Spirit to convict, cleanse, and empower you towards greater humility in the future. And that is the point of the whole thing: humility. The practice of submission is not just a road of pointless self-abnegation; it helps you develop a spirit of humble Christlikeness.

How is the fruit of our sacrifice of submission returned to us in the church? When we come to church bearing a week's worth of training in humility and obedience, we find ourselves immediately thrust into a position of unimaginable honor. The church is the main context in which we exercise our reign in Christ, using the authority of prayer as the royal priests of God's creation. This high dignity is shown in the patristic practice of standing during communal prayer, of which more will be said in chapter 14. Another sign of our position of honor appears

---

5. Saying 14.19 (Ward, *Desert Fathers*, 147).

in some ancient liturgies, in which the pastor actually bowed not only toward the altar, but toward the congregation as well, in recognition of the royal-sacramental status of the body of Christ. When we have humbled ourselves to be like Christ, God exalts us, again to be like Christ.

We also gather the fruit of mutual love and harmony in the church when believers have learned the road of humble submission to one another. The joy of a church community that has learned to practice submission against their pride is a rich reward in and of itself, and a markedly different experience from a church in which pride still runs wild in its members' hearts.

Against Greed: The Practice of Simplicity

Greed is a passion similar to pride in at least one respect: most people probably would not say that they struggle with either vice, and yet most of us actually do. We may have in mind the caricatures of a vain mirror-gazer and a greedy miser, and think that because we are not that, then it's not a problem for us. But in the classic Christian sense, greed is not just an attribute of robber barons; it is a disordered attachment to possessions and physical comforts, and every single one of us has it (and truth be told, most of us have a good deal more of it than we realize).

To see if you have this affliction, you can gauge yourself against the radical call of the New Testament: Do you lend freely to borrowers while actually expecting not to get your money or item returned (Luke 6:34–35)? Would you be truly content with nothing more than the basic necessities of food and clothes (1 Tim 6:8)? Do you give to the work of God, not just from what you can spare, but in such a sacrificial way that it requires giving something precious away (Luke 21:1–4)? Do you give to the point of selling your own possessions so that you can have more to share with the poor (Luke 12:33)? Do you view "riches and pleasures" as inherently dangerous things, with the potential to choke your spiritual life to death (Luke 8:14)? Most important of all: Do you live in wholehearted, worry-free trust in God's provision at all times, even times of fiscal insecurity (Matt 6:25–32)?

If you felt like you had to answer "No" to any of those questions, then there is something of a gap between your attitude toward money and possessions and the New Testament's recommended attitude. Now, obviously, each of the passages referenced above comes with relevant context that ought to be considered as well, and the implications of those verses will not work out exactly the same way in everyone's life. Christian doctrine has never held that everyone is called to the most radical form of voluntary poverty. That said, however, those of us modern Christians who live in relatively wealthy societies sometimes tend to jump toward trying to explain away the above passages as our first impulse. It is not uncommon for us to begin discussions of these verses with some kind of caveat, like "Now, it's not a sin to be rich"—which, as true as it might be, usually does not match the spirit of the text. It may not be a sin to be rich, but it is a fairly dangerous condition, spiritually speaking, at least if we take the New Testament teachings on wealth and possessions seriously. The patristic writers hew closely to Scripture on this mark, even those who preached to rich and privileged audiences: Basil goes so far as to say that "for many, it is prosperity of life that constitutes the greatest trial," and John Chrysostom tells us that "there is nothing more grievous than luxury."[6]

Greed can be understood as a reliance on material things for our comfort and security. It is a universal passion in the human experience, though of course some will have greater struggles against it than others. In its most acute form, the drive to possess becomes all-consuming; life becomes a quest to increase the digits of one's salary or bank balance. This is idolatry, a life of serving mammon instead of God. But even if we are not quite at that point, it is still worth asking ourselves to what degree we are captives of our possessions. Because that is what it is at bottom—captivity, an enslavement of the mind and heart which blinds us to God's gracious provision and thus leads us into even more passions and sins (1 Tim 6:9–10). The call to break the spell of greed is not a grueling course of pretending that poverty is pleasant; it is a matter of liberation. If we are not at the place where we can "joyfully accept the confiscation of [our] property" (Heb 10:34), then we are not truly free. The chains of our attachments to material things are keeping us from joy.

So what disciplines can help us grow out of this particular passion? Many in the early church actually did recommend a course of radical renunciation, if one was capable of it. Some of the most popular stories, like the conversion of Antony to his vocation as a desert hermit, tell how he simply gave away his family fortune in order to live in complete simplicity (though also, it should be noted, ensuring that his dependent

---

6. Basil, "I Will Tear Down My Barns," 1 (*On Social Justice*, 59); John Chrysostom, *First Sermon on Lazarus and the Rich Men* (*On Wealth and Poverty*, 26).

sister was provided for beforehand). We should not rule this kind of response out; it may be that in our materialistic age God will raise up a new generation of desert fathers and mothers for us. But for many of us, radical renunciation is probably not the answer, not least because we have children or other family members who depend on our continued ability to support them, and it would be a shirking of our duty to love them if we throw away the means God has granted us for their care.

The overall shape of Christian discipline in this area can probably best be described with the word *simplicity*. This is an attitude of life shaped by several different practices, foremost among which is a resolution to live fairly close to the level of what we actually need rather than what we think we want. For many of us, this would result in a practice of living below our means and devoting the excess to the nurture of those God has set in our care, to giving to the work of the church at home and abroad, and to generous practices of almsgiving for the poor. Further, it means that we resolve not to make the pursuit of money or possessions one of the main goals of our lives, and to accept poverty (if it should come) as just as much a gift of God, if not more, than any wealth that might come. It is a way of living life with completely open hands: though we practice wisdom and good management in matters related to money, we also understand that every penny of it truly belongs to God, and it is his to take if he asks for it. Further, even if he does not directly ask for it, we should be zealous about finding ways to give his blessings away, because this is the call of Scripture itself. Basil tells us not only to view the things in our possession as truly belonging to God, but as actually belonging to others, set into our hands for the express purpose of relieving their poverty.[7]

Does this ethic of simplicity mean that we can never buy pleasure purchases again? No, certainly not—remember that moderation is the key to the practice of many of these disciplines. It is not so much a matter of what we buy as it is the spirit in which we receive God's blessings, and our overall intent to be channels of those blessings rather than stagnant reservoirs. Throughout Scripture, God's people were able to joyfully use the bounty of his blessings in a spirit of celebration, delighting in his goodness. The direction of our hearts is the key: does our enjoyment of material blessings incline toward our own experience of pleasure, or toward giving grateful thanks to God for his provision? Such things take

---

7. Basil, "I Will Tear Down My Barns," 2 (*On Social Justice*, 61); cf. *Didache* 4.8 (Holmes, *Apostolic Fathers*, 350–51).

discernment, so here, as with the matter of pride and submission, a daily course of examen is advised.

But let's not look at simplicity just as a willful impoverishment, thinking in terms of what we ought not to buy. In a much more significant way, it is an invitation to freedom. It grants the joy of being untethered to the cares and worries of material pursuits. John Cassian refers to this kind of renunciation as "true riches . . . no king can grant them and no enemy can take them away."[8] John Climacus goes so far as to call the monk who lives in voluntary poverty "lord of the world," who has handed all his cares over to God.[9] One more example rounds out the picture: John Chrysostom, who preached to the imperial court itself, sums it up by saying, "If we are to tell the truth, the rich man is not the one who has collected many possessions but the one who needs few possessions; and the poor man is not the one who has no possessions but the one who has many desires. We ought to consider this the definition of poverty and wealth."[10]

The renunciation inherent in simplicity is met with the bounty of God's life in the church, just as submission was. When we come to church to bring our offering of a week's worth of simplicity, we are met with the manifest, overflowing virtues of God's community. The practices of hospitality and generosity between members of the church are there not just to be a safety net, but as our regular experience of God's gracious provision. The remarkable, self-emptying redistribution of property in the Jerusalem church (Acts 2:44–45) was not a fluke of early enthusiasm; it was a sign to the world that in this community of the people of God, the idols of humanity's hunt for mammon come crashing down, and the chains that bind us to worry and stress are shattered under the power of our generous love for one another.

Simplicity does not bind us to a pinched and austere way of living. Rather, it opens the floodgates of joy for us, granting us the ability to truly delight in God's good blessings not only for the sake of our pleasures, but for the praise of his glory, and to radiate his character by becoming givers of blessings ourselves.

---

8. Cassian, *Conferences* 3.8 (90).

9. Climacus, *Ladder* 17 (189).

10. John Chrysostom, *Second Sermon on Lazarus and the Rich Man* (*On Wealth and Poverty*, 40).

Against Wrath: The Practice of Silence

When we hear the word "wrath," many of us think of explosions of white-hot rage. The reality is more mundane and ubiquitous. Like pride and greed, it is simply an aspect of fallen human nature shared by us all, whether or not we have problems with our temper. If we were to use emotional terms to describe this passion, many of us would experience it not so much as rage, but as irritation and resentment. It is the nagging frustration of having the imagined sovereignty of our selfhood challenged. We experience wrath when someone or something else gets in the way of the idolatry we lavish on our own desires, something that pushes back against our conception of the way things should be or the way we ought to be treated. (Incidentally, "wrath" as a divine attribute is also portrayed in the Bible as a response to sovereignty challenged, but in God's case it is not a vice, because he truly is sovereign.)

If we are honest with ourselves, we will all find this kind of wrath in our hearts and our lives, probably far more often than we would care to admit. Consider how you would respond to this scene from the life of Moses the Black, a desert father who, in his early years as a hermit, had tremendous struggles against anger and wrath. When he was older, he was asked to take up a ministry position, and in order to test him, his bishop arranged to have the other clergy publicly pour out verbal abuse on him, attacking him for everything from his character to his appearance. Many people, standing in that spot, would probably feel the stirring of frustration and resentment in their hearts, and many would want to angrily jump to their own defense. But Moses, having gone through decades of rigorous training against his wrath, was able to maintain his silence. As he walked out of the building, instead of grumbling against his unfair treatment, he was overheard saying to himself, "They have spoken rightly about you." His response calls to mind the ancient Stoic advice for maintaining humble patience when one's character is attacked: respond by saying, "Yes, and you could have said even more, because you don't know the half of it!"[11]

That is the sort of virtue we are after in our journey against wrath: complete meekness of heart. Too often meekness is equated with someone who is weak, unable to stand up for themselves, and who thus becomes a doormat for everyone else. That is as far from the truth as could be imagined. Meekness is true strength of heart, and not one person in a

---

11. See Epictetus, *Enchiridion* 33.9 (*Discourses and Selected Writings*, 237).

thousand has the strength to respond like Moses the Black did. "Meekness is a permanent condition of that soul which remains unaffected by whether or not it is spoken well of."[12]

How does one acquire the virtue of meekness, over against wrath? The top answer from patristic writers was *silence*. To continue the quotation above from John Climacus, "The first step toward freedom from anger is to keep the lips silent when the heart is stirred."[13] This, like all the skills mentioned in this chapter, is one that takes a good deal of practice. Most people are not able to have this kind of automatic control when in the heat of the moment, at least not at the beginning of their *praxis*. So, once again, a habit of daily examen, of prayerfully sifting through the events of the day under the guidance of the Holy Spirit, will prove tremendously valuable to one's improvement. It is not something that will be mastered in just a few days; it is a rather long journey—a pilgrimage, even. As Abba Sisois said, "Our form of pilgrimage is keeping the mouth closed."[14]

Even after we have learned how to keep the tongue quiet when it would rather lash out in those moments when we desperately want to leap to our own defense, there is still the turmoil within our hearts to address. Silence of the tongue does not automatically translate to silence of the heart. One of the habits that patristic writers advised for dealing with this stage of the problem was to practice an act of gratitude. Give thanks to God for the person who is criticizing you, "for through [that person], we acquire patience."[15] If you find the spark of wrath rising in your heart, direct your gaze back to God and thank him for the opportunity to practice your growth into patient meekness.

One of the other fruitful practices toward this end is to make time to regularly practice silence, not only of your tongue, but of your thoughts as well. This was one of the core insights of the early monastic tradition: the intentional silence and solitude of one's cell will, if received in the right way, help us to tame the turmoil of our thoughts. "Go and sit in your cell," said Abba Moses, "and your cell will teach you everything."[16] There is tremendous power in the habit of prayerfully learning to quiet

12. Climacus, *Ladder* 8 (146).
13. Climacus, *Ladder* 8 (146).
14. Saying 4.44 (Ward, *Desert Fathers*, 27).
15. Barsanuphius and John, *Letters of Barsanuphius and John* 554 (*Letters from the Desert*, 152–53).
16. Saying 2.9 (Ward, *Desert Fathers*, 10).

our thoughts and turn the gaze of our hearts to God. We are not advising any kind of mental blankness associated with Eastern mystical meditation, but rather a patient practice of entering into the experience of the psalmist: "I have calmed and quieted myself, I am like a weaned child with its mother" (Ps 131:2).

The practice of silence and solitude, when aimed at quieting the turmoil of the mind and heart, is not an attempt to void ourselves of rational thought (of which this type of prayer is sometimes falsely accused); it is a recognition that our passions run feral through our minds until we, by the empowerment of the Holy Spirit, learn how to tame them. So take some time just to sit in silence and direct your mind toward God. It is a good deal harder than it sounds, and you'll find that your mind is wanting to pull you off in a thousand different directions, but this practice is a good step toward that "permanent condition of the soul" that Climacus spoke of, which can be calm and meek even in the midst of the fiercest attacks.

Let's address a few other issues related to silence and wrath before we move on. We should understand that this, like all other disciplines, is subject to careful discernment. While remaining silent is often to the benefit of our spiritual growth, there will be times where the proper thing to do is to speak up: to give voice to truth against lies, or to ensure the protection and safety of someone else who is being unjustly attacked. In some cases, we must even speak out as an act of love for our enemy, for to leave them in their self-destructive patterns without saying a word might amount to a cruel and cold disregard of their value.

There is also a place in the biblical model of the Christian life for what is often called "righteous anger," as displayed in the zeal of Christ and the aggressive fervency of Paul's writings. But about such things, patristic writers would advise us to be cautious: we are neither Christ nor Paul, and for us, the tipping point between righteous anger and the affronted passions of self-centered wrath can be very hard to discern. We ought to be resolute and zealous in the face of evil, but when anger is kindled, its fire can be tremendously hard to control, and we often get burned. The core issue comes down to the state of our hearts: if we speak out, it should be a movement of love for those around us, not simply because we are irked at the opposition.

One more clarification: when we talk about keeping silent in the face of criticism, we should not get the idea that we don't need love and affirmation from others, or that it is improper to want such things.

We were created as communal beings, and even in our redeemed state, united with God, we need the support of our communal relationships to be truly whole. The problem of wrath is not that it makes us upset when we are not loved; the problem is that we get upset when other people (or circumstances in general) get in the way of how we would like to reign in our lives. But we all do need love, and it is quite proper to want to receive it. The wonderful part of being a member of the body of Christ is that this need is fulfilled when the church is what it ought to be—not an arena of competing egos, each thirsty for praise in a zero-sum game for attention, but a radiant overflow of mutual encouragement, of love that does not seek its own interests. The sacrifice of silence, which we bear with us to present before God in our worship, is returned to us in the fellowship and encouragement of our brothers and sisters in Christ.

13

Disciplines: The Practice of Christian Training (Part 2)

IN THE PREVIOUS CHAPTER, we began our overview of some aspects of Christian *praxis,* looking at three sets of disciplines that early Christians put into action against the core passions of fallen human nature. In this chapter, we continue that overview, dealing with the final four of the "seven deadly sins" and the practices that enable our healing from them. At the end of the chapter, we will also look at the overarching place of prominence given to prayer and Scripture in Christian *praxis.*

Against Envy: The Practice of Confessing and Blessing

Envy is the passion that yearns for what others have. Like all the other passions, envy is something everyone deals with to one degree or another. It is so universal, and so universally problematic, that it is targeted by the sole example in the Ten Commandments of an ethical injunction aimed not only at outward actions, but at the state of one's heart: "Thou shalt not covet." Envy might even make a claim to be the definitive passion of our current society, saturated as we are in social media, which drives people to paint their lives in rosy hues and make a display of it before all their friends. This effectively drives many users to a state of incessant envy at one another's lives. But even to people who are advanced in Christian *praxis,* envy can often be a stumbling stone, because it is an easy thing to become envious not only of someone else's material things or life circumstances, but even of virtues in others' lives that you would like to acquire for yourself.

Envy shares some similarities with wrath, in that it is a reaction against the ways in which our self-idolatry is challenged. Whereas wrath reacts in irritation at these challenges, envy recognizes the hollowness of our claims to sovereignty and adulation, at least when compared with other people. But, like wrath, it still has its roots in self-centered pride. In envy, we are struck by the perception that others around us have more cause for blatant self-idolatry than we do; but rather than take that impulse and let it turn us to repentance, it simply makes us long for more ways to keep our own lives in the center spotlight.

Many of the same disciplines that apply to other passions will also help us against envy: simplicity, fasting, and silence all produce a bounty of strengths that will aid us here. But there is another common practice in patristic writings that has special force against envy: the practice of confession. Many denominations have turned confession into a rather private matter, something that either happens between you and God alone, or between you, God, and a member of the clergy. For those that practice confession publicly, it is usually done as painlessly and nonspecifically as possible, by using a liturgical prayer of general confession that everyone says together.

The early Christian view of confession was rather more radical: it was something to be done openly in one another's presence. James says, "Confess your sins *to each other*" (5:16). There are numerous instances in the history of early Christianity in which the sinner was asked to stand in front of the congregation and give a public confession of their darkest sins to the entire church (and thereafter to spend some weeks or months in acts of public repentance). With that background in view, it becomes obvious why the Christian tradition eventually opted for private modes of confession; the painfully public model drove many people to keep their sins to themselves rather than face such a humiliating ritual. But the mere fact that early Christians thought confession ought to be a public ritual is something that should give us pause. There will be cases in which it is the wiser course to opt for a private confession. But in many cases, the best way to handle confession is in small groups of trusted, mature brothers or sisters in Christ. The early Christian tradition urges us not to keep too tight a lid on the knowledge of our sins. The darkness does not go away unless it is brought into the light. Passions thrive in concealment, and bringing them into the open is very often the largest step toward victory.[1]

Envy is essentially a desire for self-exaltation, a yearning to rise to the imagined level of those around us. Confession kicks the legs right out from under this passion by lowering oneself in public humility rather than striving to rise in public acclaim. Our fallen nature craves the pleasure and attention that we see others getting for their desirable qualities, but we can counteract this by drawing attention not to our own desirable qualities, but to our failings. This radical act of honest self-abnegation hollows envy of its power and strikes down to the root of self-centered pride.

The other practice that works remarkably well against envy is that of *blessing*. The basic idea here is that when our hearts are tempted toward envy, we train ourselves to offer prayers for the other person's good as our first impulse. Envy, untempered by Christian *praxis*, can quickly lead to an abject form of cruelty, wherein we rejoice when others fall. Against this tendency, you should pray blessings upon the objects of your envy. Ask God to increase his favor over them, to lead them on to even greater bounties of grace and love, and to protect them from evils and temptations. Paul is a good model of this behavior. In 2 Corinthians 13:9, he says, "We rejoice whenever we are weak and you are strong. This is what we pray for, that you may become perfect" (NRSV). Consider those people whom you might be tempted to envy: Do you, like Paul, rejoice when their strength highlights the contrast with your weakness? If not, then perhaps the best way forward is that when we are confronted with the temptation to envy, we ought to turn it into a prayer for that person's strength to lead them to perfection.

There are many ways that the sacrifices of confessing and blessing are returned to us with joy in the life of the church. These practices lead to harmony and reconciliation, not only between us and God, but between the members of the body of Christ, as we forgive one another and learn to love each other for who we really are, not who we pretend to be. Growing beyond envy yields a harvest of joy in our communion with one another, because we begin to realize that the admirable and desirable qualities we see in other people's lives are not there to detract from our own, but to complement them. Because we are members of one body, their strengths belong to me, and mine to them. Gregory the Great writes, "Those good

---

1. See Cassian, *Conferences* 2.11 (68–70); Climacus, *Ladder* 4 (108).

qualities that we love in others, which we do not seem to be able to imitate, are, in fact, ours also. And whatever is loved in us becomes the possession of those who love them."[2] Together, as we lay aside the envy that would long to see us exalted on the throne of our own lives, we come to realize that in the church we are inheriting a far greater exaltation: together we reign with Christ, we share in his glory, and we attain a beauty of life that is incomparable to what we could ever gain on our own.

Against Lust: The Practice of Chastity

These next few passions are good examples of the way that our natural desires become twisted into sinful desires, as described in chapter 11. Lust is what our good, God-given sexual and romantic desire becomes when it exists in the darkness of separation from God. Instead of leading to an act of self-giving love, it makes our own pleasure the driving concern of our lives. Sexual and romantic desire (both of which are covered by the Greek term *eros*) was supposed to draw us toward outpourings of joy that are faithful and free, but instead of outpourings, we have warped it into a draught that we drink to slake our own fevered thirst. Now, clearly, our own pleasure was one of the intended ends for our desire, but not the only end. Eros-desire was given to us so that we might model and experience the self-giving love of God in our daily lives, and to become participants in his great work of the creation of new life. Our pleasure in this arrangement includes physical sensations and emotional delight, but it is not reducible to them. True sexuality includes layers of grace and goodness over and above our physical and emotional experiences. In addition to pleasure, we have the inexpressible joy of growing in mutual love and the incarnational embodiment of our love and joy in the lives of our children.

But as marvelous as these pleasures are, the ultimate delight of our sexual and romantic desire is the way that it draws us into a participation of the love of God, which always gives of itself to us and always desires us to come to him. Some early Christian writers, like Gregory of Nyssa and Pseudo-Dionysius, would go so far as to write about the divine *eros*—the love of God characterized by this fullness of giving and desiring, as is so often portrayed in the Old Testament prophets. It is this experience of

---

2. Gregory the Great, *Book of Pastoral Rule* 3.10 (108).

God's love that we find so deeply woven into the fabric of Augustine's life in his *Confessions,* a book that is fervent and rich with desire.

One of the points that needs to be stressed is that this highest experience of sexual and romantic desire—the way it invites us into the very love of God—is something that is not only available to those in sexual relationships. It is a heritage built into our very nature, by which even those people consecrated to a life of singlehood may experience the self-giving and always-desiring nature of the love of God, and to share in its depths. In fact, many patristic writers believed that those who lived a life of consecrated singlehood were able to experience this highest reward of sexual desire in an even fuller way than those who were married, a position to which Paul's teachings in 1 Corinthians 7:32–35 might provide some support. The wild, unfettered romance of the love of God is not something that requires one to be married in order to experience, and Paul seems to suggest that the unmarried are in the most advantageous position for experiencing it.

But in order to experience it, whether married or single, we are called to the discipline of chastity (the practice of living faithfully as sexual beings within the bounds set by Scripture). In the case of single people, this discipline was simply referred to as virginity, which was the subject of many glowing homilies and treatises in the patristic period. Now, it might strike one as odd to call chastity or virginity a "discipline"—many today tend to think about them more as a state of being than a series of actions. But at their core, they are a series of actions. We talk about chastity and virginity as something that can be lost, but in a more profound sense, they are simply something that we *do*: they are manifest in the choices we make each and every day. (One example of considering virginity as a discipline rather than a status is the fact that many early theologians taught that a victim of rape could still be a virgin, because their will had not consented to the act.) Chastity is simply our faithful daily response to sexual temptations, wherein we refuse to consent to the movement of our fallen will from natural desire to sinful acts.

How does this work in practice? A great many practical disciplines form the overall set of actions that enable us to live chastely. Fasting and confession are particularly effective, as are some forms of prayer which we will touch on in the next chapter. For those who are in faithful relationships with a romantic partner, having a dedicated and intentional program of growing together in love is a proactive measure that adds tremendous strength against temptations. The temptations themselves are not the problem, of course. Temptations will come, simply because we are wired by God's good and gracious design to be beings of desire. It is simply a matter of giving ourselves the tools to respond to temptations in a faithful way.

For those who find themselves burning with lust or romantic desire, but are not in a situation in which they can enter a marriage relationship (as Paul would advise in that circumstance—1 Cor 7:9), the patristic writers counsel a practice of directing our eros-desire toward God.[3] In the same way that a fasting person might offer their hunger up to God, we can offer this hunger up to him, too. This may sound strange to our ears, and it is certainly not intended to be taken as a sexualization of our relationship with God, but as a consistent impulse to pour out the yearning of our hearts toward him. Our longing for the union of romantic and sexual love is an expression of our deeper longing for union with God. This outpouring of our yearnings is something to be done not only in the desperate moment of trying to resist temptation, but as a regular practice of one's life. Through prayer and Scripture, we ought to develop a love for the unimaginable beauty of God, to learn to respond to his outreaching heart, so that when other longings come upon us, we can plunge into the deep and satisfying pool of God's endless romance toward us.

This, too, like all the other disciplines of renunciation, finds its reward in the communal life of the body of Christ—some will find that reward in the institution of marriage, but all have access to it in the brotherly love which characterizes our life as Christians. In the church community, we are given the opportunity to grow in love with one another as sisters and brothers, and as we do so, we come to appreciate each other not as potential objects of lust, but as whole persons. Lust short-circuits our ability to love others because it limits that love to the sexual or romantic, the physical or emotional. It is a pale half-measure of God's intended blessing for our relationships; when we give in to lust, we are short-changing ourselves of the wonder of truly knowing and loving those around us. In the life of the church, however, as we live together in bonds of love, we come to know and love each other for all that we are.

---

3. See Climacus, *Ladder* 5, 15 (129, 179); Gregory of Nyssa, *Sermons on the Song of Songs* 1, quoted in Clément, *Roots*, 175–76.

Against Gluttony: The Practice of Fasting

Gluttony is, in many respects, very much like lust. It takes one of our good, God-given natural desires, and subverts it toward a lesser end. God made us to be eating beings, and his provision and commands regarding food form one of the core features of our unfallen life in Eden. Taking food is a physical symbol of the way we receive the blessings of God and grow directly from those blessings. One of our central religious rituals, communion, is an act of eating, symbolizing the way we are spiritually nourished by our union with Jesus Christ. But these good and proper ends are twisted by gluttony, which, like lust, makes our own pleasure the central concern of our eating. It is just another aspect of that self-idolatry which seeks to reign in our hearts, where only God should reign. And like all forms of idolatry, it is ultimately unsatisfying. It falsely promises to assuage our desires but leaves us either disheartened by our overindulgence or constantly wanting more. For this reason, Climacus calls gluttony "hypocrisy of the stomach."[4]

For the writers of the early church, the main problem with gluttony was not (as we now tend to think) whether we are healthy or unhealthy, fit or obese; it was an issue of our hearts turning away from God to chase after lesser pleasures. In gluttony—especially in what we might now call "emotional eating"—we tend to seek a salve for our wounded hearts in the broken pieces of physical creation rather than in the overflowing fountain of blessing from its Maker. This is not just a vice of the overweight; it tends to be universal in our society. For some people, even an over-attachment to healthy eating, pursued for the way it makes them feel about themselves, can be just as spiritually problematic as gluttony. While food and physical health are both good gifts of our Creator, given to us for our nourishment, well-being, and pleasure, they were never meant to be a replacement for God, not even in the smallest instances. Rather, the goodness of food was meant to be part of our celebration of God, a gateway to delight in our relationship with him who alone salves our wounded hearts.

This brings us to a practice that is central to the Christian spiritual disciplines, one of the most formidable weapons in our arsenal: fasting. While I match it here against the passion of gluttony, it is by no means limited to that one application. Climacus tells us that some elders regarded it, along with obedience, as the preeminent form of *praxis*: "fasting

---

4. Climacus, *Ladder* 14 (165).

destroys sensuality and obedience completes the destruction by bringing in humility."[5] Fasting is a training ground for Christian growth that can bear fruit against any of the passions, and it has many uses even beyond one's personal spiritual growth. In the New Testament, it is often shown in conjunction with prayer, particularly during times of consecration or seasons of discernment (Matt 4:1–2; Acts 13:1–3; 14:23). Given the fact that it is clearly indicated in the Gospels as an expected practice for Jesus' followers during the church age (Matt 6:17–18; 9:15), it is striking how absent this discipline is from some church traditions. Even in those traditions where fasting is built into the church calendar, it is not uncommon to find it being practiced lightly and sparingly. In doing so, we deprive ourselves of a powerful tool in our Christian life.

When we talk about fasting, we should reset our preconceptions once again. Many Christians view it as a form of austere renunciation, an act of bodily negation, but the point of this (and all the disciplines) was actually a positive one: the building of virtue and the focusing of the heart upon God, that our prayers might be empowered. Fasting is, among other things, a course of healing, of using physical hunger to allow the Holy Spirit to tear our gaze from the things of the world and to train us to look to God instead.

Fasting is also not quite as grueling as it is sometimes portrayed, particularly when one looks at the lives of the desert fathers. Though many did fast in fairly vigorous ways, the consistent advice which they left us in their writings is that we ought to be moderate in such things. Doing a complete fast of skipping multiple meals was not generally advised. Launching directly into the most austere form of fasting is usually a recipe for a quick failure. (And it should be added here that no one should undertake a new program of fasting without consulting a physician first, particularly if there are underlying health conditions involved.) Abba Poemen was once asked his advice for a rule of fasting, and this was his answer: "I would have everyone eat a little less than he wants, every day."[6] Cassian agrees: "Too much fasting and too much eating come to the same end . . . One should take cognizance of the state of one's strength and body and allow oneself as much food as will sustain the flesh but not satisfy its longings."[7] Essentially, the desert fathers' form of fasting was to

---

5. Climacus, *Ladder* 26 (239).
6. Quoted in Hall, *Worshiping*, 245.
7. Cassian, *Conferences* 2.16, 22 (76–77).

DISCIPLINES: THE PRACTICE OF CHRISTIAN TRAINING (PART 2)   193

eat enough food for proper nourishment, but not to eat so much that we avoid the presence of hunger as a regular feature of our day. Then we can take these moments of hunger in between meals and turn to God, offering our desire up to him in prayer. Whatever our manner of fasting might be, it should present us with opportunities to offer our desire up to God.

Further, by saying no to the impulse to eat whenever the mood strikes us, we engage in a form of training whereby we develop our ability to say no even when more difficult temptations assail us. Fasting not only helps us move the gaze of our hearts from created things to the Creator, it gives us practice in standing our ground against all the passions. When the natural, bodily urges of lust or sloth or greed come upon us, we are more prepared to stand against them for having fasted. This is one of the main ways that we, like Paul, can say, "I strike a blow to my body and make it my slave" (1 Cor 9:27).

This is just a brief glance at a few of the many roles that fasting can play in the Christian life. Patristic writers also liked to emphasize the fact that fasting enabled generosity—if you didn't eat as much bread on a particular day, you would have more to give away to the poor. And it is also important to remember that in most cases, fasting was not a purely individual discipline. Even the desert fathers usually lived in loose communities, and fasting was part of their communal life. So also for lay Christians in the early church: there was a longstanding tradition, going all the way back to within just a generation of the apostles, that Christians fasted on Wednesdays and Fridays, and so fasting was something you did together.[8] It was a communal practice, and you would have the support of the community in following it. Fasting is far easier to do when you do it together, and in that context it also builds up the community in fellowship.

It is not hard to see how our act of renunciation in fasting might be given back to us in blessing in the life of the church. The sacrifice of fasting is given back to us in the joy of eating together as the body of Christ. We are invited to participate in the feast-table of the messianic king, the communion of his body and blood. Further, many church traditions incorporate regular events of feasting together, whether for liturgical holidays or potluck dinners. Across much of early Christianity, there was a practice of having a second basket of bread at church (beyond just the communion loaf), and this "blessed bread" was set out so that anyone

---

8. *Didache* 8.1 (Holmes, *Apostolic Fathers*, 354–55).

who desired could have a piece on their way out of the church service. In the life of the church, eating becomes once again what it was meant to be: a joyful, communal celebration of the gracious provision of God, which, far from turning us away from him, instead directs our hearts to him in grateful thanks.

Against Sloth: The Practice of Work

The last of the classic "seven deadly sins," as codified by Gregory the Great, was sloth. As in the case of many of these passions, though, we should begin by clearing away some misconceptions. Many Christians will think that because they are not a particularly lazy person, that the vice of sloth doesn't apply to them. Sloth is not just about laziness, though. It is a universal feature of fallen human nature, which takes our innate desire to find rest in God and instead seeks that rest in a thousand lesser things. And here is where the danger of sloth comes to bear: because we are seeking rest in our entertainment, our social media, and our diversions, we are tempted to give up our striving to grow in our relationship of unity with God. We seek rest before we have fully entered into the true rest that God alone provides, and so we are in serious danger of becoming stuck along the way of holiness.

We should also realize that sloth is not just about an absence of outward activity. It carries with it serious emotional and spiritual side effects. Resting in anything that is not God does not actually provide the deep rest we so desperately seek, and so we become ever more weary in our souls. One of the defining characteristics of sloth is a feeling of emptiness, even of despondency. Most of us have probably experienced something like this, if only in the hollow feeling we get after mindlessly scrolling through our social media feed for far too long.

If we continue to seek rest in lesser things, these feelings become rooted deep in our natures. Not only does this lead to despondency, but it makes us feel less and less able to get back up and keep walking along the road of Christian *praxis*. Sloth builds on itself, and it has a radically disempowering effect on our spiritual life. The temptation of sloth is everywhere around us in our society; all of us have faced it and we will face it again, probably on a daily basis. We need to be aware of it, because it is like quicksand to our hearts.

What spiritual discipline did patristic writers advise for counteracting sloth? The answer is simple to the point of being mundane: work. Specifically, manual labor was promoted as an effective means to keep us from the spiritual dangers of sloth. The common stereotype of early monks and desert hermits is that they just sat around and prayed all the time, but anyone with even just a passing acquaintance with their writings would know that they were famous for being hard workers at their handicrafts. Reed mats and woven baskets were among the most common products of the desert fathers and mothers, and other monastic groups worked hard at gardening and producing Bibles by hand. Benedict, who launched the greatest monastic movement in the Western church, thought manual labor was so important for spiritual growth that the catchphrase for his ethic was *Ora et Labora* (prayer and work). This was an insight rooted in Scripture: the apostle Paul also commended manual labor as one of the basic practices of Christian life (1 Thess 4:11; cf. 2 Thess 3:10; Eph 4:28; 1 Cor 4:12).

Any kind of active work has the benefit of engaging our bodies and minds in a focused task. In the case of much manual labor, these focused tasks are those which still allow us room to devote attention to prayer while we work, or even to make our work an active prayer in and of itself. In manual labor, it is easy to do what Brother Lawrence would later call "the practice of the presence of God," and to do one's work mindfully, as a prayerful sacrifice offered up to God. By focusing our minds and hearts in this way, it also prevents the eye of the mind from drifting off into the sorts of fantasies that lead so naturally into the passions. "A monk who works is tempted by only one devil," says Cassian, "but a monk who idles is tempted by a host of devils."[9] In addition to these spiritual benefits, work also carries a whole host of other blessings, not least of which is that work gives us the means to provide for our own needs and for those of the poor as well. But the bottom line is that work helps to train us in habits of activity, which is exactly what we need to press on in Christian *praxis*.

In the church, our sacrifice of labor results in blessings upon blessings. It allows us to participate in the joy of contributing to the work of the kingdom in our midst and to the relief of the poor. But even more importantly, the weekly life of the body of Christ gives us that true rest that we are really seeking. By working during the week and coming to worship God on the day of rest, a day for intentionally dwelling with

---

9. Cassian, *Institutes* 10.23, quoted in Chadwick, "Introduction," 20.

him and his people, we enter the rest he has promised for us, at least in an anticipatory way. Here we may lay down the burdens of our hearts, and here we may find rest for our souls. In our work, as in every one of the disciplines above, we are not walking a road of stern negation, but a pathway of open-horizoned joy. By the work of the Spirit in and through and around these disciplines, we are built up in the virtues; we find healing from our deepest wounds; we are trained to orient ourselves back to God, the one true good for whom our hearts are always longing; and we enter into the richness of life itself, life as it was meant to be lived.

Prayer and the Ministry of the Word

In addition to the disciplines mentioned above (and many others besides), two overarching practices form the lifeblood of both communal and individual Christian growth: prayer and Scripture (see Acts 6:4). While prayer and Scripture both entail a series of habits interwoven throughout one's life, I have chosen not to call them "disciplines" here, in order to keep them separated from the disciplines of renunciation. Whereas the disciplines are those parts of *praxis* by which a Christian learns to turn the gaze of their heart away from the darkness of all that is not God, prayer and Scripture are the active means by which one then directs that gaze back to God. Ascetic renunciation and the habits of prayer and Scripture reading go hand in hand, but they are not exactly the same thing; they are the two stages of the fundamental action of *praxis*: pulling our desires back from their disordered attachments (the role of ascetical disciplines), and turning those desires toward their proper end (the role of prayer and Scripture).

The role of prayer in Christian purgation and illumination will be covered in detail in the next chapter. For now, it is enough simply to know that many voices of the patristic age thought that the entire Christian life was, essentially, an exercise in prayer. Prayer, in its many forms, is the shape of our relationship with God. It is the way that we now walk and talk with God, as Adam and Eve had opportunity to do in the cool of the garden. Prayer is the turning of the gaze toward God in love, petition, and thanksgiving, and receiving the communication of his light into our lives. Without prayer, all our other practices and disciplines crumble away to meaninglessness.

Scripture, likewise, is a basic necessity in the Christian life. It is the foundation on which all the disciplines are built, and it gives us the structure on which to be built up in wisdom and discernment. Readers of patristic literature are often struck by just how saturated their works are in references to Scripture. Bible passages drip from patristic pages like honey from a comb; it is a hard task to find a single paragraph where there is neither an allusion to, nor an outright quotation of, Scripture. It is striking, in an age in which books were all hand-copied and were thus a rare and precious commodity, just how well these writers knew their Bibles. Hours of meditation, memorization, and even transcription of biblical books formed the framework for their practices of Christian growth. So important was the reception of Scripture to the Christian life that early Christians helped to develop and popularize the format that we now refer to simply as books—instead of carrying around armfuls of separate scrolls, they learned how to bind leaves of parchment together along one edge into a codex, a single volume capable of bearing multiple books of the Bible.

Bible reading was both an individual practice (for those who had access to biblical scrolls and codices) and a communal one. For ordinary Christian laypeople, who would have had less access than most clergy did, the weekly worship service took on an aspect of tremendous importance: it was their primary opportunity to hear the words of Scripture read and explained. Scripture was treated with the utmost respect in ancient liturgies, usually with multiple readings and special honor granted to the reading of the Gospels. As patristic theology developed in the eastern half of the Christian world, such that artistic icons came to be used as a sort of direct window to heavenly realities, the Bible was taken to be the supreme icon in and of itself. The Gospels were a literary icon of Christ, a window through which one might truly encounter his living presence.

In their sermons, patristic-era clergy advised Christians to be assiduous in studying the Bible. Jerome led home-based Bible studies for noble families in Rome before his relocation to Bethlehem, and he and many other scholars kept up a vast level of correspondence with lay believers about questions of biblical interpretation. John Chrysostom exhorted his hearers to pay such attention to Scripture that they became "interpreters even of syllables," studying everything, down to the smallest markings of the text.[10]

10. John Chrysostom, *Sixth Sermon on Lazarus and the Rich Man* (*On Wealth and Poverty*, 117–18).

In our model of Christian *praxis*, prayer and Scripture form the second stage of the process, the means by which we turn our gaze to God. It is important to note that to experience their power in all their fullness, one needs to have them active in both one's personal life and in the communal life of the body of Christ. Without these two preeminent practices, engaged through our daily practice and our weekly worship in church, everything else would be in vain. Not only do prayer and Scripture constitute the means of turning our gaze back to God in the face of discrete temptations; they also (and more importantly) form the channels of sustaining grace by which we are able to learn how to steer clear of temptations in the first place. With our endless desire for God being endlessly quenched through our relationship with him, experienced through prayer and the ministry of the word, there is simply less space for our thirsting desires to draw us elsewhere. As we grow in our Christian lives, prayer and Scripture become not only avenues of escape, but fertile gardens of rest in our growing union with God.

14

Prayer:
Royal Authority and Priestly Service

WHAT'S THE POINT OF prayer? Let's say I'm praying for the healing of a family member with cancer. Is it the case that God needs to be talked into this? Does he not want to do it unless cajoled to do so, like the unjust judge in Jesus' parable (Luke 18:1–8)? On the other hand, if he does want to do it, why does he need my prayers to do so? Why not just do it?

It seems like we are asking God to do things he should probably want to do anyway, and which he clearly has the power to do whether or not we ask him. Why would Scripture encourage us to be active in intercession, when (at least in some sense) God has no need for our intercessions? If he is omnipotent, he can do all things; and if he is sovereignly omni-beneficent, he will do all the good that he wills to do. So what place do we have in that dynamic? It seems like God has placed us in a role for which no role is really necessary—unless, that is, he has created the universe in such a way that his reign is meant to be mediated through his appointed officials.

Prayer is a foundational practice to our identity as God's royal priesthood. Intercessory prayer is but one of its forms, along with every aspect of our relationship with God: praise, thanksgiving, contemplation, rest, confession, blessing, and many more; and across the whole scope of the practice of prayer, our priestly work and our participation in Christ's reign comes to the forefront of our lives. If the work of growing in holiness is an expression of our royal commission to reclaim the territory of our own hearts for the kingdom of Christ, then the work of prayer is part of our participation in the active work of the reign of Christ. It is nothing less than the exercise of our office to its fullest extent, standing between God's broken creation and the eternal courts of his sovereign sway.

Let's think for a moment about the idea of humans, now restored to our royal priesthood in Christ, standing in our position between God and the rest of his creation. This is our role not only because we are restored to Adam's priesthood, but because we are mystically united to the incarnate Christ, who is himself the great High Priest and the only true mediator. Connected to him, we become ministers of reconciliation ourselves, as God reconciles the cosmos to himself through Jesus (2 Cor 5:17–20; Col 1:20).

Prayer can be understood as the two directions in which our participation in this relationship works. When we undertake prayers like thanksgiving, praise, or contemplation, we are expressing creation's yearning to be united to God. On behalf of our own souls and the whole of our broken world, we bring this yearning into the courts of the Ancient of Days in gratitude, worship, and desire. This movement of prayer thus bears the yearning of creation up to God. The other movement, expressed in intercessions and blessings, seeks to help bear the sovereign power and mercy of God down to creation. When we intercede for others or speak blessings over their lives, we are acting as instruments whereby the benefits of Christ's reign are brought down, as it were, and applied to creation's needs.

In these two movements, then, we see the intimate intertwining of our dual identity, both royal and priestly. There is a danger here of oversimplifying the dynamic, but one might even conceive of the priestly dimension expressing the first movement, of us bearing creation's longing up to God, and the royal dimension expressing the second movement, of us bearing the sovereign power of Christ's reign and applying it to a particular situation. This is, as I say, oversimplistic (after all, intercession and blessing were part of priestly work, too), but it may help us to understand the basic outline of our dual identity in practical terms.

But before we look at these two movements of prayer, let's pause for just a moment to examine where we are in the broader picture of the Christian life. The last few chapters have taken us through an overview of the early Christian perspective on growing in holiness, which roughly corresponds to the first stage of the journey of Christian growth. Maximus the Confessor called this stage *praxis,* emphasizing our work of putting spiritual disciplines into practice. Other parts of the Christian tradition have called the first stage purgation, thus placing emphasis on the hoped-for results of growing in our capacity to uproot the power of sinful desires in our daily lives. With this chapter, we move to an examination of the next stage (called *theōria* by Maximus, or "illumination" by other sources).

It is important to understand that while illumination is often portrayed as a second stage, it is not usually the case that a Christian is able to complete their *praxis* to the point of having no issues with sinful desires ever again, and then move on to the experience of illumination. Rather, for most Christians, these two stages overlap and intertwine throughout the whole of one's life. Ascetic disciplines form one part of the motion of *praxis* (turning away from the passions), and prayer and Scripture—which must be experienced both individually and communally—form the other part (directing our gaze to God).

In this paradigm, we can understand illumination as the result of the process of turning away from our passions. When we turn our gaze to God, having already been healed of our spiritual blindness through Christ, the light of God's radiant life can shine into the dark and empty corners of our life, and bring illumination there. Turning our spiritual gaze to God is essentially like throwing open the window-shutters of a dark house to the blazing light of day. Prayer is a necessary element of this process. In addition to its usefulness to our *praxis*—as the means by which we cry out to God, even in the midst of our fiercest battles against sin—it is also the movement by which we seek and find the transforming light of God, now available to us in Christ, thus to be transfigured in his light (2 Cor 3:18). Prayer's work will draw us further into the experience of our original *telos*: growing into an ever-greater union of love with God (which is the third and final stage, of which more will be said in the next chapter).

The "Upward" Prayers of Creation's Longing

Prayer is an umbrella term that describes every movement of the human heart toward God, and the forms of Christian prayer are a broad assortment of all the possible ways in which we seek the face of our Maker. There are a great many resources in the Christian tradition by which one may explore any of these forms of prayer, so our focus here will be to highlight just a few of the main contributions of patristic counsel. This should not be read, however, as an indication that early Christian writers did not devote significant attention to other forms of prayer as well.

Some of the forms of prayer included in the first movement (expressing creation's upward yearning to God) are confession, repentance, praise, adoration, thanksgiving, scriptural meditation, and contemplative prayer. In each of these, we offer prayer from our own hearts, but we also act as representatives of all creation. We bear in our own longings a microcosm of the brokenness of the fallen cosmos. In fact, many early Christian writers expressed a sense that their prayers not only represented the cry of all creation, but that such prayer was instrumental in God's work of sustaining and restoring all things. This idea came to be expressed by John Climacus's famous axiom, "Prayer holds the world together."[1]

In the earliest Christian texts, the most common categories of prayer (apart from the recitation of the Lord's Prayer) appear to be thanksgivings, petitions, and intercessions. The liturgical round of prayer in weekly church services, which itself centered on thanksgiving and intercessions, was the core of a Christian's priestly work. In offering a sacrifice of thanksgiving in the words of our prayers, we fulfill the prophecies about all nations bringing God true and pleasing sacrifices (Mal 1:11; cf. Isa 61:11).

Contemplative Prayer

By the third and fourth centuries there was a growing emphasis on contemplation as the apex of private prayer. The great popularizers of this form of prayer, as with the ascetic disciplines, were the *abbas* and *ammas* of the desert monastic tradition. John Cassian wrote, "A state of soul more exalted and more elevated will follow upon these [other] types of prayer. It will be shaped by the contemplation of God alone and the fire of love."[2] Contemplative prayer did not replace the other prayers, since there is always a need for prayers of gratitude and praise, but it began to be seen as the goal toward which all other prayers would draw us.

Contemplative prayer was thought to be the essence of prayer at its most fundamental level: turning one's attention toward God, and simply beholding him. It was an attempt to practice, as fully and as literally as

1. See Climacus, *Ladder* 28 (274).
2. Cassian, *Conferences* 9.18 (111).

possible, the divine injunction in Psalm 46:10: "Be still, and know that I am God" (see also Ps 131:2). In contemplative prayer, the Christian simply dwells with God, entering the infinite, eternal rest of God's abiding presence. We join with the "living creatures" around his throne (Rev 4:6–8), whose only tasks are praising and beholding—indeed, whose very being is an act of beholding the beauty of the Lord. "In the same way [as the living creatures who are covered with eyes] . . . the soul that is borne by God is no longer anything but gazing."[3]

Prayers of contemplation thus tend to be silent and wordless (at least for the most part), in an attempt to fix one's thoughts on God alone.[4] While there is certainly a place for using words in prayer, the early church fathers and mothers knew only too well how quickly our words can get in the way. If our prayers become a monologue, it leaves us unable to listen, to say nothing of patiently and attentively abiding with the presence of God, whose being no thought or language can ever fully comprehend. This understanding of the inherent limitations of human language in prayer has its roots in the New Testament, where Paul acknowledges that we do not always know what to pray for, and yet in this situation, the Holy Spirit himself is interceding "through wordless groans" (Rom 8:26).

Among some Christians, contemplative prayer is regarded as little more than new age mysticism trying to sneak its way into our prayers like a wolf in sheep's clothing. This obviously cannot be true, since Christian contemplative prayer predates the new age movement by many centuries. It is significantly different from Eastern mysticism and modern meditation techniques, though there are superficial similarities. In the Christian tradition, there is no attempt to make the mind a blank slate, nor to erase all vestige of thought. It is not an attempt to negate the turmoil of our thoughts by doing away with them; rather, it is the exact opposite of a negation. We are not entering a place of nothingness to find our peace; we are fixing our minds and hearts on the one true center of all reality. It is the farthest possible thing from an anti-intellectual act: "Prayer without distraction is the highest intellection of the intellect."[5] Instead of wiping away our thoughts or limiting them merely to our body's sensations, we turn them to God with clear-eyed attention.

---

3. Pseudo-Macarius, *Fifty Spiritual Homilies* 33.2 (PG 34:741–42c).

4. See Cassian, *Conferences* 9.25 (116).

5. Evagrius, *On Prayer* 35 (*Philokalia* 1:60).

Christian contemplation includes similarities with other meditation techniques, but this is because both sets of practices must deal with the intractable nature of the fallen human mind, not because of any shared heritage between the Christian tradition and Eastern mysticism. Simply put, the fallen mind has a fierce tendency to wander, to direct its attention to outward objects of desire or interest or fear, and so anyone who practices any kind of meditation or contemplation must learn techniques for reining in these feral habits of the mind. Whereas Eastern and modern meditation practices aim for a thoughtless calm or a mindful awareness of one's own body, the Christian tradition aims to turn all our attention toward God himself. It is an attempt to enter, in some small way, into the shape of our eternal bliss in the everlasting kingdom, where we will experience the beatific vision of seeing God face to face (Rev 22:4).

Contemplative prayer is an extraordinarily difficult practice to master. Most people simply cannot make wordless prayer work for them for any length of time; other thoughts eventually crowd in and demand their attention. For beginners, practicing contemplative prayer can be extraordinarily frustrating, as they begin to realize just how little control they actually hold over their own thought life. (But even if that frustration were the only fruit of contemplative prayer, that alone would make it worthwhile, as an encouragement to humility.) To make contemplation simpler, many patristic writers counseled the use of simple phrases or actions, by which we can find some assistance in maintaining our focus on God. For many, it was a simple repetition of the name "Jesus" whenever one's thoughts began to wander, as Climacus advised: "Let the remembrance of Jesus be present with your every breath."[6] Many would use a continuing round of the famous Jesus Prayer (of which more will be said below) for this very purpose. This is not the sort of "vain repetition" that Jesus spoke against in Matthew 6:7, but a gentle nudge that we give ourselves to turn our attention back to where it belongs.

By using this kind of contemplative prayer, which Maximus saw as the core practice of *theōria*, we anticipate the restoration of the cosmos. We become living prophecies of the destiny of all creation in the new heavens and the new earth, where Christ will reign, God will be all in all, and the light of their radiance will suffuse our whole lives (Rev 21:23; 22:5; 1 Cor 15:28). Contemplative prayer is the active practice of

---

6. Climacus, *Ladder* 27 (270).

beholding God and delighting in him, a foretaste of the fullness of the union to which we are growing.

Some other Christians, even if they don't suspect contemplation of being a new age practice, still view contemplation as something of a waste of time. Why are we just sitting here silently, when we could be accomplishing much-needed tasks of petition and intercession? Such a perspective is not wholly misguided, though it does betray something of the cult of productivity in which we in the West have been raised. While intercession is essential, no form of prayer is mutually exclusive of any other, and if you don't have time for both intercession and contemplation in your weekly practice, then your priorities may require some rearranging. Contemplation is not a waste of time; it is an active participation in the work of New Creation, by which we ourselves become fashioned and fitted for the works to which God calls us. Beholding God necessarily includes the fact that we are being transformed by that very beholding (2 Cor 3:18; 1 John 3:2). A servant of Christ who is being deeply transformed will also be deeply useful to the work of the kingdom in the world.

If we are listening to the wisdom of the patristic tradition, we should give some place to the practice of contemplative prayer, including it in our regular round of prayers along with our confession, thanksgiving, intercession, and praise. Indeed, Climacus advises us to combine them all into one prayerful ascent into the presence of God: first thanksgiving, then confession, then our requests, and then concentrated attention that leads to "rapture in the Lord."[7] Meditation on Scripture is another way that leads us naturally to contemplative prayer: if, in our prayerful reading, we come across a word or phrase that seizes the full attention of our soul, then we should stop on that idea, dwell with that phrase and bring it with us into the presence of the Lord. As Evagrius said (concerning praying the psalms), "A single word in intimacy is worth more than a thousand at a distance."[8]

The "Downward" Prayers of Jesus' Reign

The second major movement of prayer involves asking for the dispensation of God's blessings into particular situations in our world. We usually call this intercessory prayer, whereby the person praying intercedes on

---

7. Climacus, *Ladder* 28 (275–76).
8. Evagrius, *Pareneticus*, quoted in Clément, *Roots*, 202.

behalf of another person or community. As noted at the beginning of the chapter, there is no obvious reason for intercessory prayer unless God intends for us to serve in a role of administering the works of his kingdom. The fact that we are told over and over again in Scripture to pray in this way is strong evidence that God has called us to a participatory role as officials in his kingdom's administration. To be a Christian is much more than simply being a sinner saved by grace; we have a noble identity and a high commission. We have work to do here which no one else can do. If we, his royal priests, are not active in intercession, then we have shirked our duty. Intercessory prayer is the clearest practical way in which we participate in the reign of Christ here and now. It is one of the ways that we Christians fulfill our original commission: made in the image of God, and tasked with ruling, filling, and subduing the earth (Gen 1:26, 28).

Asking Great Things of God

One of the astonishing aspects of early Christian intercession was just how big their prayers were. While there is plenteous evidence of highly specific prayer requests from early Christianity, dealing with the most mundane and personal matters imaginable, there is also a broad tradition of praying "for all people everywhere."[9] The earliest Christian prayers are full of these intercessions, asking God to pour out his grace upon all Christians in every part of the world, on all humanity, on the worst and most dangerous of people, on our very own enemies, and on all nations.[10] Many of these broad-scope prayers eventually became part of the ancient liturgies, and thus became part of the normal round of Christian prayer week in and week out, for centuries upon centuries. To the eyes of the early Christians, there was no limiting horizon to what God might do among the nations in their own day.

There's a marvelous example of this tendency from the life of Polycarp, one of the leading figures of the second-century church. When he was eighty-six years old, after having served as a pastor in Smyrna for decades, the Roman magistrate issued a warrant for his arrest. Polycarp acceded to the requests of his followers and fled the city, out to the refuge

---

9. Justin Martyr, *First Apology* 65 (*ANF* 1:185).

10. See Clement, 1 Clem. 59.2, 4; Ignatius, *To the Ephesians* 10.1; *To the Smyrnaeans* 4.1; Polycarp, *To the Philippians* 12.3 (Holmes, *Apostolic Fathers*, 122–25, 190–91, 250–51, 294–95).

of a little cottage in the backcountry. But the Roman officers closed in quickly, and Polycarp calmly gave himself up. The manner of his arrest was striking, though. He began by welcoming his persecutors warmly, and then laying out a feast for the hungry men. When they had finished eating, he asked if he could pray before they took him into custody. Upon their agreement, Polycarp stood up and prayed out loud for two full hours, astonishing the watching men with the grace, joy, and godliness of his prayer. The men finally had to arrest him, but only after he had prayed for "everyone who had ever come into contact with him, both small and great, known and unknown, and all the universal church throughout the world."[11]

As we look back on these broad, wildly confident prayers, we can see that their prayers were not in vain. Within the patristic age itself, the whole vastness of the Roman Empire came to hear the gospel of Jesus Christ (to say nothing of its incredible spread beyond imperial borders), and an entire system of pagan religion that had stood for millennia came crashing down in submission to the reign of Christ. The same is true of our own day. Much of the power behind the jaw-dropping global spread of Christianity in the past two centuries no doubt comes from the fact that Christians have once again dared to ask great things of God. A concerted series of efforts to pray for all nations, which went hand in hand with the Protestant mission movements of the nineteenth and twentieth centuries, has borne tremendous fruit for the kingdom, such that those parts of the world that were almost completely non-Christian for 1,800 years are now positioned to be the heartlands of the faith in the centuries to come. We have come to learn what the earliest Christians knew well: that in the face of kingdom-sized prayer and full-hearted labor, even the mightiest strongholds of the enemy will crumble and fall.

Praying toward Each Other: The Practice of Blessing

Intercession in the patristic age wasn't only aimed at large-scale targets, though; it was also a fit instrument for the finest of work, and could be directed to the benefit of just one person or situation. One of the most intimate and lovely forms of intercession was a kind of prayer known as a blessing. Most of us are familiar with this form of prayer, though we probably do not use it as much as some early Christian communities

---

11. *Martyrdom of Polycarp* 7.1—8.1 (Holmes, *Apostolic Fathers*, 312–15).

would have. It derives directly from Jewish tradition, in which prayers of blessing were commonplace. Many of these blessings were directed at God, such as the classic prayer of thanksgiving: "Blessed art thou, O Lord our God, King of the universe, who bringeth forth bread from the earth."

But there is another form of blessing, unique in that it is a prayer *not* directed to God as its primary audience. This kind of blessing is an intercession spoken aloud in the presence of God, but directed to the person being prayed for. Such a prayer calls on the power and mercy of God, but it addresses itself to the person who will actually receive the benefits of the prayer. Consider, for example, the famous priestly prayer of Numbers 6:24–26: "The Lord bless you and keep you; the Lord make his face shine on you and be gracious to you; the Lord turn his face toward you and give you peace." While this prayer invokes the actions of God, it is actually addressed to the recipients of the blessing. Other examples of this type of prayer include the benedictions often used at the conclusion of worship services, which are prayers that usually address the congregation: "May the grace of God go with you," etc.

The proclamation of blessings over the people of God was one of the main responsibilities of Old Testament priests, and it must have been one of their most pleasant tasks. There is a wonderful quality that grows from speaking blessings aloud: it is a form of prayer that not only invokes the power of Christ's reign for another's sake, but it binds us actively to that person for whom we pray. The person who receives the blessing is a participant in the act of praying itself; they know they are being prayed for, and they receive the prayer as an act of love, poured out directly upon them in the intimacy of a shared space and time with the one who prays for them. The practice of blessing brings intercession out of the silence of prayer-closets and sets it to work in our relationships. It is an ancient Christian practice well worth recapturing in our daily lives.

Prayer from the Center: The Cry of the Heart

There is a set of prayers that does not easily fit into the schematic we have been examining of either "upward" prayers expressing the yearning of creation toward God, or "downward" prayers which claim and apply the blessings of Christ's reign onto particular situations. Prayers of personal petition bridge both categories. These prayers, in which we bear ourselves as living sacrifices before God, are both an expression of our yearning for him and an act of beseeching his sovereign power to act in our behalf. When we pray for ourselves, our prayers combine both movements into one impassioned cry of the heart.

There are, of course, as many ways to pray personal petitions as there are persons to pray them. In addition to what we might consider normal, free-flowing prayer from our hearts, as well as the universally recommended usage of the Lord's Prayer, patristic writers advised a few specific forms of personal prayer. We will look at two of them here, one that was used as an in-the-moment defense against temptation, and another that formed a continuous foundation for one's prayer life: arrow prayers and the Jesus Prayer.

Arrow Prayers

Arrow prayers are short lines or phrases that can be easily memorized and put into action when one has need of them. They appear to have developed out of the ancient monastic tradition of praying through the book of Psalms (though the term "arrow prayer" itself may be a later development). As monks learned all the psalms by heart, praying them day in and day out, they found that a few of the lines were particularly helpful in moments of temptation. They would take some of David's pleas of desperation and turn them into bursts of prayer that could be used at a moment's notice. The most popular was Psalm 70:1: "Hasten, O God, to save me; come quickly, Lord, to help me." When faced with a temptation that they just could not get away from, they had lines of Scripture in their arsenal to use as prayers, shooting up quick petitions for assistance from God. (Other examples can be found in Psalms 3:7; 6:4; 54:1; 57:1; and 59:1, just to name a few.) In this form of prayer, the memorization of Scripture becomes a powerful bedrock on which to build our prayer lives.

The Jesus Prayer

The Jesus Prayer, for its part, has a long and influential history, and it is most often practiced today by using this short phrase: "Lord Jesus Christ, Son of God, have mercy on me, a sinner" (based loosely on the tax collector's prayer in Luke 18:13). It is particularly important in Eastern Orthodox prayer, but it has been growing in popularity in Roman Catholic and Protestant circles as well. The roots of this prayer practice go back to the patristic period, drawing from at least two sources. First, the "Lord, have mercy" sections, which constitute the irreducible core of this prayer, go back to the ancient liturgical prayers of the Christian church: *Kyrie eleison,* "Lord, have mercy." (This Greek phrase remained unchanged even as Christian liturgies were written in other languages, which is a testament to just how foundational this short prayer was to the practice of early communal worship.) This standard refrain of early Christian worship stands as a needful but confident plea for the Lord of mercy to be true to his nature and his promises, and to pour out his mercy on us again.

The second source of the Jesus Prayer goes back once again to the early monks. Some of the monastic movements in the patristic period were working on ways to keep Paul's injunction to "pray continually" (1 Thess 5:17). In addition to praying the psalms, many monks would use the invocation of the name of Jesus as a prayer, repeating it over and over as a simple way to keep the mind focused on God. Over time, these two traditions came together, forming a practice of taking the liturgical prayers of the church, based on the prayers of Scripture itself, and turning it into the constant refrain of one's life. When used as an exercise in continual prayer, the Jesus Prayer helps us enter into a sense of peace rooted in the gospel itself: that though we are sinners, we can always call on Christ's mercy.

The Jesus Prayer is usually prayed many times over in succession. Again, this should not be seen as a "vain repetition," but as a way of bringing the cry of our heart before the Lord, even when we have no words of our own, and keeping the gaze of our spirit continually on him. The repetition of the prayer helps it become like an instinct of our souls, an ingrained tendency to run to the fountain of Christ's mercy as our first impulse whenever our own sinfulness confronts us. The prayer is simple but powerful, expressing in just a few words our faith in Jesus' lordship and divinity, the brokenness of our fallen nature, and our hope for his help. It is the theology of the gospel in the form of a prayer. Most of our desperate prayers for God's help would fit quite well into the mold of the Jesus Prayer. Whatever may be the problem we are wrestling with, and whatever our hopes for God's intervention in our lives, they can all usually be summed up just by saying, "Lord Jesus Christ, Son of God, have mercy on me, a sinner."

How to Pray with Your Whole Self

To Christians of the patristic age, prayer was not just a matter of the words that we say, and not even just a matter of the different patterns of prayer we could learn to use. They knew very well that we were holistic beings, with bodies as well as souls, and so the body's part in prayer mattered a great deal to them. Early Christians had several bodily habits of prayer that are worth exploring, even if you choose not to use them yourself. They provide an insightful glimpse into the symbolic theology of prayer, into the themes and truths that early Christians considered important in their acts of devotion.

Standing in Prayer

As was mentioned back in chapter 1, standing was the default position for prayer in much of the early Christian tradition. There were other things one could do in prayer, of course—numerous variations of bowing, kneeling, or lying prostrate, all of which matched particular attitudes of prayer. Kneeling in prayer was a good way to express the humble contrition appropriate to a confession of sin. But kneeling was not the standard position for prayer, and neither was bowing. In fact, across most of the early Christian church, kneeling in prayer was prohibited on Sundays, and not only on Sundays, but for whole periods of the liturgical calendar. This prohibition is attested not only in the decrees of the ecumenical councils, but in the testimony of the church fathers as well. Tertullian writes, "We consider fasting or kneeling in worship on the Lord's Day to be unlawful. We rejoice in the same privilege also from Easter to Pentecost."[12] Peter of Alexandria concurs: "We have received it as a custom not even to bow the knee on [Sunday]."[13] Why would kneeling be prohibited? The answer leads us to the first of three symbolic ways that standing in prayer helps us understand our identity and our duties in the Christian life.

Sunday was the day of resurrection, the day of New Creation, and it was a day for standing in our new identity as God's royal priesthood. The first symbolic message of standing in prayer is that we have been given a position of dignity and honor. When we stand in prayer, we are recognizing as true what God has said about us: that we are more than

---

12. Tertullian, *Chaplet* 3; cf. *On Prayer* 23 (ANF 3:94, 689).
13. Peter of Alexandria, *Canonical Epistle* 15 (ANF 6:278).

merely sinners now, we are God's own daughters and sons, co-heirs with Christ (Rom 8:15–17). The normal posture of beloved children in the presence of their father is not to bow or kneel. The throne room of God has become our native home, the place of meeting with our Abba, and we can approach the throne of grace with confidence. As kings and queens of the New Creation, we stand in the authority granted us by the King of kings himself.

The second symbolic message in this prayer posture has to do with the idea that when we pray, we are in the presence of God. Standing, as opposed to bowing or kneeling, means that we are looking at God (at least in a symbolic sense) rather than turning our faces away. In the standard form of prayer-posture, a Christian would stand with arms upraised (cruciform-style) and face looking to the heavens. By contrast, when we bow or kneel or close our eyes, we are actually doing the opposite set of motions from the normal practice of early Christian prayer, and turning our faces away. Standing and lifting one's face to heaven was a physically symbolic act of beholding God, of meeting with God "face to face," as Moses was said to have done (Exod 33:11). If one was to put a physical posture to Paul's description in 2 Corinthians 3:18—"We all . . . with unveiled faces contemplate the Lord's glory"—it would be awfully hard to match those words with any posture of bowing or kneeling.

The third symbolic message of standing as a prayer posture is that it is a position of readiness. In Luke's account of the garden of Gethsemane, when Jesus entreats his sleeping disciples to "get up" and pray with him (Luke 22:36), the word he uses is not one of the words usually used for "wake up," but for "stand up" (it is also sometimes used of the physical action of "rising up" involved in resurrection). Standing in prayer sets our minds ready for action. When we are standing, the body conveys a message to the mind that the work to be done calls for focus and attention. (This, incidentally, is the psychological reason why so many people find combining walking with praying a helpful thing to do.)

Bowing and kneeling do have their place, of course. It is not an insignificant thing to enter the presence of the King of the universe, and bowing or lying prostrate is more than appropriate there. Kneeling, similarly, expresses a sense of humility, reverence, and contrition, and it has its place in confession and repentance. Standing, however, was considered the normal way for the royal priests of God to go about their work: a position of honor, of direct communion with God, and of readiness for the labor ahead.

Facing East

Another traditional part of early Christian practice was to face east when one prayed. Nowadays, we tend to associate praying in a particular direction with the practice of Muslims, but it actually goes back to ancient Jewish tradition. Jews would face the direction of the temple in Jerusalem when they prayed, as demonstrated by Daniel (Dan 6:10). For Christians, though, there was an early tradition (unanimous in the sources that mention it) in favor of praying toward the east.

This may simply have developed as a natural consequence of the events of Jesus' ascension. The last place the disciples saw Jesus was as he ascended into heaven from the Mount of Olives, east of Jerusalem, and the angels said that when Jesus returned, they would see him coming in the same manner that he left. It would seem natural, then, to face the place where you would expect the Savior to appear; and for the mother church in Jerusalem, facing the Mount of Olives meant that they worshiped in an eastward orientation. For many centuries, it was not only individual Christians who oriented themselves eastward to pray; it was also the custom to build each church so that the worshiping congregation would face the east.

As the patristic era progressed, a theological rationale began to attach itself to the practice of facing east. Praying toward the east continued to be conceived as turning in the direction of Christ himself: he had ascended to the east (from the perspective of Jerusalem), and he himself had referred to an easterly orientation of his return, saying "just as the lightning comes from the east . . . so will the coming of the Son of Man be" (Matt 24:27 NASB).[14] It was not only about Jesus' ascension and return, however. Once again, as we have seen so many times, patristic theology found symmetries between Jesus' story and the garden of Eden. Jesus had opened the gates of paradise for us, giving us access to the tree of life through his death on the cross. And where was this paradise located? According to Scripture, it was "in the east" (Gen 2:8).

In this way, the manner of Christian prayer became a physical representation of our restored identity. By standing and facing east, the direction of Eden, we symbolize the fact that we are taking up the duty given to humanity there, to serve as the royal priests of God's creation-temple. As Basil put it rather poetically, "We all look to the east at our prayers

---

14. See John of Damascus, *Exact Exposition* 4.12 (*Writings*, 352–54).

... we are seeking our own old country, paradise, which God planted in Eden in the east."[15]

Now, clearly, this is not a binding rule that requires following; any Christian may pray in any direction they please, seeing as we serve a God who is omnipresent, existing beyond all our concepts of space and direction. Even if it is not required, however, you may still find it helpful. When Origen defended the practice of facing east in prayer, his case amounted to saying that there is really no good reason not to.[16] You have to face somewhere when you pray, so why not join the great apostolic tradition, take your stance as a priestly king or queen of the New Creation, and pray toward the east?

The Sign of the Cross

One of the most noticeable differences between the prayer practices of low-church and high-church traditions nowadays is whether or not they use the sign of the cross. In my low-church tradition, you will never see anyone doing it. In my sister's high-church tradition, you will see people doing it every single time they pray. My Protestant forebears did away with the sign of the cross long ago, suspecting it of being little more than a superstitious act, and, truth be told, they were not all wrong. A lot of Christians throughout history have used the sign of the cross as little more than a magical wave of the hand, an attempt to ward off evil. What my Protestant forebears might not have recognized, however, was that the act of making the sign of the cross in prayer was a tradition rooted in Scripture itself, and that it could be—if used properly—a powerful way to incorporate the body as well as the mind into one's prayers.

There are at least two places in the Old Testament where a physical application of the sign of the cross was performed (though of course the original audience would not yet have known the significance of the action). The first instance comes from the Passover tradition. God provides a way for the people of Israel to have freedom from the judgment of the tenth plague by applying the blood of the Passover lamb to their doorposts. In Exodus 12:22, when Moses relates God's instructions for this ritual, he tells the Israelites to 'take a bunch of hyssop, dip it into the blood in the basin, and put some of the blood on the top and on both

---

15. Basil, *On the Holy Spirit* 27.66 ($NPNF^2$ 8:42).
16. Origen, *On Prayer* 20, referenced in Bunge, *Earthen Vessels*, 58.

sides of the doorframe." The word translated here as "basin" is probably not a vessel; it likely refers to the shallow depression in the earth at the base of the doorframe, where the dirt floor would get worn away by foot traffic at the threshold of the house (thus the ancient Greek Septuagint translated this term as *thyra*, "door" or "gate," not as "basin"). In essence, then, Moses is telling the people to let some of the lamb's blood to collect in the depression under the door, then to dip the hyssop down into that blood, take it up onto the top of the doorframe, and then across to either side. He was telling the Israelites to make the sign of the cross over their doorways. A similar application of blood would later be used in the ritual of priestly consecration, when this same set of motions (or a part thereof) would be used to apply blood to the righthand side of Aaron's body: on his ear lobe, thumb, and big toe (Exod 29:20).

The second instance comes from one of the visions of the prophet Ezekiel, in which God executes judgment against his faithless people for their idolatry. Before judgment is carried out, however, God sends a messenger throughout the city to place a mark on the foreheads of all the righteous people who had grieved because of their neighbors' idolatrous acts. Anyone with the mark was safe from the coming judgment (Ezek 9:3–6; cf. Rev 7:3). What most readers might not realize, though, is that we know what that mark looked like: it was the sign of the cross. In the manuscript tradition for this passage, the mark is identified as the letter *tav* (roughly corresponding to our letter "T"), often shaped like a plus sign or cross in Old Hebrew script.[17] Perhaps most remarkably of all, the scribal tradition of using this cross-like mark apparently became an accepted way in some traditions of intertestamental Judaism to highlight passages (usually by means of a mark in the margins) relating to the deliverance of the righteous and the coming of the Messiah, as can be seen in some of the Dead Sea Scrolls.[18] For centuries before Jesus, then, Jews had been using the sign of the cross as a way to mark out texts that pointed to the Messiah, and it all began with Ezekiel's vision of the physical application of this symbol on the bodies of the righteous.

With this biblical background in place, it is hard to come away with any conclusion other than that using the motion of the sign of the cross should be considered entirely appropriate for prayer. Within the Christian tradition, the practice appears to have developed very early on, and

---

17. See Origen, *Selecta in Ezechielem* 9 (PG 13:800–801c); Skarsaune, *In the Shadow*, 370–71; Bunge, *Earthen Vessels*, 179.

18. See Skarsaune, *In the Shadow*, 182.

to have grown organically from the prayer life of the church, not as a superstitious symbol accruing on top of apostolic practice. It was universally commended as a natural part of the Christian prayer life throughout the patristic age, and Basil attributes it to the unwritten, orally transmitted practices of worship that went all the way back to the apostles themselves.[19] Indeed, one can easily imagine it as an early practice of the Jerusalem church, which had many members who were steeped in the Old Testament scribal traditions (see Acts 6:7; 15:5), whereby they took the sign of the cross from Ezekiel's vision and applied it to themselves as the mark of the crucified Messiah. Cyril of Jerusalem passionately advocated for his baptisands to use it, as a way of boldly staking out their identity and not being ashamed of the cross of Christ.[20]

In its most ancient form, Christians appear to have simply used a finger or thumb to draw the shape of the cross on their foreheads, much as in Ezekiel's vision. This method is still practiced by many denominations on Ash Wednesday or for anointings with oil. Gradually, the motions came to be applied to more of the body, such that the cross was drawn over the head and the chest. In its traditional form, a person makes the sign of the cross with their right hand, bunching the thumb, forefinger and middle finger together while keeping the other two fingers folded down into the palm. Using the three bunched fingers, one begins by tapping the forehead, then down onto the torso, before doing the lateral movement. In the ancient patristic method, still followed by the Eastern Orthodox today, the lateral movement goes from the right shoulder to the left; medieval Roman Catholic tradition, widely adopted in the West, changed this to a left-to-right movement.

Many people have proposed theological symbols for the positioning and motions of the sign of the cross, though it's not clear that these meanings were originally intended as part of the symbolic act. For example, the three fingers bunched together are said to be a sign of the Trinity, and the two fingers pressed to the palm are a sign of Christ's dual nature as God and man. The vertical motion might relate to how the Son of God came down from heaven to earth for our sake, and the lateral motion to how the gospel progressed from Jerusalem to the ends of the earth (or, in the Western method, how Jesus drew those who were far from God near). If

---

19. Basil, *On the Holy Spirit* 27.66 (NPNF[2] 8:41).
20. Cyril of Jerusalem, *Catecheses* 4.14; 13.36 (*Cyril of Jerusalem*, 102, 160–61).

these ideas are helpful to one's prayer life, then they may prove useful, but they are not a necessary element of the sign of the cross.

As with all these practices of prayer, there was no legalistic rule which said that Christians had to use the sign of the cross. You may use it if it is helpful, or choose not to use it, all at your own discretion. The practice of the sign of the cross, however, does have a beauty all its own, such that those who begin to use it in their prayer life seldom find reason to stop. It is a marvelous way to incorporate the body in one's prayers. Since we are not just disembodied spirits, but holistic beings with souls and bodies, there is something fitting about having ways, like the sign of the cross, to use our body in prayer. Unlike other bodily movements of prayer, like bowing, kneeling, lying prostrate, dancing, or raising your arms, the sign of the cross can be done very discreetly and very easily, even if you have no room to move around. The sign of the cross, at its most basic level, is simply a way for the body to pray, to express faith in Christ through its movements. There are times when the sign of the cross may enable one to "speak" silently in prayer, even when we can find no words to say.

Praying the Hours

In addition to postures and gestures of prayer, early Christians also practiced distinct prayer habits related to time. There was a longstanding tradition that Christians should, if they were able, keep the three times of prayer each day. This was a tradition rooted in Jewish practice: the prophet Daniel is shown praying three times a day (Dan 6:10), and the Psalms may also reference the practice (see Ps 55:17). Thrice-daily prayer formed the basis of the worship schedule at the temple in Jerusalem. One of the earliest postapostolic Christian documents, the *Didache,* teaches that Christians should follow this tradition and pray three times a day, specifically with regard to saying the Lord's Prayer.[21] These are referred to as the "hours" of prayer (and "hour" here indicates the time of day at which prayer begins, not that people had to pray for a full hour each time).

The normal times for these classic hours of prayer were at the third, sixth, and ninth hour of the day (that is, 9 AM, 12 PM, and 3 PM).[22] The

---

21. *Didache* 8:2–3 (Holmes, *Apostolic Fathers,* 354–57).
22. See Tertullian, *On Prayer* 25 (ANF 3:689–90).

book of Acts shows the early Christian church continuing to follow the traditional schedule of Jewish daily prayer (Acts 3:1; cf. 2:46). Indeed, prayers at each of these particular hours are attested in the book of Acts—the miracle of Pentecost happened while the church was praying at the third hour (2:1–4, 15); Peter's vision on the rooftop came while he prayed at the sixth hour (10:9); and Peter and John attended prayers at the temple at the ninth hour (3:1). These three hours also happened to overlap with three major events in the crucifixion of Jesus, which no doubt gave added poignancy to their daily observance for Christians. According to Mark 15:25–37, Jesus was crucified at the third hour (9 AM), darkness fell over the scene at the sixth hour (12 PM), and Jesus died at the ninth hour (3 PM). Thus the practice of praying the hours upheld both a continuance of Jewish tradition and a thoughtful daily observance of Jesus' passion.

It was not uncommon for two further hours to be added to these three: a set of prayers upon waking and another before going to bed, thus making five prayer times in total. (Islam's practice of five daily times of prayer was likely inherited from early Christians in the Middle East.) Some monastic movements went even further, expanding the practice from five hours to seven, thus following the model of Psalm 119:164: "Seven times a day I praise you."

While many early Christians appear to have practiced the traditional three hours of prayer, it was treated as a healthy and treasured tradition, not as a legalistic rule. Prayers could, of course, be said at any time of the day, whenever one's heart was moved to pray. Having set times of prayer during the day, however, guarded against the possibility of a slow slide into laxity. When there are no fixed prayer times, then prayer becomes just an added activity to be wedged into our already-too-full schedules. For this reason, even those traditions with no fixed prayer times have still tended to encourage their adoption, though they usually call it by a different name (like a morning quiet time).

The practice of the hours of prayer builds reminders into our day that prayer is as needful to us as any of our other daily rituals. To the early Christian, it was the most reasonable thing in the world to have three times a day to devote to one's relationship with God, just as it probably strikes us as a reasonable thing to have three times a day to nourish ourselves with food. Prayer is the daily way that we eat and drink from the fountainhead of life, and the power and privilege of praying should never be taken for granted.

15

Union: Participating in the Divine Nature

IN THE OPENING SECTIONS of this book, I talked about the familiar "melody line" of the gospel that I had grown up knowing and loving: salvation in Christ through the forgiveness of sins. This melody line thunders through the books of the patristic era, just as we might expect of a theme so central to the biblical proclamation. That melody, however, was not the only line of music they played. As we have seen, there were harmonies of creation, temple, and kingship interwoven with the melody, forming one great symphony together. But if we are to do justice to the patristic vision of the Christian faith, we can't even stop there, at hearing this full-throated symphony of salvation and the restoration of human identity in Christ. There is more to the picture than just the melody and the harmonies. The more one reads the works of the church fathers, the more one gets the impression that the melody line we thought we knew so well was not actually a fixed theme, existing in and of itself; it was always in motion, drawing us toward the final movement of the symphony, when salvation would sound forth not only in notes of what we were saved *from* (our sins), but of what we were saved *to*: union with God.

To readers who come to this juncture from the same background that I do, the voice of the patristic age suddenly takes on an aspect of wildness that we are not quite prepared to handle. Theologians talk about *theosis*—and if your Greek isn't quite up to speed, the same term can be rendered as "deification" or "divinization"—that's right, a theology of human beings becoming, in some sense, divine. If you are hoping that this is just a case of rhetorical terminology that has run a bit too far ahead of the actual concepts involved, then you might not want to read Irenaeus or Athanasius. The former says that Jesus "became what we are, that he might bring us to be even what he is himself"; and the latter that "the Son of God became man so that man might become God [or gods]."[1] Before we write off the church fathers as blasphemous heretics, though, it would be good to pause and think about this for a bit. This kind of language appears very early in the Christian tradition, so early that it appears to be a natural outgrowth of biblical theology itself. Further, it is hard to get a higher standard of early Christian orthodoxy than Irenaeus and Athanasius, so we might not want to boot them out the door too quickly.

What, then, do they mean by this startling language? To begin with, I can hopefully offset some of the alarm these quotes might cause by assuring you that neither Irenaeus nor Athanasius (nor any of the other host of patristic writers who taught on this subject) meant that we could become God in an ontological sense. They are not saying that we can become what God is in his essence. Patristic theology was crystal clear on this point: the eternal, ineffable being of God is always set apart from us. In philosophical terms, God will always be the "necessary Being" on whom we contingent beings depend, and there is no possible fusion between those identities.

Nevertheless, there is still a sense in which we may share in God's nature, and it is not just patristic writers who talk about this in eyebrow-raising ways; the Bible itself does so. Jesus quotes Psalm 82:6, in which the voice of the Lord says, "You are gods," and Jesus applies this identity to the human recipients of the Scriptures (John 10:34–36).[2] Before his arrest, Jesus prays for all Christians, and after describing the intimate union of the Father and the Son in the life of the Trinity ("just as you are in me and I am in you"), Jesus goes on to include Christians with the very same language: "may they also be in us" (John 17:21). Second Peter 1:4 is one of the classic expressions of this theme: "through [God's promises] you may participate in the divine nature." Paul also uses similar ideas, though his wording is not quite as provocative to our theological sensibilities. He speaks about us being "united with the Lord" (1 Cor 6:17; Phil 2:1) and builds a whole theology of the church around the notion of Christians being the mystical union of the body of Christ. One of his basic formulations of the nature of Christian life is that we are "in Christ," a turn of phrase that appears on nearly every page of his writings. He also says that

---

1. Irenaeus, *Against Heresies* 5, preface (*ANF* 1:526); Athanasius, *On the Incarnation* 54 (*NPNF*[2] 4:65); see also Cyprian, *Treatises* 6.11 (*ANF* 5:468).

2. See Clement of Alexandria, *Miscellanies* 4.23 (*ANF* 2:437).

UNION: PARTICIPATING IN THE DIVINE NATURE

we share in Jesus' glory (Rom 8:17; 2 Thess 2:14), which, if read with an eye toward what the idea of "glory" meant in a temple context, may tread close to the idea of union with the divine radiance of Christ.

Some Christians are so used to thinking of themselves in the humble position of sinful brokenness that they have a tough time wrapping their minds around the grandness of this vision of our destiny. The story that Scripture is telling about who we were meant to be—and who, in Christ, we are becoming—is not just that we are "sinners saved by grace," though of course that is the necessary first step. The Bible paints a picture of us being raised up and glorified with Christ, transformed in the radiance of his likeness, suffused with his glory and effulgent with the overflow of his character and life (see 2 Cor 3:18; 1 John 3:2; Rev 22:4–5). This vision of eternal life is not so much "a mansion just over the hilltop" (as the old song would have it), but something rather like the transfiguration: a radiant brightness surrounding and transforming us with the power and glory of God. It is a vision not only of what we get to enjoy in the life to come, but of who we will be; and it is a vision of such grandeur that we cannot fully put it into words. It is "Christ in [us], the hope of glory" (Col 1:27). Or, as Jesus described the ultimate end of our life in the age to come: "The righteous will shine like the sun in the kingdom of their Father" (Matt 13:43).

Maximus the Confessor expresses the idea in this way: "He who became man without sin will divinize human nature without changing it into the divine nature, and will raise it up for his own sake to the same degree as he lowered himself for man's sake."[3] We do not become God in his essence, but we do become, to the fullest extent possible for us, what we were made to be in the beginning: the image and likeness of God. We become a visible reflection of his nature as the operations of his grace transform us into radiant examples of divine character. All this is accomplished through our union with Christ in the Holy Spirit, a union already enacted by our incorporation by faith into his body, and which is being worked out in our lives in ever-increasing glory. This is a real union, accomplished by God's grace (later Orthodox thinkers would describe the working of God's grace as his *energies*, as opposed to his *essence*), by which we truly participate in the attributes of God and are spiritually enlivened by his overflowing life. We remain very much ourselves, but

---

3. Maximus the Confessor, Various Texts 1.62 (*Philokalia*, 2:178).

ourselves as we were meant to be: a billion unique mirrors of the radiance of God's character.

One of the classic images of this dynamic was of a piece of iron being heated in the forge. The iron loses none of its properties, and the fire loses none of its properties—both remain what they are in essence—and yet the iron begins to glow with the light of the fire inside it. "As iron united with light becomes light not by nature, but by union with fire and participation, so what is being deified becomes god not by nature, but by participation."[4] So it is by participation—that is, by growing in that holiness that marks the very character of God—that we become transformed into a divine life, but not by fusing our being with God's essence.[5]

This union, in the minds of the patristic writers, was the ultimate stage on the spiritual journey of the Christian life (the climax of the prior stages of purgation/praxis and illumination/*theōria*). While salvation obviously includes the idea of redemption from the consequences of our sins, the idea of salvation is also much broader and grander than swapping eternal fire for golden streets. It involves a salvation from what sin has done to us in the depths of our very nature, a healing of sin's blindness so that we can be filled with the light of God. The biblical idea of salvation in Christ invites us to behold a destiny of radiant and radical transformation, a transfiguration of our humanity into a vessel of God's own glory. All this is done through Christ: through his atonement of our sin, his remaking of humanity, and his act of incorporating us into his mystical body by faith. Now, united to the very life of God by our union with Jesus, we cannot but be transformed, as the Most Holy makes us holy. This transformation will not be seen in its fullness until Christ comes again, but it can be experienced in an anticipatory way even now.

Images of Divine Union

Scripture and tradition use a number of different metaphors to describe this union between God and humanity, a union we experience both individually and communally as the body of Christ. One prominent example is the biblical image of marriage, of a union of a lover and his beloved becoming one flesh. This most intimate example of human union is taken as

---

4. John of Damascus, *On Those Who Reject*, 1.19, quoted in Alfeyev, *Mystery of Faith*, 191; cf. Pseudo-Macarius, *Fifty Spiritual Homilies* 4.14 (56).

5. See also Boethius, *Consolation of Philosophy* 3.10 (63).

a type of God's union with his covenant community, referenced throughout the prophetic literature of the Old Testament. It also appears in Paul's theology of the church (Eph 5:25-32), as well as in the final visions of Christ's triumph, where the messianic feast is described as the wedding supper of the Lamb, and Christ and his church are portrayed as bridegroom and bride in the new heavens and new earth (Rev 19:6-9; 21:9). This imagery carries over into the postapostolic generation of Christians, where some of the earliest hymns pick up the theme. One such hymn calls Christians to celebrate their identity as "brides and bridegrooms" in the presence of Christ the bridegroom.[6] Another hymn connects the idea of loving Christ to being united with him, and then with being transformed into a child of God because of that union of love.[7]

Other biblical metaphors of our union with God abound. Some we have already seen in earlier chapters, such as Jesus' image of the vine and the branches, and our call to abide in him. Maximus the Confessor expands on the biblical notion of entering God's rest (Heb 4:1-11) and sees in it an image of coming to be united with that goal for which we were always searching.[8] The idea of eating as a physical expression of union is also worth noting. This is an image we have seen many times already, from God's provision of food in Eden, to the covenant feasts of Scripture, to the practice of communion. As the royal priests of God's New Creation, one of the ways we incarnate that identity is by eating both the physical food of this world and the spiritual food of Christ's own life (represented in communion), and building up our lives, physically and spiritually, on both kinds of food. We exist as creatures who are united with both God and his creation, and we exemplify this unique state by eating what he has given us to eat and making it a part of ourselves.

A popular biblical image of our union with God is that of the temple, familiar to us both from Paul's use (Eph 2:19-22) and from Peter's (1 Pet 2:4-5). In this image, we as stones are being built into the temple in which God dwells; we are united to him as the purified and holy vessel of his presence.[9] Ignatius, writing at the turn of the second century, expands this temple imagery in a winsome way, talking not only about

6. Hymnus Liturgicus (fragment), Papyrus Bodmer XII (Hamman, *La Prière dans l'Eglise Ancienne*, 128-29).

7. *Odes of Solomon* 3.5-7 (*OTP* 2:735).

8. Maximus the Confessor, *Ambiguum* 7.1 (*On the Cosmic Mystery*, 46, 53).

9. See *Epistle of Barnabas* 6.15; 16.6-10 (Holmes, *Apostolic Fathers*, 398-99, 430-33).

Christ as the cornerstone and us as building blocks, but also about Jesus' cross as the crane and the Holy Spirit as the rope that swings our stones into place, such that we, having our place as part of the temple, become "God-bearers" and "Christ-bearers."[10]

Patristic writers make frequent use of all these metaphors while underscoring that our so-called "divinization" is not due to any merit or glory of our own, but arises solely from our union with Christ. "This comes of his own grace, not from any property in us. For it is he alone who can make gods" (so says Tertullian, writing in reference to Jesus' quote on "gods" in John 10:34–36).[11] The theology of *theosis* is rooted not in ourselves, but in the incarnation of Jesus. God desired us to grow into ever greater union with him, but we could not do that on account of our sin; so he did it for us, uniting himself to humanity in the person of Jesus Christ.[12]

Since we are incorporated into Christ by faith, and since the Holy Spirit dwells in us as the new temple, we are now able to experience the journey of becoming what we were always meant to be. The Son of God and the Holy Spirit, working in a dynamic that Irenaeus refers to as God's "two hands" in creation, are at work in humanity right now, in the mystical union that we call the body of Christ. The Son, the *Logos* of God, has brought forth the *logos* of the new humanity (the meaning and form of redeemed personhood), and the Spirit does the sustaining and carefully crafting work of guiding each of us into that inheritance.[13]

Mirrors of God's Light

The dominant patristic metaphor for union with God is that of light. This follows directly from the biblical use of the imagery of light/darkness and sight/blindness as theological models. If we have been saved by Christ through faith in his finished work on our behalf, then our spiritual blindness has been healed. Now, through the continuing work of the Spirit, we can train our newborn vision to turn and behold the radiance of God's

---

10. Ignatius, *To the Ephesians* 9.1–2; cf. 15.3 (Holmes, *Apostolic Fathers*, 190–91, 194–95).

11. Tertullian *Against Hermogenes* 5 (*ANF* 3:480).

12. See Irenaeus, *Against Heresies* 3.18.7 (*ANF* 1:448).

13. See Irenaeus, *Against Heresies* 4.20.1; 4.38.3; 5.1.1 (*ANF* 1:487–88, 521–22, 526–27).

own beauty. By turning our hearts away from the passions through the Spirit-guided work of *praxis*, and then turning our spiritual gaze toward God as the one great goal in whom all our desires rest, we become filled with his light, and we are able to see in a whole new way. This act of beholding the light of God includes an element of transformation: not only are we able to see God's light and behold the ultimate end of our desires in him, but we also become filled with his light, like a closed-off room whose windows are suddenly thrown open. "God's influence irradiates the soul . . . like a ray of sunlight."[14]

Gregory of Nyssa expands on this idea and adds a mirror to the metaphor. Not only are we filled with God's light, he says, but we ourselves become mirrors of his radiance, and we reflect it by the acquisition of the virtues which match his divine attributes.[15] This is the sort of analogy the fathers and mothers of the early church have in mind when they speak of "divinization," or *theosis*. Just like a mirror can send out the blinding radiance of a light, even though it is not the source of the light itself, so we too, though we are not God in essence, can become so transformed by his transfiguring light that the radiance of his character pours out through us. The fruit of our union with God should be obvious to the onlooker, just like light from a mirror. When outsiders look at us, they should come to know more and more what the character of God is like. "What is Christianity?" Basil asks. "Likeness to God as far as is possible for human nature."[16]

How is this light, this union, actually experienced in the everyday lives of Christians? To answer this question, we should first note that the patristic tradition holds that our *theosis* will only be fully experienced in the life of the age to come. That said, we are on the journey in that direction right now, and the everyday experiences of the Christian life can and should attest to our process of transformation, at least in a small and anticipatory way.

As we examine a brief overview of these experiences, keep in mind that our union with God, like our holiness, is something that is already accomplished for us by Christ, and at the same time something that is still in progress. We *are* united to God right now, through our incorporation

---

14. John Chrysostom, *On the Incomprehensibility of God,* Sermon 5, quoted in Clément, *Roots,* 163.

15. Gregory of Nyssa, *Sixth Homily on the Beatitudes,* quoted in Clément, *Roots,* 237; see also Boersma, *Seeing God,* 78–82.

16. Basil, *On the Origin of Humanity* 1.17 (*On the Human Condition,* 45).

into Christ and into the temple of the Holy Spirit, but the transformation of our hearts which follows from that union is usually experienced as a slow and gradual ascent. As Gregory of Nazianzus said, "God meant it to be by piecemeal additions . . . by progress and advance from glory to glory, that the light of the Trinity should shine upon [devout Christians'] souls."[17]

There are three kinds of experiences that we will examine here, each of which can be considered the fruits of our journey into *theosis*. The first kind often commands the most attention, but is actually the least important: the experience of mystical events, ecstatic phenomena, or constant bliss. The second kind is the counterintuitive fact that our progress into union with God's light very often feels like a journey into darkness. And the third kind is the normal, basic way in which *theosis* shows its presence and its progress: our gradual acquisition of the virtues of God's own character. We will describe these as the experiences of *theosis* on the heights, in the depths, and on the daily pathway of life.

The Experience of *Theosis* on the Heights

There are some fascinating and compelling stories of mystical and ecstatic phenomena associated with *theosis* in the lives of the *abbas* and *ammas* of the early monastic communities. We have multiple anecdotes about saintly Christians who were observed to radiate light, or appear to be suffused with flame, while engaged in private prayer. Here is one of the more famous stories, in which a person who experienced such things gave a rare public glimpse of it, in the form of an invitation:

> Lot went to Joseph and said, "Abba, as far as I can, I keep a moderate rule, with a little fasting, and prayer, and meditation, and quiet: and as far as I can I try to cleanse my heart of evil thoughts. What else should I do?" Then the hermit stood up and spread out his hands to heaven, and his fingers shone like ten flames of fire, and he said, "If you will, you can become all flame."[18]

Here we see not only a miraculous display of *theosis* in action, but an encouragement to press on to attain it. "You can become all flame." If we recall that fire was a prominent image of the nature of God throughout

---

17. Gregory of Nazianzus, Oration 3.26 (*On God and Christ*, 137).
18. Saying 12.8 (Ward, *Desert Fathers*, 131).

Scripture, then this little saying rings out as a startling and beautiful example of what union with God might look like in the rarest and highest moments. Stories like this should be an inspiration, a spur in our side as we press on in our work of *praxis* and prayer, helping us to realize just how much of the adventure of knowing God still lies ahead of us. If our everyday Christian life does not yet look or feel like the burning bush on Mount Sinai, mystically aflame with God's power and light, then it should serve to sharpen our yearning, reminding us that we have unseen vistas of God's glory still ahead of us if we but press on to know him more.

Having said that, the consistent advice of the patristic writers (and of most Christian theologians thereafter) was that we should not make too much of ecstatic phenomena, mystical experiences, visions, and the like. To become obsessed with such things, or to make them the goal of one's Christian life, was seen as a beginner's mistake. Soaring emotional states and miraculous events are dispensed as blessings of God, but they were never seen as the normative experience of Christian life. Mystical phenomena were never intended to become an idol to be sought after; and their relative rarity, even in the lives of the most devout Christians, ought to give us pause. Those who did experience such things, like Paul (2 Cor 12:1–5) and the desert fathers, who underwent mystical illumination in prayer, tended to be very private about their experiences. To make those experiences the goal of one's Christian progress can be a dangerous stumbling block. It means that we are giving our own feelings and desires a place that only God himself should have. If God sees fit to give you ecstatic gifts, miraculous events, visions, or mystical bliss, all well and good. God must intend it as a blessing. But if God gives the painful ache of empty desolations instead, that is all well and good too, and God must intend it for your growth.

The Experience of *Theosis* in the Depths

This brings us to the second kind of experience associated with *theosis*. For many people, the journey into God's light is actually experienced as a kind of darkness. You can think about it this way: imagine that you have spent several hours in a building that only has dim lighting on the inside, like a movie theater. Your eyes adjust to the dimness, and you can see everything perfectly well on the inside. But now you open the door and step out into the blazing light of midday sunshine. Your eyes, forced to adjust from the false light of the inside world to the true and radiant light outside, will probably be overcome for a few moments, and the brilliance of the light will strike you as a kind of sightlessness. This kind of darkness, which often feels unexpected and disorienting, is part of the normal experience of learning to direct our spiritual gaze toward God.

This darkness of drawing closer to God is thus not the darkness of sin, not the benighted state of our fallen souls; it is rather the darkness of what Christian tradition has often called "unknowing."[19] A journey of knowing God more, who is infinitely beyond our comprehension, will ultimately lead us ever more into the realization of all that we do not know, all that we cannot envision or comprehend of God's unbounded existence. "This is the true knowledge of what is sought," writes Gregory of Nyssa, "this is the seeing that consists in not seeing, because that which is sought transcends all knowledge, being separated on all sides by incomprehensibility as by a kind of darkness."[20] This language is directly drawn from Scripture, from the way that Moses' ascent on Mount Sinai into the presence of God was an ascent into "the thick darkness where God was" (Exod 20:21; see also Ps 18:11).

As we are weaned off our dependence on our physical sight and the wandering gaze of our mind's eye, turning our desires from their accustomed consolations to seek God instead, we may come to discover that the God we are looking for can be very hard to find. While we can behold the light and glory of his presence, Scripture also teaches that, at least in a certain sense, the infinite essence of God's being cannot be seen (see John 1:18; 1 John 4:12). We should not get the sense, then, that all this talk of being filled with the light of God necessarily implies a constant upward trajectory of clear-sighted delight in the one great goal of our desires. To know God, who is always beyond our comprehension, requires that we step into the darkness of our own unknowing and allow him to speak to us not in thunder and light, not in wind or earthquake or fire, but in "sheer silence" (1 Kgs 19:11–12 NRSV).

Instead of the consolations we expect from growing closer to God, we may actually find emotional desolations in our path. This has led, in the Christian tradition, to the development of an idea called "the dark night of soul." While this term is now casually thrown around to talk about any period of emotional or spiritual difficulty, it originally referred,

---

19. See, for example, Pseudo-Dionysius, Letter 1 (*Complete Works*, 263).
20. Gregory of Nyssa, *Life of Moses* 2.16 (80).

quite specifically, to a season of being weaned off the false light of all that is not God. This weaning is not a pleasant process, and even the emotional blessings we are used to receiving from our daily walk with God might be removed. This is not because those emotions were bad, but because God desires us to seek him for his own sake, and not merely for the emotional consolations we receive from him. The dark night of the soul is a passage of growth into a greater experience of our union with God, but it is often a difficult passage. Instead of an abiding sense of God's presence with us, we may instead be confronted with what feels like a vast and impenetrable silence. Christians ought to be aware that such stages are not abnormal, and that they may in fact be a doorway toward knowing and experiencing God in a deeper and truer way than they ever could have before.

The Experience of *Theosis* on the Daily Pathway of Life

The third experience associated with *theosis* is the one that characterizes most Christians' daily lives. This experience is the long, slow road of growing in virtue in all the ordinary moments. Many Christians may never experience the heights of mystical phenomena nor the valleys of the dark night of the soul, but they will all walk the road of learning to participate in the attributes of God. Some of these become aspects of our lives that are simply given to us in full upon our salvation in Christ, like our inheritance of eternal life. To many early Christian writers, it was this immortality which we receive from God that constitutes the clearest sign of our *theosis*. Since death has been defeated for us, we have left behind the condition of mortal human life and have been welcomed into everlasting life by our union with God's eternal existence, and thus we are, in a sense, divinized. As Hippolytus writes, "You have been deified and begotten unto immortality."[21]

It is not just the immortality of the divine life that we share, however. We are also called to grow in our manifestation of God's character, becoming more and more like him in our progress in virtue. In systematic theology, this is often referred to as a participation in the communicable attributes of God (that is, those attributes that can be incorporated into Christian life, like righteousness and faithfulness, as opposed to incommunicable attributes like infinitude and omniscience). The idea here is

---

21. Hippolytus, *Refutation of All Heresies* 10.30 (ANF 5:153).

that we can catch some of God's communicable attributes in the same way we might catch a communicable disease. This seems to be what 2 Peter 1:4 has in mind when it speaks of our participation in the divine nature, because the passage goes on to describe a list of virtues like goodness, perseverance, and love (1:5–8). This also forms the basis of Justin Martyr's understanding: "We know that only those who have lived near to God in holiness and virtue are deified."[22]

Those who have not been raised to think in terms of divinization may want to take this as an opportunity to pull back to more comfortable terminology. "Well," they may say, "if it's really just a matter of growing in holiness and virtue, then it's not quite as big a deal as a word like 'divinization' suggests." Such a reaction is understandable, but it misses the point. Growing in holiness is a staggering transfiguration into the very character of God, and the astonishing grandeur of this change should not be understated. There is nothing ordinary about it. Maximus the Confessor speaks about this process in a Christian's life as the receiving of "the unparalleled divine radiance of blessed glory appropriate to him."[23] When we speak of growing in the virtues, then, it is not just about gaining a few good habits here and there. God himself is the source of all goodness, "the substance of the virtues," and so a participation in Christian virtue is a participation in God.[24]

Among patristic sources, several virtues were thought to be preeminent for the Christian life. Humility and wisdom (or discernment) were lauded as essential foundations of a rightly ordered life. But none was spoken of more highly than love. Love is the ultimate aim of the whole course of Christian *praxis*, for the virtue of love is quite probably the fullest possible way to participate in the divine nature. Peter puts it at the apex of his ladder of virtues (2 Pet 1:4–7), and John uses it as a substantive definition of the entire character of God: "God is love" (1 John 4:8, 16). Clement of Alexandria takes God-directed love as the means by which *theosis* happens: "The more one loves God, the more he enters within God."[25] It is this love, even in the darkness of our unknowing, amidst all our inability to see God in his infinite essence, that allows us nonetheless to have him and to know him. "You do not see God," Augustine writes,

---

22. Justin Martyr, *First Apology* 21 (ANF 1:170).
23. Maximus the Confessor, *Ambiguum* 7.3 (*On the Cosmic Mystery*, 63).
24. Maximus the Confessor, *Ambiguum* 7.2 (*On the Cosmic Mystery*, 58).
25. Clement of Alexandria, *Who Is the Rich Man?* 27 (*ANF* 2:599).

"[but] you love and you possess him . . . Love me, he cries to us, and you shall possess me."[26]

The desert fathers and mothers recognized love as the true goal of ascetic labors. Asceticism was not an end in itself. One elder noted that many ascetics have gone astray by making the means an end, and although they may fast more rigorously than anyone else and know the Scriptures by heart, "[they] still lack what God is looking for—love and humility."[27] Love is the antithesis of the self-centeredness that leads us away from God. It transforms us from beings who are wired by sin to take things for ourselves (which is essentially what the very first sin was), into beings made ready to give of ourselves for others. Love is the restoration of our truest selves, made alive in the life of God, a condition in which the self is characterized not by its appetites, but by its overflowing graces. As Maximus wrote in his *Centuries on Charity*, "Only love overcomes the fragmentation of human nature."[28]

That God May Be All in All

Our growth in the experience of our union with God is fundamental to our identity. If we truly are the royal priests of God, it is only because we are united to Christ, the great High Priest and the King of kings. We inherit together a share in his identity as the new Adam, and we are thus restored to our original office. So the more we come to manifest our union with Christ in our daily lives, the more we will be equipped to serve in the duties to which he calls us. This is a high and glorious calling: not only to serve in this exalted office, but to be transformed into the very character of God. To quote Maximus the Confessor again, "Nothing can be imagined more splendid or lofty than this."[29] We ourselves become, once again, a microcosm of the cosmos. As Christ is formed in us (Gal 4:19), we prefigure the day when the New Creation will encompass all things, when the light of God and the Lamb will illuminate all nations, and when God will be all in all (Rev 21:5, 23–24; 1 Cor 15:28).

---

26. Augustine, Sermon 34, on Ps 149, quoted in Clément, *Roots*, 243.
27. *Anonymous Sayings of the Desert Fathers* 90, quoted in Clément, *Roots*, 153.
28. Maximus the Confessor, *Centuries on Charity*, quoted in Clément, *Roots*, 136.
29. Maximus the Confessor, *Ambiguum* 7.3 (*On the Cosmic Mystery*s, 63).

16

Mission: The Earth Shall Be Filled

THE VERY FIRST COMMAND God gave to humans was, "Be fruitful and increase in number; fill the earth and subdue it" (Gen 1:28). This was an order to multiply, expand, and rule. But it is not just our own rule that we are called to establish. As royal priests of God, endowed with the authority of his image, we subdue the earth by inviting it to enter fully into the delight of God's reign. With this original commission in mind, consider how a pair of Old Testament prophecies envision its fulfillment: "The earth will be filled with the knowledge of the glory of the Lord as the waters cover the sea" (Hab 2:14; Isa 11:9). The earth *will* be filled. Our original mission will be accomplished, but not just in the sense of a world filled with humans; no, the completion of our mission will be a world that has been utterly transformed into a temple of God's glory, where the knowledge of God runs deeper than all the depths of the sea. This is the mission in which we have been called to participate. This is the vocation in which we become our truest selves.

Over the past few chapters, we have looked at ways in which God's plan of New Creation is being worked out in our individual hearts and lives. By the process of growing in holiness and virtue, we become equipped to stand and serve ever more fully in our restored identity as God's royal priesthood. But the story does not end with just what is happening in our individual lives. New Creation is cosmic in scope, culminating in the day when "the creation itself will be liberated from its bondage to decay and brought into the freedom and glory of the children of God" (Rom 8:21). As such, our work does not end with our own growth in holiness; that growth is woven into a far grander story, in which the culmination of God's promises will end with the renovation of the entire universe.

Our labors, then, point toward God's original intent for his creation, in anticipation of the day when the whole cosmos will truly be a temple of his glory. Not only are we a microcosm of the redemption of the cosmos, we are active participants in that great work of God. When Jesus sent out his followers to spread the knowledge of his kingdom to the nations, he was restoring humanity to its original office as a missional race, engaged in the ever-expanding work of calling the world into the joy of submitting to God's universal reign.

The Original Commission and the Great Commission

One of the curious things about the dual accounts of our creation (Gen 1:1—2:3 and 2:4–25) is that, when taken together, they appear to give human beings both a local role and a global role. Many Christians read the stories of the garden of Eden and assume that if Adam and Eve had not fallen into sin, they could have stayed right there in their earthly paradise forever, and the human race would never have experienced anything except the bliss of knowing God and working the garden. However, when we combine this sense of the story (which derives from the second creation account, that of Gen 2) with the picture of our creation in Genesis 1, a more complex portrait emerges. In Genesis 1:28, God speaks his original commission to the newly created man and woman: "Be fruitful and increase in number; fill the earth and subdue it." How, then, could human beings have possibly stayed in their original state in the garden of Eden and also filled and subdued the whole earth? They or their descendants would have had to take that commission and move out of Eden to the ends of the earth.

God's original commission to humanity seems to point us toward the fact that the temple-like state of Eden, as well as humanity's role in creation, were not static realities with fixed boundaries in one location. Unfallen humanity had a job to do that would eventually take Adam and Eve (or their descendants) beyond the original limits of the garden, in order to bring all creation into submission to the reign of God through his chosen ambassadors. If Eden was the holy of holies in God's great creation-temple, then it was the work of the priesthood to go out and take up their service in the sanctuary and courtyard areas (those areas of the earth beyond Eden), so that the whole temple could be administered in a fitting and beautiful way. In this original commission, it is not only a command to grow the human population such that the whole earth is filled, but also to rule the earth (v. 29), exercising our sovereign office over all other creatures. It is, then, an aspect of our royal-priestly identity, standing as the official representatives of God's reign, between him and his creation.

Now let's jump ahead to the New Testament. When Jesus is about to ascend and begin the period of his heavenly messianic reign, he gives his disciples a commission that restores humanity's original commission in several striking ways. The Great Commission texts, like the accounts of Eden, have both a local and a global vision of humanity's work. In the Lukan version, Jesus tells his disciples that the message of the Messiah's gospel "will be preached in his name to all nations, beginning at Jerusalem" (Luke 24:47; cf. Acts 1:8). The work of humanity begins in our local situation, but is also meant to extend to the ends of the earth, just as the original work of God's royal priests would begin in Eden and then go on to fill the earth.

The Great Commission also echoes our original commission by focusing on the issues of authority and rulership. In the original commission, the first humans, made in the image of God, were sent forth to rule and subdue the creation. In the Great Commission, it is Jesus—who is not only made in the image of God, but is himself the image of God—who claims "all authority," and then delegates his followers as his representatives, serving as witnesses of his reign to all nations (Matt 28:19). This idea of authority and rulership is deeply interwoven in both texts. In the Great Commission, the instructions to Jesus' followers do not simply end with an obligation to preach the good news, but to make disciples of all nations and to teach them to observe his commands (28:19–20). In effect, Jesus calls them to take up the original commission of "rule and subdue" by bringing all nations into submission to the reign of the new Adam, the image of God, the true Priest-King of all creation. This submission, of course, is not brought about by the forceful or violent ways of the world's kingdoms, but by the peaceful proclamation of the forgiveness of sins, by baptizing, and by teaching.

Some might object at this point, however, and say that while the Great Commission is aimed at bringing people into the joyful freedom of submitting to the reign of Christ, the original commission very clearly aimed at subduing animal creation. "Rule over the fish of the sea and the birds in the sky and over every living creature that moves on the ground" (Gen 1:29). This is true, but it seems natural enough that people would be included as an object of that commission after humanity's fall into sin. After the fall, humans themselves were in desperate need of being restored to full submission to the reign of God. It is no surprise, then, that Jesus' commission to his followers begins by aiming for a restoration of the ones who were meant to be the royal priests of the first commission.

Further, the early Christian church seemed to understand that Jesus' Great Commission had something even larger than the global evangelization of human beings in mind, because when Christian scribes summed up its essence in the "long ending" of Mark, they took its aim as being broader than just people: "Go into all the world and preach the gospel to all creation" (Mark 16:15). In some early patristic writings, the proclamation of the gospel is portrayed as the cosmic declaration of the glory of God, extending to all creation.[1] Early Christians saw in the gospel the fulfillment of humanity's original commission, whereby the whole world, to the very ends of the earth, would submit to the reign of the messianic king (cf. Ps 2:8–9 LXX; Rev 2:27; 3:14; 12:5).

The Christian commission to proclaim, baptize, and teach is thus a restoration of our original office. In all our work, we are carrying out the original task of the royal priests of God's creation-temple: to fill the earth and subdue it to the reign of God. This is primarily done in our labors of evangelism, which is the focus of the Great Commission texts, but it also includes all the practical works of justice, mercy, and love for our neighbors that fall under the broad task of teaching the nations to observe all that Christ has commanded us (Matt 28:19–20).

The Nations Belong to Him: Mission as Declaring the Victory of Christ

One of the striking things about Christianity's rise is the optimism of its ascendancy. Even in the early centuries, when Christianity was a persecuted and despised minority, their writings reveal unlimited confidence that their faith would constitute the eventual destiny of the entire world. Rising in an age when nearly all religions were content to be parochial affairs—Roman paganism, for instance, was well inclined to accept foreign gods as having power in foreign places, and to simply add them to

---

1. See, for example, Origen, *Against Celsus* 1.62 (ANF 4:424).

their pantheon—Christianity made startling claims to be the one true universal religion. Even ancient Judaism, which made overarching truth claims about the entire world, did not expect other nations to accept those claims or live by them (at least not until the advent of the Messiah). But Christians, from their earliest beginnings, confidently expected that the entire world would prove to be the scope of their Messiah's reign, not only in the age to come, but in the very age of the church itself. Origen, despite his own experience of being brutally tortured as a member of this persecuted minority, could nonetheless write in total confidence, "Every form of worship will be destroyed except the religion of Christ, which alone will prevail. Indeed, it will one day triumph."[2]

Early Christians expected God to be true to his word, and so they saw signs of the messianic prophecies of the Old Testament coming true all around them. The nations would come to believe in Christ—even if not as a unanimous totality of all people, certainly at least in a representative fashion, with believers in Christ coming from all nations, because that is what the prophecies said. While some patristic writers allowed for a future millennial state on earth, and most acknowledged that the full culmination of Christ's reign would not appear until his second coming, the broad tenor of their work reflected the idea that the messianic reign had already begun with Christ's ascension and that its effects could be seen and felt all around them.

In Justin Martyr's dialogue with his Jewish interlocutor Trypho, he wrestles with Trypho's objection that Jesus, rather than being crowned with glory and ushering in the messianic kingdom as the prophets foretold, was instead last seen publicly when he was dying on a cross like a common criminal.[3] Justin offers a rebuttal of the idea that Jesus' crucifixion would disqualify him from being the Messiah, and ultimately comes around to argue that, in point of fact, the messianic kingdom has obviously begun to appear through Jesus, because the prophecies about it were being fulfilled before their very eyes. "If all nations are blessed in the Messiah [Ps 72:17], and we who are from all nations believe in him, then he is the Messiah, and we are they who are blessed through him."[4] Justin's argument still holds true today, and one might say that it holds far more forcefully today, when Christians can be found in every corner of the

---

2. Origen, *Against Celsus* 8.68 (ANF 4:666).
3. Justin Martyr, *Dialogue with Trypho* 32, 36, 39 (ANF 1:210, 212, 214).
4. Justin Martyr, *Dialogue with Trypho* 121; cf.109–10 (ANF 1:260; cf. 253–54).

globe. Even the last remaining unreached people groups may well have a witness of the gospel in their midst within this decade, which would constitute an incredible milestone in Christian history. Anyone who has observed the international array of Christian pilgrims traveling to the biblical sites in Israel can attest that the prophecies of Isaiah are coming true right before our eyes, as the nations stream to the mountain of the Lord (Isa 2:2; 60:1–3; see also Mic 4:1). Jesus Christ has accomplished and established one of the central hallmarks of the prophesied messianic age: the nations of the world have come to worship the God of Israel. As Athanasius writes, "The whole earth is filled with the knowledge of God, and the Gentiles . . . are now taking refuge in the God of Abraham through the Word, even our Lord Jesus Christ."[5]

The triumphalism of early Christianity's view of the world is firmly rooted in Scripture. Critical to their understanding of Jesus' messianic office were texts like Psalm 2, which speaks to a character identified as the king, as Christ ("anointed"), and as the Son of God (vv. 2, 6–7, 12), and which says to him, "I will make the nations your inheritance, the ends of the earth your possession" (v. 8). Another foundational text was Psalm 110, which speaks to a character identified as "lord" and as a priest in the order of Melchizedek (vv. 1, 4), and portrays this character's reign as being an absolute triumph over his enemies: "Sit at my right hand until I make your enemies a footstool for your feet" (v. 1). So ingrained was this triumphalist perspective in early Christian writings that it is common to find them referring to the global spread of the Christian faith as a *fait accompli*, as if the gospel had already reached to the ends of the earth. "The whole world," writes Clement of Alexandria, "has already become the domain of the Word."[6] Tertullian agrees: "Christ's name is extending everywhere, believed everywhere . . . reigning everywhere, adored everywhere."[7]

While some modern readers might regard this triumphalist attitude as an unhealthy kind of overconfidence, it is hard to downplay the scope of early Christianity's achievements in evangelism and mission. Some groups were better than others at launching cross-cultural mission movements—the Church of the East in central Asia, for instance, far outperformed the church in the Roman Empire in planting the faith across

---

5. Athanasius, *On the Incarnation* 40 (*NPNF*² 4:58).
6. Clement of Alexandria, *Exhortation to the Heathen* 11 (*ANF* 2:203).
7. Tertullian, *An Answer to the Jews* 7 (*ANF* 3:158).

cultural and national borders—but even within the Roman Empire, dramatic transformations appeared. The traditional pagan religions of the Greco-Roman world had undergone a popular revival by the second century CE, so it is not the case (as some popular histories have assumed) that Christianity simply swept over the remains of an exhausted system of belief that was already in decline. Rather, Christianity triumphed over a resurgent and all-pervasive paganism in rather remarkable ways. Well before the rise of Christianity as a Roman state religion, it was already on its way to being the empire's dominant faith simply because of its effectiveness in bringing new converts to faith. Writing at the end of the second century (more than a full century before Emperor Constantine's conversion), Tertullian could already claim "We are but of yesterday, and we have filled every place among you . . . Almost all the inhabitants of your various cities are followers of Christ."[8]

One of the regular refrains of early Christian apologetics was simply to point out that the pagan cults appeared powerless to stop their rise.[9] In fact, one of the reasons that the desert fathers and mothers went out into the deserts to pray was that they felt that the gospel had already effectively conquered the demonic powers that lay behind pagan temples in the cities, and so they were chasing the demons out of their last places of safe retreat in the wilderness. These desert hermits were not simply seeking a life of quiet contemplation apart from the world; they conceived of their work as spiritual warfare, in which they continued to push back the routed powers of Satan.

Much of early Christianity's evangelistic efforts have this spirit of triumph about them. When one plumbs the church fathers for references to Christian motivations in evangelism and mission, one finds very quickly that the motivations we might put at the top of the list are rarely mentioned. No doubt early Christians did feel a real concern for the salvation of individual souls, but this is hardly ever brought up as a motivating factor. Far more often, the victory of Christ and the extension of his reign is put forward as the driving force behind early Christian mission. One of the dominant motifs in the Christian artwork that emerged in the patristic period was an abbreviation applied to images of Christ: *IC XC NIKA*, which is short for "Jesus Christ conquers." This conquering should not be thought of in terms of military conquest, colonialism, or

---

8. Tertullian, *Apology* 37 (ANF 3:45).
9. See Athanasius, *On the Incarnation* 8.46–47 (NPNF[2] 4:61–62).

imperialism; it was an expression of Jesus' complete and total victory over the powers of evil in the spiritual realm and the ongoing spiritual progress of his reign (Col 2:15; 1 Cor 15:25). This set of ideas—often called *Christus Victor* theology—was at the center of the way the early church went about its missionary labors. They were making manifest in the world what was already true in a cosmic sense: Jesus Christ was the reigning King of the universe, and his kingdom would continue to spread through the preaching of the good news and through acts of love and justice until it had reached to the ends of the earth.

In fact, if properly understood, this kind of *Christus Victor* missiology would never lead to imperialism or military conquest. An imperialistic Christianity is openly and obviously incompatible with the teachings of Christ, who told us to love our enemies, who consistently declined to seize power by force, and who taught that the way his kingdom operates is different from the kingdoms of this world. In *Christus Victor* theology, the enemy is always and only a spiritual enemy—Satan, demons, and the spiritual powers and authorities that lie behind all systems of oppression. The enemy is never another human being, not even if they happened to be a passionate adherent of another religion or a committed persecutor of the Christian faith. Rather, those humans are the very people to whom God has sent us to serve as his royal priests.

This leads us to an important consideration. The theology of Christ's victory does not lead to a militaristic mindset, in which atheists and the adherents of other religions are arrayed against us in a competition for society's soul. There is no sense in which we are entrenched against hostile enemies who are trying to achieve Christianity's destruction. Rather, we simply know, with the purity of faith exhibited by the early church, that Christianity cannot be destroyed, because Christ has already won the victory and secured his reign. Those people who seem so hostile to our faith are not our enemies. Only the spiritual powers of evil in this world are the enemies of our faith, and they have been beaten decisively and are even now being pushed back by the advance of the gospel.

This means that those we might otherwise regard as opponents are, in fact, our very own people, the nearest and dearest objects of our concern. The neighbors around us who base their lives on godless pursuits, sometimes in open rebuke of Christianity, are not in competition with us. They are not "the other"; they are our very own, to be the recipients of our love, care, witness, and intercession. They are the ones for whose sake we minister and strive in the office to which God has appointed us. We belong to them, and they belong to us. We are their priests, whether they know it or not. The unbelieving world is tied to Christians like the body to the soul, as the postapostolic *Epistle to Diognetus* puts it:

> [The Christians] live on earth, but their citizenship is in heaven . . . They love everyone, and by everyone they are persecuted . . . In a word, what the soul is to the body, Christians are to the world . . . The soul loves the flesh that hates it, and its members, and Christians love those who hate them . . . Though Christians are detained in the world as if in a prison, they in fact hold the world together . . . Such is the important position to which God has appointed them, and it is not right for them to decline it.[10]

One more note on the confident, all-encompassing vision of the patristic age: many readers today will look at the triumphalist streak in those early centuries and think that it was mistaken. After all, Christianity has been around for 2,000 years, and many people today cannot shake the feeling that it is now in a period of decline. This feeling, however, is quite probably in error. In point of fact, the early Christian attitude was based almost entirely on Scripture, and cannot really be faulted on that mark. If they were mistaken about anything, it was simply that they underestimated the scope of the work that lay before them in the progress of world missions and the time it would take to achieve such a work.

Some Christians today are probably guilty of the opposite errors, by not taking seriously the triumphal confidence of Scripture and by underestimating the staggering global expansion of the Christian faith in the past two centuries, which now appears to be accelerating in much of the world. The writers of the patristic age would probably look at our world today and feel even more confident (if that were possible) of the triumph of their faith. They would see a world on the brink of realizing, for the first time in 4,000 years, the actual fulfillment of God's promise to Abraham: that all the thousands of ethnic people groups in the world would be blessed through his faith (Gen 12:3).

Indeed, for Christians convinced that they have a role to play in the great mission of God to all peoples, this may be the most exciting period of history in which to be alive. God's work of reconciling all things to himself is in progress through the reign of Christ, and there are some indications that it may be accelerating around the world in our own day. If the New Creation has already begun with the re-creation of a new

---

10. *Epistle to Diognetus* 5.9, 11; 6.1, 6-7, 10 (Holmes, *Apostolic Fathers*, 702-5).

humanity in Christ, as this book has argued, then we can see signs of that re-creation at work all around us. The first stage in the reconciliation of the cosmos to the reign of God is the reconciliation of humanity to him, and even now we are at the brink of seeing—for the first time ever—the actual and literal undoing of Babel's dissolution of humanity through the reconciling work of the church of Jesus Christ. Whereas the tragedy of Babel, an after-effect of the fall, resulted in the disunion of all peoples because of sin, now through the gospel of the messianic King, representatives from every tribe and tongue and people and nation are being gathered back together again in one body. This has been the vision of the new humanity all along: a vast crowd of people from every language and nation gathered around the throne of God, worshiping him (Rev 7:9–10). Today, as missionaries both local and foreign press on with their labors, and as the Scriptures are being translated into all of humanity's tongues, we are seeing in our own day a fulfillment of all these ancient prophecies. We can see this milestone just ahead of us on the horizon, but we are not yet there, and great labors still await us. The call to be a royal priest of God is a call to be part of his work of mission to the nations, whether in prayer, in giving, or in going, and there has never been a more exciting time to take up the mantle of that calling than right now.

Ministers of Reconciliation

The progress of the Christian faith throughout the world is based primarily on the proclamation of the gospel message, so that others might hear and come to faith. The missional work of the church, though, is not limited to evangelism alone. Or rather, it is not limited to the evangelism of the word alone. By undertaking acts of love, mercy, and justice in our society, Christians also manifest the message of Christ and grant to the watching world an ever-clearer picture of his kingdom. In fact, most of the stories of conversion that come to us from the patristic age have more to do with the impact of Christians' deeds than the impact of their words.

One of the main avenues of evangelism, strangely enough, was public martyrdom. In story after story of early Christian martyrs, from Polycarp to Perpetua, we have accounts of people in the crowd being so struck by the Christians' calm courage in the moment of their death that they went and sought out the faith for themselves. We might call this "evangelism by character," because it was the public display of ordinary

Christian virtue—the way that Christians came to share in the radiant holiness and love of God's own character—that struck the witnesses of these events.

Acts of mercy and justice came to be one of the hallmarks of the early Christian witness. Despite malicious rumors that circled about Christians for centuries (they were variously called cannibals, atheists, and an outright threat to the safety of the empire), they came to be known for their sacrificial love. Early Christians would do things that no one else had ever dared to do, nor even considered doing. They were known for saving abandoned infants who had been left to die, paying manumission fees to set slaves at liberty, and caring for plague victims instead of fleeing the cities when disease struck. Some even went so far as to sell off family estates in order to give the money to the poor. Julian the Apostate, the last Roman emperor to try to oppose the rise of Christianity, used to complain that it was impossible to tear down the Christians in the public's eyes, because they not only cared for their own poor people, but for everybody else's too.

All these things lie at the core of our office and identity. As God's royal priesthood, part of our work is the administration of the blessings of God upon his world, based on the authority given to us at our first commission.[11] Since we serve as ambassadors of a God of love, mercy, and justice, it is our duty to do the work of love, mercy, and justice in every situation we can. As royal priests of the New Creation, Christians cannot simply withdraw themselves and wash their hands of the world as it runs to its ruin. Kings and priests are people who cannot help but be deeply involved in the working of society, and the work of justice is at the core of both offices (see Deut 17:8–20).

Paul encompasses these missional labors in his beautifully poetic description of his office, "the ministry of reconciliation." Immediately after linking this idea to the New Creation, Paul says that "God was reconciling the world to himself in Christ" (2 Cor 5:17–19), and that he has a share in that very ministry by the proclamation of God's forgiveness. While Paul speaks only about his own ministry in the passage, what he says is applicable to the office of all Christians. As royal priests of the temple of God's New Creation, serving in union with the great High Priest and the King of kings, part of our service is to be agents of Christ's work in pulling God's broken creation back together. By our work in the

---

11. See 1 Clem. 61.2 (Holmes, *Apostolic Fathers*, 126–27).

evangelism of word, character, and deed, we serve to help reconcile the world back to God, and thus to apply the restoring work of Christ to the situations around us.

Paul's description in 2 Corinthians 5 is focused on the reconciliation between God and humans because of forgiveness through Jesus, but it would not be amiss to include one more extension of our labor of reconciliation. We human beings are not only the priestly go-betweens in the work of bringing other humans to faith, but we are also the go-betweens for the whole physical world as well. We were created in the image of God to rule over animal creation and to tend the garden, and so our original commission, now restored in Christ, will necessarily include those elements as well. The Christian office thus includes creation care, exercised alongside our first priority as witnesses of the gospel of Christ. We were created to serve in a position of care and oversight for the whole earth, and that office remains today. Environmental concerns ought not to be a pawn of political platforms, but a genuine interest of all Christians. This world is the handiwork of our beloved King, and if we love him who made it and proclaimed it good, then we should also seek its good.

Paul, writing in Romans 8:18–21, even connects the coming restoration of all creation with "the glory that will be revealed in us." In other words, there is some aspect of our destiny as redeemed human beings that is directly linked to the restoration of all creation. Some early Christian groups, like the Ethiopian Orthodox Church, made this theme a major part of their congregational life by intentionally cultivating patches of forest and garden around their churches, so that the physical church itself might be a sign of the restoration that is to come. We do not yet know all the details about what the restoration of natural creation will look like in the end, but we do know that we, like our forefather before us, can do our part by tending the garden spot where God in his grace has placed us.

The Symphony of the Ages

As we consider the scope of the work we undertake as God's royal priests, it is time now to come back to that concert hall in which we began this book. Perhaps, like me, you have had the privilege of learning the instrumental parts one by one, and hearing the wonder of how they all fit together. Or perhaps you have had the blessing of knowing and growing with all these musical themes, melody and harmonies, for quite some time. In either case, it is the same symphony which we have tuned our ears to hear. The runs of notes and musical themes that fill out the picture of creation, temple, and kingdom have woven themselves around the song of "Christ in [us], the hope of glory" (Col 1:27), and the final setting of that score is breathtaking. God has done something in our hearts that ties into his plan for the restoration of all things, a plan that culminates in the entire cosmos being transfigured through Christ into a temple of divine glory.

One of the main points of this book, however, is that this is not just a symphony which you have the great honor to hear; it is a symphony in which you are invited to play a part. You are not merely a member of the audience. There is a seat reserved on the stage for you, with an instrument you have been fitted to play. We Christians are the royal priesthood of God, the active agents of his plan to bring all things into joyful submission to his reign. This was our first commission (Gen 1:26–28), and it is even now being enacted in the reign of Christ (1 Cor 15:24–28), of whose kingdom we are ambassadors. Through your worship, your prayers, your ascent in holiness, and your labors in service and love, you play an indispensable role in the work of Jesus' messianic reign. God has called you to be a part of the symphony of the ages.

This symphony, as stunning and marvelous as it already is, is not finished yet. We have heard its interweaving themes rise to a thunderous climax in the work of Christ and the establishment of his reign, but there is still a grand finale yet to come. For those who have spent time with the fathers and mothers of the early church, or even for those acquainted with liturgical Christian traditions, these hints of a coming finale are everywhere. In many English translations of the old liturgies, certain texts (like the *Gloria Patri*) end with the words, "world without end." It's a curious turn of phrase, but even in its sparse English form one can hear echoes of God's eternal plan for his created order. "World without end" goes back to Greek and Latin phrases which say "unto the ages of ages." This is a common way to end prayers in many churches which have roots in the ancient traditions: "now and forever, and to the ages of ages."

These words remind us that we stand at the turning of the ages even now. As officials of the messianic reign of the great Priest-King, whose kingdom is already on the march but has yet to come to its final consummation, we stand astride two different ages in the salvation history of the world. Much like humans are a microcosm of the cosmos, uniquely made to have one foot in the physical world and one in the spiritual world, we Christians are a microcosm of the turning of the ages, with one foot in the age that is passing away and another already planted in the coming age of the New Creation. Maximus the Confessor, writing about the theme of the eighth day, would sometimes say that we who lived in the eighth day were already living the life of the age to come.

One of the great surprises in the story of Jesus is that many of the elements that God's people assumed were going to happen only at the end of history have jumped ahead in the timeline. Resurrection, messianic reign, the outpouring of the Spirit, and the transformation of humanity to have "a new heart and new spirit" (Ezek 36:26) were all generally thought to be events that came at the end. But the resurrection of Jesus and the inauguration of his messianic kingdom have overturned that expectation. The great restoration has already begun, here in the midst of history, and we are part of it. God's New Creation is already in motion, and in the work of Christ's reign, all things in heaven and earth are being brought back together in him (Eph 1:10). The fallen priesthood is being restored, and the desolate temple rebuilt. We who live as God's royal priests already know the joy of dwelling with God and serving him wholeheartedly, and we are part of his plan to invite the whole created order into the experience of that joy. The part that we play is leading directly up into the symphony's grand finale. On that day, as the age to come finally becomes our "world without end," God will be all in all, we will behold the light of his face, and the joy of his presence will be forever ours.

Appendix

On Reading Patristic Sources

WHY SHOULD WE STUDY the writings of the patristic age, or care about the opinions of the early church fathers and mothers? I believe there are very good reasons to do so, even if one does not come from a liturgical or sacramental tradition that draws directly from roots in the patristic age. But one of the dangers of a book like this is that it might subtly suggest that patristic writers are an authoritative standard unto themselves, and that we ought to adopt everything they might have said on any given subject. That is not a suggestion I hope to make, despite how deeply grateful I am for the witness, guidance, and insight of the patristic writers. They were men and women of faith, just as we are, indwelt by the same Holy Spirit and striving to study and apply the same sacred texts. God used many of them in tremendously powerful ways to protect his churches from the dangers of heresy and false teaching. But it would be a mistake to suppose that everything they said or taught is worth accepting; like anyone, they made errors in interpretation, occasionally entertained truly bizarre ideas, and they frequently disagreed about peripheral matters.

So if they are not a gold standard of fully reliable interpretations, why lean on them at all? There are two good reasons for doing so. The first is that our own traditions of theology and biblical interpretation have all descended from them, to a greater or lesser degree. Regardless of what denomination of Christianity you hold to, the patristic age is your patrimony, and you can learn a great deal about why you believe as you do by studying the way those writers and thinkers navigated the theological issues of their day.

The second reason is one of proximity: those first centuries of Christianity after the apostolic period were far closer to the production of the biblical texts than we now are. They shared many similarities of language and culture with the world of the Bible, and while that was not a sure defense against any and all errors, they tended to be able to understand the cultural perspectives of Scripture (and the New Testament in particular) better than we can. Their cultural similarity gave them an innate ability to get to the heart of what biblical writers were saying in a way that we, who are more distant in time and culture, sometimes have more difficulty doing. Here's the bottom line: if you want to know if there is some glaring, unconscious area of biblical or theological interpretation that you are missing because of the limitations of your cultural perspective, reading patristics is one of the best ways to discover that answer. The contrasts between their thought and one's own can be illuminating.

I should include a caveat here for those who might wonder about my selection and use of sources, and how representative they are of the shape of patristic interpretation as a whole. One of the dangers of a book like this is that it might lead one to think that there was a well-ordered, fully organized system of theological thought among the early church fathers and mothers, known and followed by all. This is simply not the case. The theological writings of the patristic era are much more like a vast, unscripted dialogue, with wandering conversations that went in all directions. That's not to say there was no common ground. Against the currently fashionable presumptions in some academic circles, early Christianity was not merely a wild no man's land of conflicting theological opinions, where gnostics and docetists had an equal voice at the table. To the contrary, there was a definite body of common theology held by confessing Christians within the churches that had descended from apostolic labors. Within the communal fellowship of the church, which even in the New Testament period showed clear signs of solidarity and intentional organizational structures, even across as vast a space as the Roman Empire and beyond, there was indeed a body of doctrine that constituted "the faith that was once for all entrusted to the saints" (Jude 3 NRSV). This common core of doctrine was, and always has been, the basic outline of biblical theology derived from the New Testament documents, and which substantially still exists in the classic early creeds of the church, such as the Apostles' Creed.

But even with that common core of doctrine in place, we should not get the impression that major, comprehensive systems of theological thought existed in the early church, at least not in the same way that we might hold them today. There was nothing so fully fleshed as Calvinism or Thomist philosophy in the early church. One can certainly find individual thinkers with well-thought-out systems of doctrine, even very early on, such as Irenaeus of Lyons. But such systems did not represent fully orbed schools of theological thought. Even in those times and places where one could speak of "schools" of theological interpretation, such as the Antiochene school or the Alexandrian school, it was not so much a matter of systematic doctrine as it was a general inclination toward a particular kind of biblical interpretation or a common pattern of theological sensibilities. So when a reader encounters a book like this one, which by necessity must try to systematize some of the insights of early Christian theologians, they should at least be aware that this systematization is drawn from lines of thought that occur across many sources, and that it does not represent a discrete deposit of doctrinal data that can be found, fully formed, in any particular theologian or school of thought.

Nonetheless, the theological ideas and themes considered herein were all generally present across a representative swath of major patristic writers, and many of the broader outlines I have presented are drawn from the emergent consensus of the Greek-speaking Christian world, particularly as it began to be systematized in the later centuries of the patristic period. In doing so, I have made every attempt to show that these themes were faithful parts of the earliest Christian witness, and thus many of the insights which form the foundation of this book are taken from earliest generations of writers, like the apostolic fathers, Justin Martyr, and Irenaeus, as corroborated by biblical theology and ancient Jewish traditions. If one were to trace the arc of this book's theological vision, one can find it anchored in (just to name a few) the New Testament writings of John and Paul, Irenaeus, Athanasius, the Cappadocian fathers, and Maximus the Confessor.

Thus the shape of this vision of the Christian life—the royal-priestly vision, based on humanity's calling and office from our creation onward—is not something cherry-picked or fabricated from contrasting sources, but leans on common themes and insights that have been present in the Christian witness from the very beginning, and which later came to be dominant in some of the most significant schools of Christian thought.

For those who might wish to read further along some of the themes presented in this book, or simply to learn a little more about the writers I mentioned, I offer the following list of recommended resources, accessible even to beginners in patristic studies:

Patristic Theology & Spirituality:

Worshiping with the Church Fathers, by Christopher A. Hall
Reading Scripture with the Church Fathers, by Christopher A. Hall
Living Wisely with the Church Fathers, by Christopher A. Hall
Dangerous Passions, Deadly Sins, by Dennis Okholm
The Roots of Christian Mysticism, by Olivier Clément
Early Christian Doctrines, by J. N. D. Kelly

Books Relating to Creation and Temple Themes:

In the Shadow of the Temple, by Oskar Skarsaune
The Temple and the Church's Mission, by G. K. Beale
God Dwells Among Us, by G. K. Beale and Mitchell Kim
The Lost World of Genesis One, by John H. Walton

Series with Translations of Patristic Sources in Contemporary English:

Popular Patristics Series (St Vladimir's Seminary Press)
The Classics of Western Spirituality (Paulist Press)
The Early Church Fathers (Routledge)
Ancient Christian Devotional (IVP)
Ancient Christian Commentary on Scripture (IVP)
The Philokalia (Faber & Faber)

Reference Works:

David W. Bercot, *A Dictionary of Early Christian Beliefs*
Henry Wace and William C. Piercy, *A Dictionary of Early Christian Biography and Literature* (Available as a free PDF at Christian Classics Ethereal Library, ccel.org)

Bibliography

Alfeyev, Hilarion. *The Mystery of Faith: An Introduction to the Teaching and Spirituality of the Orthodox Church*. London: Darton, Longman and Todd, 2002.
Athanasius, et al. *The Paradise of the Holy Fathers*. 2 vols. Translated by Ernest A. Wallis Budge. London: Chatto & Windus, 1907.
Augustine of Hippo. *Confessions*. Translated by R. S. Pine-Coffin. London: Penguin, 1961.
Barker, Margaret. *Temple Theology: An Introduction*. London: SPCK, 2004.
Barsanuphius and John. *Letters from the Desert*. Translated and edited by John Chryssavgis. Popular Patristics Series. Crestwood, NY: St. Vladimir's Seminary Press, 2003.
Basil the Great. *On Social Justice*. Translated by C. Paul Schroeder. Popular Patristics Series. Crestwood, NY: St. Vladimir's Seminary Press, 2009.
———. *On the Human Condition*. Translated by Nonna Verna Harrison. Popular Patristics Series. Crestwood, NY: St. Vladimir's Seminary Press, 2005.
Benedict of Nursia. *The Rule of St. Benedict in English*. Edited by Timothy Fry. Collegeville, MN: Liturgical, 2019.
Boersma, Hans. *Seeing God: The Beatific Vision in Christian Tradition*. Grand Rapids: Eerdmans, 2018.
Boethius. *The Consolation of Philosophy*. Translated by Richard Green. New York: Macmillan, 1962.
Bunge, Gabriel. *Earthen Vessels: The Practice of Personal Prayer According to the Patristic Tradition*. Translated by Michael J. Miller. San Francisco: Ignatius, 2002.
Cassian, John. *Conferences*. Translated by Colm Luibheid. The Classics of Western Spirituality. New York: Paulist, 1985.
Chadwick, Owen. "Introduction." In *Conferences*, by John Cassian, 1–36. Translated by Colm Luibheid. The Classics of Western Spirituality. New York: Paulist, 1985.
Clément, Olivier. *The Roots of Christian Mysticism: Texts from the Patristic Era with Commentary*. Translated by Theodore Berkeley and Jeremy Hummerstone. Hyde Park, NY: New City, 1993.
Climacus, John. *The Ladder of Divine Ascent*. Translated by Colm Luibheid and Norman Russell. The Classics of Western Spirituality. New York: Paulist, 1982.
Cyril of Jerusalem. *Cyril of Jerusalem*. Edited and translated by Edward Yarnold. The Early Church Fathers. London: Routledge, 2000.
Ephrem the Syrian. *Hymns*. Translated by Kathleen E. McVey. The Classics of Western Spirituality. New York: Paulist, 1989.

———. *Hymns on Paradise*. Translated by Sebastian Brock. Popular Patristics Series. Crestwood, NY: St. Vladimir's Seminary Press, 1990.

Epictetus. *Discourses and Selected Writings*. Translated by Robert Dobbin. London: Penguin, 2008.

Gregory of Nazianzus. *On God and Christ: The Five Theological Orations and Two Letters to Cledonius*. Translated by Lionel Wickham and Frederick Williams. Popular Patristics Series. Crestwood, NY: St. Vladimir's Seminary Press, 2002.

Gregory of Nyssa. *The Life of Moses*. Translated by Abraham J. Malherbe and Everett Ferguson. San Francisco: HarperCollins, 2006.

Gregory the Great. *The Book of Pastoral Rule*. Translated by George E. Demacopoulos. Popular Patristics Series. Crestwood, NY: St. Vladimir's Seminary Press, 2007.

Hall, Christopher A. *Worshiping with the Church Fathers*. Downers Grove, IL: IVP Academic, 2009.

Hamman, Adalbert Gauther. *La Prière dans l'Eglise Ancienne*. Traditio Christiana 7. Bern: Peter Lang, 1989.

Holmes, Michael W., ed. *The Apostolic Fathers: Greek Texts and English Translations*. 3rd edition. Translated by Michael W. Holmes. Grand Rapids: Baker Academic, 2007.

John Chrysostom. *On Wealth and Poverty*. Translated by Catharine P. Roth. Popular Patristics Series. Crestwood, NY: St. Vladimir's Seminary Press, 1981.

John of Damascus. *Writings*. Translated by Frederic H. Chase, Jr. Washington, DC: Catholic University of America Press, 1958.

Josephus. *The Complete Works*. Translated by William Whiston. Nashville: Thomas Nelson, 1998.

Lewis, C. S. *Mere Christianity*. San Francisco: HarperCollins, 2001.

Maximus the Confessor. *On the Cosmic Mystery of Jesus Christ*. Translated by Paul M. Blowers and Robert Louis Wilken Popular Patristics Series. Crestwood, NY: St. Vladimir's Seminary Press, 2003.

———. *On the Ecclesiastical Mystagogy*. Translated by Jonathan J. Armstrong. Popular Patristics Series. Crestwood, NY: St. Vladimir's Seminary Press, 2019.

The Philokalia. Edited by Nikodimos of the Holy Mountain and Makarios of Corinth. Translated by G. E. H. Palmer et al. 4 vols. London: Faber & Faber, 1979–95.

Pseudo-Dionysius. *The Complete Works*. Translated by Colm Luibheid. The Classics of Western Spirituality. New York: Paulist, 1987.

Pseudo-Macarius. *The Fifty Spiritual Homilies and the Great Letter*. Translated by George A. Maloney. The Classics of Western Spirituality. New York: Paulist, 1992.

Skarsaune, Oskar. *In the Shadow of the Temple: Jewish Influences on Early Christianity*. Downers Grove, IL: IVP Academic, 2002.

Ward, Benedicta, ed. *The Desert Fathers: Sayings of the Early Christian Monks*. Translated by Benedicta Ward. London: Penguin, 2003.

www.ingramcontent.com/pod-product-compliance
Lightning Source LLC
Chambersburg PA
CBHW050846230426
43667CB00012B/2174